Teaching in the Field

✳

Teaching in the Field

Working with Students in the Outdoor Classroom

Edited by

Hal Crimmel

The University of Utah Press

Salt Lake City

The Defiance House Man colophon is a registered trademark of The University of Utah Press. It is based upon a four-foot-tall Ancient Puebloan pictograph (late PIII) near Glen Canyon, Utah.

Printed on acid-free paper
08 07 06 05 04 03
5 4 3 2 1

LIBRARY OF CONGRESS CATALOGING-IN-PUBLICATION DATA

Teaching in the field : working with students in the outdoor classroom / edited by Hal Crimmel.

   p. cm.

Includes bibliographical references and index.

 ISBN 0-87480-762-X (pbk. : alk. paper)

 1. Field work (Educational method) 2. Outdoor education.

3. Literature—Study and teaching (Higher) I. Crimmel, Hal, 1966–

  LB2394.T43 2003

  371.3'84—dc21   2003006424

The excerpt in Fred Taylor's essay from "The Summer Day" in *New and Selected Poems,* copyright © 1992 by Mary Oliver, is reprinted by permission of Beacon Press.

The excerpt in Fred Taylor's essay from "Lost" in *Traveling Light: Collected and New Poems,* by David Wagoner, is reprinted by permission of the University of Illinois Press.

Terry Gifford, "Teaching Environmental Values through Creative Writing with School Children." An earlier version of this essay first appeared in *English in Education* 36:3 (UK) and is reprinted by permission of the author.

R. Edward Grumbine, "Going to Bashō's Pine: Wilderness Education for the Twenty-First Century." This essay first appeared in *ISLE: Interdisciplinary Studies in Literature and Environment* (Summer 1999) and is reprinted by permission of the author.

11049

❋ CONTENTS

❄ ACKNOWLEDGMENTS

A s this collection goes to press, I am aware of many personal and professional debts.

First, I want to thank those involved in the project from its origins. The guidance and insight of Dawn Marano, University of Utah press acquisitions editor, seamlessly moved this book from concept to publication. Her gracious manner and hard work made this endeavor a pleasure for everyone involved. Don Scheese helped get the ball rolling during some good talks around Lake Calhoun in Minneapolis, where I sketched out my ideas for the book. Cheryl Glotfelty suggested putting the request for proposals out on the ASLE e-mail distribution list, and did so.

Many others helped in completing the project. The peer reviewers, and especially W. Scott Olsen, provided an insightful critique of the manuscript. Ricki Degges, the copy editor, lent a keen eye to the project. I am grateful to the College of Arts and Humanities and the Department of English at Weber State University for their financial assistance in the production of this book. And I especially want to thank the contributors for their diligent work in making this collection a success.

A few good professors whose commitment to teaching stimulated my interest in the subject are Rob Farnsworth and the late John Mizner at Colby College, and Jeffrey Berman and Helen Regueiro Elam at the University at Albany, State University of New York. Once I began teaching, others lent their wisdom and friendship, including my former colleagues at Gustavus Adolphus College in Minnesota and those in the English department at Weber State University who have made me feel warmly welcomed in a new place. And thanks to all those members of the Association for the Study of Literature and Environment (ASLE) and the Western Literature Association (WLA) for giving me a scholarly and creative camp in the otherwise cold wilderness of academia.

Sticking to writing and editing requires quality recreation with quality people. Thanks to those who kept my passion for the outdoors alive while skiing, hiking, biking, camping, and running rivers with me over the years. You know who you are.

Lastly, thanks to my parents, Henry Crimmel and Ann Goodwin Elmer, and my sister, Catharine, for their encouragement over the years. I am also grateful to my wife, Ingrid, for her support, and to my sweet little daughter, Natalia, for bringing so much joy into my life.

November 1, 2002
Salt Lake City, Utah

Teaching in the Field

An Introduction

NOTES FROM THE PAST

Tavernier Key, Florida, January, 1976.

Outside a soft breeze was blowing in off the Gulf, but the air in Captain Gay's living room smelled musty, as old Florida bungalows sometimes do. His house, filled with charts, compasses, mounted fish, spoke of the sea. A big nickel-plated revolver lay on a side table that, like the rest of his furniture, was finished with a heavy marine varnish that gave off an amber glow in the dim light. The small gold ring in his ear glittered as he chatted and flirted with the students. He was lean and brown, an older man embodying the raffish atmosphere of the Florida Keys in the 1970s— a little run down, a little dangerous. The students, who had befriended him the previous week at a local tavern, found him charming and full of local color. Too young to care about such things, and since no one was paying attention to me, I decided to pick up the gun. I had never held a real pistol before, and its heavy weight felt good in my hand, like a tightly packed snowball ready to be thrown. The polished steel of the trigger, cool and smooth against my finger, begged me to pull it, as triggers do, and so I turned and pointed that shiny gun at Captain Gay's chest.

I was just a ten-year-old kid, tagging along with my Dad during his January term philosophy course, but I did know the students' interest in Captain Gay was becoming a distraction. There had been other complications, too: our already Spartan fishing camp turned out to be badly rundown and infested with cockroaches. There were disputes with students about late nights at the tavern. There was a deep-sea fishing charter with a dilapidated vessel and a bleary-eyed captain; far offshore a heavy swell developed, and the students became too seasick to fish.

But so far this month no one had been seriously hurt, and since the revolver did not seem loaded, I thought we could have some fun. I came closer to Captain Gay and prepared to pull the trigger. I decided to say "Bang! You're dead," as the hammer came down with a loud click, as it did on my friends' toy guns at home, which would cause all the students to laugh. As I started to pull, though, someone reached out, took the pistol from me, and shook out six gold-plated shells. At that moment I felt that our group, quite literally, had dodged a bullet.

In retrospect, despite these real-world intrusions, the course provided a rare opportunity for students to absorb the special magic of the Keys, while thinking about the formation of values, the focus of this month-long course. Here, on an isolated key, thousands of miles from the distractions of campus, a course could be modeled on a life in a monastery, where study had a physical as well as an intellectual dimension. Students would be freed from the pressures and temptations of residential college life, and as a result might reflect more faithfully on the values they held. Here, students might be able to focus and attain clarity of thought in the elemental beauty of the Keys. There were deserted groves of key lime trees filled with tiny tart fruit, schools of barracuda off the end of the dock, ghostly translucent shrimp feeding by moonlight. Maybe it was just the warmth of the January sun, the gentle trades, the crunch of coral underfoot, the soft subtropical sky and gentle blue hues of water stretching in all directions. Maybe it was pure relief at having escaped the harsh northern New York winter. But I somehow understood that spending time outdoors had a beneficial effect on students and that the Keys had created a positive learning environment for them.

I did not know it then, but these days would serve later as a benchmark for my own undergraduate courses. Most of these, naturally, took place indoors in classrooms and laboratories, and I did not feel any connection to my studies until I went on a geology field trip. We loaded up a bus and headed out into one of those heartbreakingly beautiful New England fall afternoons: scarlet red sugar maples against crisp blue sky, fleeting late September sun warming the shadows in the cooling woods. As we absorbed the elegiac farewell to summer from our seats on fallen trees and glacier-scoured outcrops of Canadian Shield granite, these ancient rock formations, the subject of our trip, suddenly seemed a tangible part of a larger whole. Interactions with peers seemed relaxed and natural, far from the classroom. And I wanted more. The intellectual abstraction of my other courses was a receding tide that left me high and dry, far from the ebb and flow of the rest of the world.

On a gloomy October day a few weeks later, we traveled to Popham Beach, one of the few beaches on Maine's rocky coast. We came to see a rare geological feature known as a tombolo, a sandbar created when waves wrap around an island, collide, and deposit enough sand to form a land bridge between island and shore that becomes exposed at low tide. I remember the shadowy conifers at the edge of the deserted beach, the damp lick of heavy salt air, the dark wet overcast sky, the looming Maine winter. Here, place dissolved geology's scientific parameters: the poetic transcended the technical, raw nature absorbed science, and books finally met the land.

But I soon abandoned geology, for its demanding quantitative aspects—memorizing rocks, formations, crunching numbers, and so forth—erased from the equation the emotional impact of particular landscapes and places. And though English seemed a classroom discipline, one where eccentric types read depressing books and then met three times a week in a stuffy room to discuss them, I joined their ranks. Thus, aside from an occasional class on the steps outside the library in early fall or late spring, my undergraduate career took place indoors.

After graduation I began working on rivers in the summer and in the mountains in winter—physically and emotionally inspiring places. When I later turned to graduate school, I wondered if literature and writing courses could include a healthy dose of these outdoor environments and whether they could both enhance learning or even be the focus of a class. Being outdoors had seemed to stimulate and motivate students in Florida, and it captivated me in Maine, I recalled. Why not try it in a literature class? So as a graduate teaching assistant, I started taking my classes on short field trips—a Saturday morning here, an afternoon or evening there. These were not the traditional humanities field trips to theaters and museums and poetry readings, but rather trips into the outdoors. The other TAs, mostly theory-addled types addicted to the latest trends, smiled patronizingly when I shared my experiences.

But the students and I winter hiked in the Helderberg Mountains just south of the city of Albany. We explored how different forest ecosystems—clearings, mature stands of White Pine, brushy third growth—affect the imagination, and how sun, clouds, temperature, and wind change perceptions of place. Later we would read Hawthorne's "Young Goodman Brown," and take night walks through pockets of remaining forest near campus to a small clearing. There we would discuss the author's use of setting and his portrayal of wilderness.

Ernest Hemingway once said that he wanted his readers to feel more than they understood, the basis for his famous "iceberg principle," in which seven-eighths of the meaning of a story lies beneath the surface. It becomes the reader's task to articulate emotion, seek out the textual sources that give rise to it, and make sense of them. I like to think that during our nighttime classes in the woods, students felt the imaginative power the northern forest had on the population of colonial New England. Urban students, particularly those from New York City, were clearly apprehensive about going into the woods at night—and rightfully so. Many New Yorkers know that Central Park can be dangerous after dark. But the students from rural areas semed excited, perhaps because this little pocket of woods reminded them of places where they once escaped from the prying eyes of adults during their childhood and teenage years. Maybe they viewed the forest as a place to subvert the conventions of society, as do the inhabitants of Salem in "Young Goodman Brown." Perhaps both urban and rural students came to feel in these woods more than they understood, and found this sufficient motivation to work at developing a closer reading of the story.

But these were hunches. In 1991 there was little written about teaching arts and humanities outdoors, especially literature and writing courses. No English professors I knew took students on such trips, and I frequently wondered if doing so was a fringe practice with little precedent or justification. Only those in the sciences took students on field trips, and they conducted empirical studies on site. Imagine, I thought, if biology professors tried to make students feel more than they understood, say, by burning them with coals from a campfire as a way to motivate them to understand neurological processes. Unlikely. However, we do know that marrying pathos with logos is an important component of scientists' education, a notion that stretches back at least to the 1970s. As David Orr has more recently noted, "Often those who do comprehend our plight [the ecological crisis] intellectually cannot feel it, and hence they are not moved to do much about it."[1] In a similar fashion, I hoped my students' emotional engagement with the places we visited would stimulate them to engage intellectually as well.

And so, in succeeding years, during a series of one-year appointments in Minnesota, I worked in field trips each semester. The Mississippi River bluffs became a favorite site for nature-writing exercises. A creek on campus became the focus of a segment on environmental action, and my classes hauled out several dump trucks full of trash, mattresses, and construction debris. The next year we discussed Willa Cather's *My Ántonia* surrounded by a sea of restored tallgrass prairie on the campus arboretum.

Certainly we could have dissected the text in the classroom, under the fluorescent lights, as one might a frog in a laboratory. But a short walk let us experience the numinous spirit of the Great Plains found in the novel. In the late afternoon, when the setting sun fell over the tallgrass, students could glimpse the Great Plains as they seemed a century ago, and share in the characters' deep affection for the living prairie.

At other times, the challenges of teaching outdoors seemed to overshadow any benefits. During a "Literature of Winter" course held in January, for instance, we camped along the North Shore of Lake Superior. We tried to hold class as a powerful storm blew in off the lake, turning glassy calm into towering eight-foot waves that pounded the shoreline with heavy, shuddering blows. Discussion and writing both became impossible in the wind-driven snow and bitter temperatures. Starting a fire and cooking began as major challenges and quickly grew into a desperate undertaking.

The students' safety was another nagging concern. They skittered over ice-caked boulders along the shoreline, the heart-stopping cold of the clear water just feet away. Later, deep in the snow-cloaked woods along the Baptism River, one student sprained her knee and barely made it back to the trailhead. Another fell into the freezing water after breaking through thin ice on a small lake.

Failure to work as a team also created problems. As temperatures dropped, and the snow deepened, I could see many were in trouble because of inadequate outdoor gear. Despite workshops, a checklist, and a pre-trip inspection, the determined still smuggled in jeans and other cotton clothes, which quickly became sodden. The misery of a few vocal students began to affect the morale of the entire group. Then, at night, the rainfly blew off one tent. No one wanted to brave the storm to reattach it, and the heavy wind-driven snow quickly soaked the tent, its occupants, and their precious sleeping bags. The next day, a rogue faction spoiled the afternoon by whining about not being able to watch the Minnesota Vikings playoff game on TV at a nearby ranger station, then nearly skidded the van off the road and into a snowy ravine. At such moments one's meditations alternate between patience and vengeance.

GROUNDS FOR THE COLLECTION

I tell you these stories because the idea for this collection, like several of the essays presented here, grew out of personal experience, not library research. I wanted to gather ideas about teaching outdoors and organize them in such a way that college professors and graduate students alike, both those currently teaching in the field and those who would like to begin, could turn to one resource. I further wanted to work to establish broad-based pedagogical support for teaching non-science-based courses outdoors. It is my hope that this collection can help continue to legitimize field-based learning for those who are teaching literature or writing, or writing intensive courses across disciplines, or who are teachers of environmental studies or courses addressing human relationships with nature. It is my hope also that this collection can serve as a text for practitioners who wish to enlighten students, colleagues, and administrators to the value of teaching outdoors.

There are many more of us now than just a few decades ago, when few instructors outside of geology, anthropology, botany, forestry, or zoology were likely to venture into the field. But today, perhaps in a reflection of the ever-growing passion for the outdoors, teachers in many disciplines are venturing outside. In English and writing, for example, this interest is reflected in the growth of the Association for the Study of Literature and the Environment (ASLE) to over one thousand members worldwide, who are dedicated to the study of literature and the environment. As well, there are now over four hundred environmental-studies programs at U.S. and Canadian universities, and dozens of field institutes dedicated to outdoor-based higher learning.

But still, those who take or would like to take students outdoors must face a number of tough questions: Why take students outside the classroom as part of their learning? What are the justifications? How do students benefit, and why? What are some strategies for facilitating effective learning outside the classroom? How does taking students into the field benefit teachers, who have to serve on these trips as professor, dean of students, dining services director, counselor, and campus police, all rolled into one? What settings work best—urban, suburban, pastoral, wilderness? How does one go about planning field trips, running them smoothly, and bringing everybody home safely?

Outdoor education is well established at primary and secondary levels and in the area of field-based wilderness educational programs such as the National Outdoor Leadership School (NOLS) and Outward Bound. And though much continues to be written about these areas in such publications as the *Journal of Experiential Education*, there are relatively few resources for college-level practitioners—especially for those in the humanities—and most are scattered widely. In the summer of 1980, for instance, *The Journal of Environmental Education* ran a special section on wilderness education, with an editorial by Roderick Nash. In 1985 Fred Waage's *Teaching Environmental Literature*[2] appeared, containing a four-essay section on field-based teaching in the context of environmental literature. *Ecopsychology: Restoring the Earth, Healing the Mind,*[3] published in 1995, contained three essays relevant to the practice of teaching outdoors. Then, in 1999, as part of its nature literacy series, the Orion Society published *Into the Field: A Guide to Locally Focused Teaching,*[4] a collection of three instructional essays. In 2001, several pertinent essays appeared in the collection *Ecocomposition: Theoretical and Practical Approaches.*[5] The annotated bibliography found at the end of this collection provides information on these and other relevant texts.

It is my intention to build on that base of knowledge. The following essays discuss courses taught at a variety of institutions, and all use the outdoors as a site or subject of instruction. Not every class was perfect or an immediate success—an important lesson for new practitioners as well as for the experienced. Taking students out of the classroom has some similarities to a child finding a loaded pistol and then wanting to fire it: in outdoor settings it is impossible to predict what students will find, whether the pistol will be loaded, and whether someone will be shot. Group dynamics, automobiles, weather, terrain, and illness all affect field learning in ways they do not in four-walled classrooms. Behavioral issues also are magnified in the field, where the freedom of being off campus and away from home can create temptations too great to resist. Students have been known to drink to excess, wreck motel rooms, set fires, trash government property, and generally misbehave. I do not gratuitously mention such behavior. These are serious concerns that have legal and professional implications for the faculty members who are accountable for their students' actions. Teaching outdoors presents a set of new challenges for even the most veteran instructor. But with skill, grace, and a little luck, one can prevent most such situations from occurring and manage those that do.

THE COLLECTION

From the English Lake District to the Appalachian Trail, from tidewater Maryland to the Maine woods, from the north shore of Lake Superior to the Big Bend of Texas, from the Colorado Plateau to the streets of Cincinnati, the essays in this collection are as diverse as the geography from which they spring. Topics range from gender and the north woods, to wilderness education, to natural history, creative writing, and environ-

mental literature, to teaching urban nature, and others. Though many selections are directed at teachers of writing and literature, their crossover
appeal is great. Any instructor who uses writing as a tool in the field,
whether teaching in the humanities or social sciences, will find these essays
valuable. Readers also will find authors take diverse approaches to their
topics. Several essays are written as works of narrative scholarship, an exciting genre of writing rapidly gaining acceptance in the academy, while
others are more traditional works of scholarship.

The collection is organized into three parts. Part I, "Why Go?: Justifying Teaching Outdoors," addresses the question of whether there are
sound reasons for taking students outdoors. Those in the sciences have an
easier time answering this, says Alan Brew, but the endeavor is "more
troubling for those of us teaching in the humanities," in part because colleagues see "field courses as elaborate contrivances for a good time."[6] Part
I seeks to dispense with that notion by discussing the many benefits of
teaching beyond the classroom. We begin with Robert E. Burkholder's
essay "'To See Things in Their Wholeness': Consilience, Natural History,
and Teaching Literature Outdoors." The author describes his experiences
teaching on the Appalachian Trail to argue that "teaching literature and
related courses outside may be the last preserve of natural history, a pre-
technical engagement with the natural world that creates a sense of
wholeness for its practitioners."[7] We move to more arid climates in
"Teaching the Desert: The Literature of Landscape in and out of Place,"
by Charles Mitchell. The essay traces his "exploration of the literature of
landscape," through a discussion of "the desert as metaphor, analogy, and
case study" in the works of Austin, Abbey, Silko, and Ruess, and through
a field course taught in the American Southwest based on those authors.
Mitchell shows us how taking students to the places they read about provides a deeper critical appreciation for these texts. The next essay, by
Sierra Institute director R. Edward Grumbine, is entitled "Going to
Bashō's Pine: Wilderness Education for the Twenty-first Century." It provides a short overview of wilderness education, followed by a discussion of
the importance of educating "the whole person" by "connecting across
boundaries in four key relationships": place/learning, doing/knowing,
individual/group, and reflection/action. Alan Brew follows with "Where
Passions Intertwine: Teaching, Literature, and the Outdoors," a meditation on the passion that fuels his love of teaching outdoors, and one that
he hopes to instill in his students in order for them to make connections
between self, place, and text. This section concludes with "Engaging Nature: A Canadian Case Study of Learning in the Outdoors," by Brent

Cuthbertson, Janet Dyment, Lesley P. Curthoys, Tom G. Potter, and Tim O'Connell. We learn of four different course models for engaging nature in the Canadian outdoors, from those taught almost entirely in wilderness settings to short trips to "near nature," natural areas close to human settlement. The essay provides an excellent introduction to the range of outdoor teaching opportunities available to the college instructor, along with a rationale for each.

Part II, "Strategies for Teaching," provides readers with suggestions for field-based assignments, class sessions, and semester-length courses. From tidewater Maryland Katherine R. Chandler writes with ideas for helping students focus during outdoors sessions in environmental literature and composition courses. Her essay, "Can't See the Forest or the Trees: Finding Focus," gives us ideas for using drawing, tree shrines, and walking to help students zero in on their surroundings as a prerequisite to writing. Laird Christensen's essay, "Writing the Watershed," provides a community-focused, hands-on approach to solving environmental problems. He describes a course where students learn about Michigan's Pine River bioregion, a once-pristine watershed utterly fouled by agricultural and industrial pollution. The course seeks to deepen students' and area residents' knowledge of this watershed, with the hope that new understanding might bring about "profound changes" in the way local ecosystems are treated. Terry Gifford, in "Teaching Environmental Values through Creative Writing with School Children," then discusses steps in the creative writing process. He describes a weekend-long project designed to "raise awareness of environmental values" through creative nonfiction and poetry writing in the English Lake District. Liz Newbery and Bob Henderson contribute "Going Out as a Way In: Social, Cultural, and Ecological Learning and the University Field Trip," an essay suggesting teaching outdoors can lead students to critical awareness, which can then lead to personal and social change. The authors describe three separate field trips to illustrate how transformation might occur. In "On the Path, Off the Trail: Teaching Nature Writing as a Practice of the Wild," Fred Taylor explains four practices of writing—attentiveness, freedom to explore, receptivity, and openness to sharing—as central to teaching nature writing. An account of a weekend trip to a nature center on Cape Cod completes the piece. Part II concludes with an essay describing the links between students and the area where they live. Andrew Wingfield's "Road Trip: Self-Directed Field Work as a Learning Journey" asks students to conduct research in Virginia and elsewhere, as part of an independent fieldwork project tied to a course on roads and rivers.

Part III, "Field Considerations: Issues to Consider in Planning and Execution" is organized around the issues instructors face when planning and teaching courses with field components. How do we treat all students equally and ensure they treat one another in the same fashion? What factors should we consider when deciding on a suitable location and length of stay? How do we secure administrative support, plan menus, prepare for emergencies? This section begins with "Facing the Challenge: Overcoming the Common Obstacles to Running a Successful Field Studies Course," by Corey Lee Lewis. It provides readers with a step-by-step plan for "planning and executing a field studies course" by focusing on the five areas instructors must address: administrative, logistical, managerial, academic, and ethical. But even the best-laid plans can implode, as Allison B. Wallace cautions us in her essay "In Thoreau's Wake on the West Branch." In her recounting of a canoe trip on Maine's West Branch of the Penobscot, Wallace provides a reminder that field trips are not all sunshine and camaraderie. Next is Britain A. Scott and Steven M. Hoffman's discussion of an environmental studies program in Minnesota's north woods as a context to explore "the implications of outdoor education's 'manly' beginnings for educators working with coed or women's groups." Their essay, "Woodswomen and 'Super Studs': Gender Issues in a Northwoods Environmental Studies Program," then addresses the question of how to overcome gender stereotypes in outdoor education. This is followed by Barbara "Barney" Nelson's "Building Community on a Budget in the Big Bend of Texas," which explores how questions of environmental justice impact teaching literature and writing outdoors. The final essay in this section, and the last in the collection, is by John Tallmadge. His essay, "Urban Nature as a Scene of Instruction," explores the value of "urban landscapes as outdoor laboratories for exploring the interactions—physical, historical, and spiritual—between humans and other beings in nature" on the streets of Cincinnati. This important essay awakens us to the possibilities for taking students into urban environments and serves as a reminder that experiencing cities is also an important part of taking students outdoors. An annotated bibliography of sources relevant to the practice and theory of teaching outdoors completes the collection.

In closing, many readers will remember field trips that were important parts of their primary and secondary education—the field trips to look at bugs, trees, rivers, clouds, or historical sites, and then draw or write about them. But somewhere in the leap to university-level education this sun-on-the face, wind-in-the-hair, cold-feet-and-dirty-hands approach to learning vanished. This collection shares approaches for recovering that aspect of teaching and bringing it back into the main pedagogical current at colleges and universities. In so doing we can introduce the practice of field-based learning to new practitioners and continue to legitimize it for those teachers who have taken and will continue to take their students outdoors.

Notes

1. David W. Orr, "Reinventing Higher Education," in *Greening the College Curriculum: A Guide to Environmental Teaching in the Liberal Arts*, edited by Jonathan Collett and Stephen Karakashian (Washington, D.C.: Island Press, 1996), 11.

2. Fred Waage, ed., *Teaching Environmental Literature* (New York: MLA, 1985).

3. Theodore Roszak, Mary E. Gomes, and Allen D. Kanner, eds., *Ecopsychology: Restoring the Earth, Healing the Mind* (San Francisco: Sierra Club Books, 1995).

4. Clare Walker Leslie, John Tallmadge, and Tom Wessels, *Into the Field: A Guide to Locally Focused Teaching* (Great Barrington, Mass.: The Orion Society, 1999).

5. Christian R. Weisser and Sidney I. Dobrin, eds., *Ecocomposition: Theoretical and Practical Approaches* (Albany: State University of New York Press, 2001).

6. Alan Brew, e-mail to author, September 26, 2001.

7. Robert E. Burkholder, e-mail to author, Fall 2001.

References

Orr, David W. 1996. Reinventing higher education. In *Greening the College Curriculum: A Guide to Environmental Teaching in the Liberal Arts*, edited by Jonathan Collett and Stephen Karakashian, 8–23. Washington D.C.: Island Press.

PART I: Why Go?
Justifying Teaching Outdoors

Introduction to Part I

The essays in Part I, "Why Go?: Justifying Teaching Outdoors," explore the rationale for leaving the traditional classroom behind and heading outdoors. These five selections help to explain why teaching about the environment, the relationship with nature, and literature and writing is productive in the field. We begin with Robert E. Burkholder's "'To See Things in Their Wholeness': Consilience, Natural History, and Teaching Literature Outdoors." Burkholder maintains that immersing students in an outdoor experience helps them to understand textual abstractions in an "immediate and profound way." Further, he reasons that teaching outdoors can help to bridge the gap between theory and practice, and between the sciences and arts and humanities, through natural history, a neglected discipline that allows its practitioners to "see a thing in its wholeness."

Charles Mitchell follows with "Teaching the Desert: The Literature of Landscape in and out of Place," which asserts the fundamental importance of landscape in literature and in life. Mitchell tells us that though students' education prepares them "to deal with abstract ideas and feelings," they are "less well-prepared to engage the immediate, material contexts that give some of those ideas shape and resonance." Through an account of courses taught in the desert, he maintains we need to teach students to react to place as well as to texts and intellectual abstractions.

In the next essay, Sierra Institute director R. Edward Grumbine explains how wilderness education can be just that. "Going to Bashō's Pine: Wilderness Education for the Twenty-first Century" directs our attention to the value of experiential learning, in a world that privileges the traditional "empty vessel" model of higher education, where professors fill passive students with "expert knowledge." Grumbine asserts we must learn both by doing and by knowledge assimilation; to do so most effectively in academic wilderness education, instructors must work to connect "across boundaries in four key relationships: place/learning, doing/knowing, individual/group, and reflection/action."

Alan Brew takes a different path in "Where Passions Intertwine: Teaching, Literature, and the Outdoors." He tells us that teaching literature outdoors permits him to "teach fully and vulnerably from the heart," and that it permits a "vigorous connection between individuals and literary expressions of the human condition." Taking students on field courses in the southwestern deserts and the Minnesota north woods builds enduring links between self, place, others, and text, says Brew.

Such courses, whether taught wholly or partially in the outdoors, can contribute to human wellness, as Brent Cuthbertson, Janet Dyment, Lesley P. Curthoys, Tom G. Potter, and Tim O'Connell note. But the focus of their essay, "Engaging Nature: A Canadian Case Study of Learning in the Outdoors" is to work to refute the notion that "serious study and the 'distraction' of the outdoors are not compatible." They discuss four different course models for engaging nature in the Canadian outdoors, from "near nature" to wilderness, and they explain the value of each of these in facilitating student learning.

※ ROBERT E. BURKHOLDER

"To See Things in Their Wholeness"

Consilience, Natural History, and Teaching Literature Outdoors[1]

". . . [W]e see literature from the midst of wild nature, or from the din of affairs, or from a high religion. The field cannot be well seen from within the field."

—Emerson, "Circles"

It's 3:30 A.M. on Saturday, April 7, 2001, at the Dahlgren Backpack Campground near Boonsboro, Maryland. I am sound asleep in my tent, deep inside the peace that comes from drifting off to the rhythmic thumping of rain on a waterproof nylon tent fly. But I am called away from that restfulness by a whispered but persistent female voice coming from just the other side of the thin nylon tent walls: "Dr. B., Dr. B., Angelique is really sick." This was repeated over and over by Angelique's worried tent mate, Stacy, until I groggily muttered that I'd be there in a minute. When I emerged from the tent, Stacy led me to the cinder-block restroom where Angelique was crying, unable to stand, sit, or lie down because of an incredible pain in the middle of her back. I talked with her for a few minutes, asked her if she wanted to try to fight through the pain, and she said she would try. She took a few Tylenol and headed back to her tent. But twenty minutes later, just as I was about to fall off to sleep again, I could hear Angelique crying nearby. This time, I was far quicker in responding to Stacy's worried call. And this time Angelique said that the pain was too intense; she wanted to go to the hospital.

I was section-hiking the Appalachian Trail through Maryland, the easiest stretch of the entire 2,167-mile trail according to most guidebooks, as a capstone experience to a Penn State English Department Senior Seminar on "The Literature and Culture of the Appalachian Trail" that had been figuratively thru-hiking the trail since classes began in early January. We were using *The Appalachian Trail Reader* as our central text, had begun at Springer Mountain, Georgia, with James Dickey's poem of that title, and had read our way northward, with pauses in our progress toward Mt. Katahdin for reading Annie Dillard's *Pilgrim at Tinker Creek*, poetry by Whitman and Frost, Stephen King's *The Girl Who Loved Tom Gordon,* and three thru-hike narratives, including Bill Bryson's *A Walk in the Woods* and Robert Alden Rubin's *On the Beaten Path.* We had, in fact, begun our field trip at the Appalachian Trail Conference Headquarters in Harper's Ferry, West Virginia, where Rubin himself, now the editor of the ATC's *Appalachian Trailway News,* had greeted us, given us a pep talk, autographed copies of his book, and sent us on our way.

With me were thirteen students, all English majors, who would be graduating at the end of the semester. Many in that thirteen had limited or no exposure to hiking or backpacking, and despite my best efforts to prepare them for the physical and mental demands of a fairly long hike and to make sure they all were at least marginally fit for the trek, I could tell from the start that the trek wasn't going to be easy. This was a group that needed frequent cigarette breaks and time for lengthy discussions of whether the golden sunset we saw at Weverton Heights that sunny and warm first day out actually constituted "the sublime." We had, by the way, already rejected Thomas Jefferson's claims in *Notes on the State of Virginia* that the view from what is now called Jefferson Rock in Harpers Ferry is "one of the most stupendous scenes in nature" (quoted in Emblidge 1996, 176). We were, I think, actually practicing as a class what John Tallmadge calls "reading natural history" by bringing our reading and class discussion to a direct and fully engaged experience of the Appalachian Trail in the mid-Atlantic at the beginning of its spring blossoming. But the potential hazards seemed much less significant than our cumulative joy that we had actually pulled this trip off, had escaped from State College and classes for a few days and were going to be outside at the very moment that spring seemed to be announcing its arrival.

I had tried a similar hike, although not nearly so ambitious, in the spring of 1998 in a Senior Seminar on wilderness literature, hiking a fourteen-mile loop around the Hickory Creek Wilderness in the Allegheny National Forest in northwestern Pennsylvania. Then my group had been much smaller and decidedly more experienced, including a male student who had lived in Alaska and explored some of its wilderness, and a female veteran of an Outward Bound course. Even though most of the students in the Appalachian Trail course were novices, we were still optimistic that we could hike the forty miles between Harpers Ferry and the Mason-Dixon Line between Thursday afternoon and Sunday afternoon. In that way, we would experience some of the distance demands placed on thru-hikers (who have to average eleven miles a day for six months to complete the AT in a single hiking season) but also have enough leisure to enjoy ourselves and to learn a little about the history and ecology of the area through which we planned to hike, an area that has historical connections to the Revolutionary and Civil Wars and is now rumored to be criss-crossed with secret radar and communications facilities associated with Camp David in the nearby Catoctin Mountains.

That's what we had hoped.

But the hike up Weverton Heights (an elevation gain of about one thousand feet over two miles of switchbacks) left about a third of the student hikers gasping and sweating at the top of the grade and not wanting to take the time to hike the short distance to the scenic overlook that allowed one to survey the four miles or so we had just hiked along the Potomac River from Harpers Ferry. Then, that first night in the newly built Ed Garvey Shelter, some students grumbled when they discovered that it was a quarter-mile hike to the nearest water source, and a few of the least prepared shivered through a chilly April night in the open-fronted shelter. The next morning, as we prepared for our first full day of AT hiking, the clouds began to roll in, and five minutes down the trail from the shelter, it began to rain. Mostly it was a drizzle, but periodically it seemed as if the clouds opened up, so that by the time we reached Gathland State Park and stopped for lunch, we built a fire in the fireplace of the picnic pavilion to get warm and fight off the effects of the chilling rain. Needless to say, some students' cheap rain gear failed them almost immediately, so a few hikers needed to change clothes and dry out before we could head for the Dahlgren Campground, our destination for that day. Already, the warm sunshine and joy of only eighteen hours before were forgotten, and despite the end of the rain and the arrival of the sun in midafternoon, several of the students were suffering the realization that a forty-mile hike is no picnic. That evening as we ate our dinners and assessed how everyone was doing, it became clear that several of the students could not go much farther; in at least a couple of cases, tender feet were sore and bedeviled by blisters. We agreed as a group to modify our goal, to hike only to the next shelter the following day and then be picked up early on Sunday.

So even if Angelique had not gotten sick, we had already decided to acknowledge our newly understood capabilities and be happy with our modest accomplishments to that point and cut back on our expectations:

Over the mild objections of a few students we would cut our hike to about twenty-five miles. So ending the outing after Angelique's trip to the hospital was not of enormous consequence. Still, as I waited for the ambulance to arrive in the parking lot of a restaurant on U.S. Route Alternate 40 in the darkness at 5:00 in the morning; and later, as I struggled to answer questions from hospital personnel about how I was related (or not related) to the patient I had accompanied to the hospital in the ambulance; and as I sat in the hospital waiting room in my smoky clothing and scraggly two-day beard, I did ask myself just why I insisted on taking my students on these class treks. The field trips invariably cost me time and money, and English majors often seem genetically predisposed to the coffee shop, bookstore, and library. I was lucky this time: Angelique had had a kidney-stone attack and would be just fine when she was re-hydrated and the morphine wore off. As soon as I worked out the logistics, I would be able to take her and the students packing their gear and awaiting word from me at the soggy Dahlgren Campground back to State College. Still, it could have been worse, and that thought alone led me to consider the reasons for wanting to teach courses that contain an outdoor, experience-based component, whether that component is the focal point of the entire course, as it is with The Penn State Wilderness Literature Field Institute, a summer course that I began three years ago, or a standard course that "piggybacks" outdoor experience, to borrow John Elder's term (1999, 27), like "The Literature and Culture of the Appalachian Trail" course I've been describing.

While the reasons I do such courses may have seemed less than apparent to me in my wee-hours-of-the-morning exhaustion in the emergency room of a county hospital, in my more alert moments those reasons are never far out of mind. Of course, to me and to others who do them, such courses are personally rewarding. Right now I can turn from my computer screen and look at a collage of photographs taken with students in a variety of beautiful natural places. What's more, I actually like the deprivations and inconveniences of the trail. I don't mind not having access to a shower for a few days or missing a shave for a week or two. I have considerable tolerance for less-than-five-star cuisine and, in fact, don't mind at all a sustained diet of food that almost always makes a post-trip stop at a fast-food restaurant something to look forward to. But beyond my personal tolerance for and love of roughing it, I am always rewarded by my students' responses, as they are recorded in their trail journals.

After the aforementioned Senior Seminar trip to the Hickory Creek Wilderness in spring 1998, I decided I'd devote the first class after our return to a post-trip wrap-up, asking each of the students who went on the hike to summarize the experience and its value to him or her. This group of students had been at times hard to get through to—"senioritis," more than one of them explained when I expressed my frustration—and my expectations for their responses to the field experience weren't high. The trip itself had been a relatively quick one (only about thirty-six hours); it had rained the first and only night out, forcing everyone into their tents early without the community-building benefit of a campfire. Not long after we started our hike the next morning we had to crawl over more than a half mile of blown-down trees in order to get back to the trailhead and our cars without backtracking. All in all, it didn't seem to be the makings of a life-changing experience to me, but to most of them it was. The comments that David Jarecki wrote in his journal were unexpectedly typical:

> I still have a sense of spiritual lift whenever I find myself in isolation in the woods, along a stream, near the ocean, or under a pink sky at sunrise. At times I could feel God's breath on my neck. When I stopped to sit on the big rock during the hike, I heard God whispering in the thick silence. I don't really know. I'm just glad I took so many pictures with my mind's camera and not with a Kodak. Paper and film are no ways to relive the experience!

For many reasons, then—the pertinence of the experience to the subject matter of the course, the chance for students to get to know their classmates, the defamiliarizing effect of the outdoor experience itself and the solitude it can afford—most students have positive feelings about trips to the field, and many stay in touch with me and with each other years after the trip has ended, suggesting that it's a part of their college experience that is both unforgettable and important to them. In other words, I'm convinced that teaching outdoors enhances whatever effectiveness I might have in the classroom by giving students an experiential hook on which to hang ideas and assumptions arrived at through the conventional course activities of assigned reading and lecture and discussion in the classroom.

A final reason, and one that I want to explore at greater length in this article, is that of filling a gap in the education offered by most American colleges and universities. My university has scores of majors and other programs, and it prides itself in part on its comprehensiveness. However, it offers very little beyond my own courses and those of a handful of colleagues that bridges the gap between theoretical and practical education or between the concerns of the arts or humanities and those of the sciences. What I'm describing is, according to a number of recently published essays,[2] a space that was for more than a century filled by natural history, a discipline and practice no longer recognized by science and one largely ignored by the liberal arts. I for one believe the practice of natural history to be important, even a necessity, and I believe that in my own field-study courses I'm at least opening the unifying possibilities of natural history to my literature students.

First, though, I want to consider why those of us who teach courses outdoors generally represent them, in articles like this one, as though there are no liabilities in teaching such courses or risks involved in taking a group of adult or near-adult students to the mountains, or rivers, or deserts. Was my experience with Angelique's illness unique, or are risks inherent in outdoor education? Obviously, I don't intend to critique the teaching strategy of combining the study of literature with outdoor experience; I have personally found the combination to be a highly effective pedagogical tool, especially when the goal of helping our students to consider or even to imaginatively project themselves into the place of the Other they are trying to learn about and to understand is so difficult. Simply stated, taking students into the field gives them a context and experience from which to challenge "the deepest held mythologies of the dominant culture" that C. A. Bowers says are inherent in public school and university education (1997, 18). There are few pedagogical methodologies that are more effective than immersing a student in an experience that engages all the senses in a manner that helps him or her to understand the abstraction of the text in a much more immediate and profound way than one can hope for in a classroom. David W. Orr has referred to this as "a merger of landscape and mindscape" and suggested that such a merger is one of the goals of ecological education" (1992, 86). However, I do believe that any prospective teacher of such courses should judiciously consider why he or she wants to adopt such an approach and understand at the outset that as with any technology there are liabilities and benefits to this one. There are, after all, few courses in the standard curriculum in which the instructor must know something about post-structuralism, CPR, romanticism, and how to stretch a few packages of Ramen noodles into a tasty, filling, and nutritional dinner for ten.

In his fine account of the successes of the field-based courses of the Sierra Institute, Greg Gordon proves my point by neglecting to mention that those successes always come at the cost of accepting and dealing with the risks of taking a class outdoors. "Nearly 30 percent of the students state on the evaluations that it changed their lives," institute director R. Edward Grumbine is quoted as saying. "Students also respond that it helps them understand their place in nature and helps focus their academic track, often directly relating to subject matter they were exposed to on the program" (quoted in Gordon 1999, 14). I have had similar successes in the field-study courses I've taught; however, what I find most interesting in Gordon's article is the suggestion that his rhetorical approach is occasioned by the lack of respect given to field-based teaching within the university. Gordon says, "While students consistently respond that they learned more on Sierra Institute than any other course in their academic career, field studies programs remain on the periphery of academia because of their interdisciplinary approach and wilderness setting" (1999, 14). In so saying, Gordon indirectly articulates one of the greatest liabilities of teaching a course with a field-studies component—the substance of the course itself is devalued, and it is viewed as a less than serious academic endeavor. One reason for this is, as David W. Orr tells us, our cultural belief that "education is solely an indoor activity" (1992, 87).

My point is simply this: Those of us who have adopted teaching outdoors as a component of our pedagogy have found it to be so effective that we want to convince our colleagues of its value, but that has proven difficult for reasons similar to those that Orr believes serve as roadblocks to teaching ecological literacy. Besides the generally held belief that education can occur only indoors, the other obstacles Orr cites include the emphasis on specialization in higher education, a decline in aesthetic appreciation that has desensitized us to the ugliness of abused and disordered landscapes, and the political threat that seeing things "in their wholeness" presents to the established order (1992, 87–88). Teaching a literature class outdoors is so far beyond the accepted paradigms for the way in which literature is taught in universities that I don't have to go out of my way to point up its risks or liabilities or otherwise emphasize how a given field-study course varies from the conventional course. In my interaction with other departments in the university, their response has been to look on the endeavor of teaching literature outdoors with considerable skepticism, both as to my motives and the potential effectiveness of my pedagogy. That is clearly what the administrators in the Geology Department thought when one of their graduate students on stipend signed up for the first of my Penn State Wilderness Literature Field Institutes in spring 2000. Ordinarily, this graduate student's departmental support would have covered the tuition for any 400-level course, and that is how the Field Institute was designated—English 497. The student was noticeably excited at the prospect of studying literature related to his interests while backpacking, something he had loved doing for years. And his disappointment was just as noticeable when he called me a few weeks later to tell me that his department wouldn't pay for him to take my course because it wasn't serious enough.

The first fumbling attempts I made at incorporating outdoor experience into my courses were met with skepticism, if not disdain, from many of my colleagues in the English Department. One of the first of these attempts, a wilderness literature course for American Studies students in the fall of 1997, included a weekend hike in the Hickory Creek Wilderness, the only federally designated wilderness area of any size in the entire state of Pennsylvania. Even though we read all of Roderick Nash's *Wilderness and the American Mind,* Abbey's *Desert Solitaire,* Leopold's *A Sand County Almanac,* Thoreau's *The Maine Woods,* Anne LaBastille's *Woodswoman,* and substantial portions of David Rothenberg's collection, *Wild Ideas;* even though the class met in a classroom three times a week for fifteen weeks, wrote papers, and took exams, the course was, I believe, generally viewed as a "camping course." When I took this course to Penn State's Schreyer Institute for Innovative Teaching, I got the support I sought but also the suggestion that I should lead my class into the woods during blizzards or other life-threatening conditions in order to teach my students how risky wilderness experience can be. I took the Schreyer Institute's grant to pay for a graduate assistant, but I didn't take all of the advice offered. I have no doubt that the advice was meant to be constructive, but it also rather transparently reveals the way in which the innovative teachers on the institute's board understood and valued my course and my methodology. To them a literature course with a backpacking component must be about extreme behavior and taking physical risks and not about considering language, ideas, and even behavior that points one beyond the assumptions of the dominant culture toward a world where healthier human/nature relationships are possible. In other words, the intention of my course was to give my students what David W. Orr has labeled the brief chance "to see things in their wholeness" (1992, 88). Obviously, such an intention makes any course a very serious endeavor.

The Sierra Institute director, R. Edward Grumbine, has implied as much in defending his program's field-based courses from the charge that they are experiential and, therefore, without academic substance or merit: "There is an immediate value judgment placed on field studies programs that they are 'experiential.' . . . The dichotomy between experiential and

academic education is false. . . . We try to wed them into a seamless whole
. . . to engage the head as well as the heart and change the mind-set that
breeds this dichotomy" (quoted in Gordon 1999, 11). Grumbine's thinking suggests David W. Orr's idea that the mission of the Liberal Arts is "to
develop balanced, whole persons" (1992, 100–101), a mission that Orr
believes goes unfulfilled because of higher education's almost obsessive
concentration on educating only students' intellects:

> Technical education and liberal arts have been consigned to different insti-
> tutions that educate different parts of the anatomy. What passes for higher
> learning deals with the neck up and only half of that, technical schools the
> remainder. This division creates the danger that students in each, in [J.
> Glenn] Gray's words, "miss a whole area of relation to the world."[3] For lib-
> eral arts students, it also undermines an ancient source of good thought:
> the friction between an alert mind and practical experience. Abstract
> thought, "mere book learning," in Whitehead's words, divorced from prac-
> tical reality and the facts of life, promotes pedantry and mediocrity. It also
> produces half-formed or deformed persons: thinkers who cannot do, and
> doers who cannot think. (Orr 1992, 101)

Orr's argument provides a rationale for the place of field-study courses
or courses that have a field-study component in the contemporary college
or university, but it also clarifies why my own courses are misunderstood,
devalued, or dismissed as not serious. Moreover, Orr's comments seem to
me to have resonances of an intellectual tradition that values a pedagogy
that aims to both see things in their wholeness and produce whole persons. It certainly seems to echo Emerson's assessment in "The American
Scholar" of the monstrous results of a society that has fragmented human
wholeness: "The state of society is one in which the members have suffered amputation from the trunk, and strut about so many walking mon-
sters,—a good finger, a neck, a stomach, an elbow, but never a man"
(1957, 64). Similarly Orr's comments seem related to Paul Shepard's observations in *Nature and Madness* that our culture inhibits us from reaching biological maturity, thus leaving us alienated from and maladjusted to
the world in which we live (Shepard 1998, 14–15).

Orr's argument also echoes Thoreau's critique of education. Clearly concerned that education in his time tended to focus too much on the student's
intellect, Thoreau wrote in the "Economy" chapter of *Walden* that he believed that colleges should teach students how to live in a world that demands our physical engagement as well as engagement with our intellect:

"But," says one, "you do not mean that students should go to work with their hands instead of their heads?" I don't mean that exactly, but I mean something which he might think a great deal like that; I mean that they should not *play* life, or study it merely, while the community supports them at this expensive game, but earnestly *live* it from beginning to end.

(1973, 51)

It may, of course, seem as though Thoreau is suggesting a sort of vocational component for higher education, something that seems reinforced by asking us to think about who learns more, "the boy who had made his own jack-knife from the ore which he dug and smelted . . . or the boy who attended lectures on metallurgy at the Institute in the mean while, and had received a Rodgers' penknife from his father?" (Thoreau 1973, 51). In light of Thoreau's description of his own vocations in the "Economy" chapter—that is, a keeper of a journal, an inspector of thunderstorms, a herdsman of the town's wild stock, etc.—isn't it reasonably clear that Thoreau is not advocating vocationalism at all but rather as full an engagement with the experience of living as possible, physical as well as mental? In other words, isn't he, like Orr, demanding an education that aims at wholeness?

In fact, while Thoreau places most of his emphasis on the necessity of physical engagement and action in expressing his thoughts on what constitutes the most effective education, he doesn't ignore the intellect, implicitly suggesting that the best education occurs in the middle ground between the theoretical and vocational, a space that also unifies the concerns of the poet and scientist. To Laura Dassow Walls, Thoreau's imagining of such a space where all knowledge is unified marks Thoreau as one influenced by the work of William Whewell, the nineteenth-century philosopher of science who invented the term "consilience" to name the process by which science and poetry are united (Walls 1995, 11). This term was used, then, by E. O. Wilson, as the title of his 1996 book that, like Whewell's work, aims to describe a process that unifies knowledge. On a much less ambitious and less abstract level, the field-study course has similar aims. When I am in the field with my literature students we bring our discussions of poetry, history, and other products of culture to nature, and the context makes all the difference in showing the students how the linkage of those seemingly disparate things actually provides a very real way to pursue and even glimpse the goal of wholeness.

From my own observations and the written comments of my students, I am convinced that "consilience" is at least a possibility and that such possibility is revealed in the way in which my students react in and to the natural world. As one might expect, sometimes short trips into the backcountry breed a sort of immediate homesickness, the kind of longing for music or television most often revealed in the conversations students have among themselves during breaks along the trail or around a campfire. But it's surprising too that students invariably find ways not related to consumerism or electronic pop culture to relate to each other and the world beyond human culture.

Despite the fact that my ill-fated Appalachian Trail field trip occurred only a few weeks before the end of the spring semester, many students reported feeling good about the trip because they were given the opportunity to know and get closer to classmates. Ryan Peterson, one of the students in the group, wrote in his journal that he "believed that the trail managed to create several friendships among my classmates in a very short time. Perhaps it was the campfire atmosphere that pulled everyone together, or it may have been the fact that we all stunk and if we were going to stink, by golly we were going to stink as a group." This sense of group identity was expressed by many in the seminar after the field trip, and I wondered just what was lost—how alienated students must be—in the all-too-typical large lecture courses. In mega-universities like Penn State even our small classes do little to instill a sense of community and so our students graduate without that sense and without the means to find community with other people or with the natural world. After one of my trips with a wilderness literature class to the Hickory Creek Wilderness, a student wrote on a trip evaluation form that it was "a great experience where I got to meet all the people in my classroom in a different setting. Since then the students act and speak to each other differently (in a good way)."

One of the small miracles of the Appalachian Trail trip was finding a veteran thru-hiker, David Atkinson (a.k.a. "Fannypack '96"), at the Ed Garvey Shelter our first night out. Fannypack, a student of AT literature and lore, loved my students because they had read and wanted to talk about books about the Appalachian Trail experience that he had also read. He was tuning up, testing new gear and hiking long distances each day, for a Pacific Crest Trail hike that he would start in a couple of months, and so the second day he hiked ahead of us, got to the Dahlgren Campground long before we did, and hitchhiked to a grocery store to buy the ingredients to treat the class to hot dogs, chips, and cookies. Fannypack was not only a thru-hiker, but a "trail angel," someone who goes out of his way to contribute to the bond that AT hikers feel for each other. As the members of my class walked or stumbled into camp, they were greeted by Fannypack, sitting on a picnic table, a couple of pounds of hot dogs cooking in a pot on top of his propane stove and a welcoming smile on his face, inviting them to eat. *Voila*, instant community!

Community, of course, is not limited to human company, but certainly plays a role in the ways in which students engage with their natural surroundings. Students have sometimes expressed to me a fear of having nothing to do and of being bored out on the trail. To be truthful, occasionally they are. But I'm frequently pleased when students engage the natural world enough to entertain themselves, a first step, perhaps, in developing a sense of community with that world, a movement toward that middle ground where self and nature, science and poetry, are unified. Examples of this sort of engagement usually involve a student's curiosity about the flora and fauna encountered on the trail. I've had students stop along the trail to study salamanders or to examine a mountain laurel flower. On a spring trip to the Hickory Creek Wilderness, we ate our lunch the first day in a meadow dotted with vernal pools. Several of the students sitting by one of those pools discovered that it and all the others were loaded with gelatinous clumps of frog eggs that literally hummed with new life. On our return, a student wrote, "The whole trip was great, but seeing the frogs was best."

A few summers ago, during the Wilderness Literature Field Institute, which features a week-long backpack trip into the Dolly Sods Wilderness in the Monongahela National Forest in West Virginia, I happily watched my students attentively observing, as though it were a television soap opera, a battle between an injured moth and some ants. Perhaps after nearly a week outside the students were starved for dramatic conflict of some sort, but I'd like to believe that their interest in that insect battle was part of a process of reaching out of themselves and beyond their culture to establish a sense of community with nature.

Recently, there have been numerous articles lamenting the demise of natural history, especially in higher education. One of the first of these, David S. Wilcove's and Thomas Eisner's "The Impending Extinction of Natural History," argues that the "deinstitutionalization of natural history looms as one of the biggest scientific mistakes of our time" because it is accompanied by an ever-increasing emphasis on laboratory work that doesn't allow the scientist to see a thing in its wholeness (2000, B24). In his essay "The Rise and Fall of Natural History: How a Science Grew that Eclipsed Direct Experience," the ecologist and nature writer Robert Michael Pyle takes the concerns of Wilcove and Eisner a bit further in his expression of fear over a loss of direct experience and "a nuanced, responsive awareness of the very earth we inhabit."[4] According to Pyle, "As the distance grows between a tiny priesthood who know small parts of nature very well and a massive population who know next to nothing about the whole and not even the names of their neighbors, a right relationship with the world seems more and more elusive" (2001, 23). In his essays on the need to restore natural history to the college curriculum, the naturalist Thomas Lowe Fleischner has argued that natural history is the parent of several modern sciences, of psychology, and of literature (1999, 82; 2001–2002, 11), thus implying that it is, in fact, that middle ground between science and poetry where wholeness is indeed possible. In defining natural history as "a practice of intentional, focused attentiveness and receptivity to the more-than-human world" (2001–2002, 11), Fleischner suggests the same sort of attentiveness that I have observed time and again among the students I take outdoors to study. Whether we are teaching literature or biology, the most important thing we can do as teachers in the "post-natural world," as Bill McKibben calls it, is to afford our students the opportunity to experience nature directly. And that direct experience, as I have tried to argue here, may give them a kind of perspective on our world and its future that is becoming increasingly rare in today's university.

Any questioning I may do of the reasons for and benefits of taking my Penn State literature students outside is resolved in knowing that in an increasingly fragmented world—a world reflected in and perpetuated by the preponderance of what our students take away from college—the opportunity to glimpse the sort of wholeness that one can see only when things, including ourselves, are viewed within their larger, natural context is rare. I certainly have my occasional doubts that teaching literature outside is worth the effort. My trip in an ambulance down South Mountain from the Appalachian Trail to a hospital emergency room one early Saturday morning in April 2001 was one of those occasions. I was concerned, then, that in having to end our trip early and in exposing my students to a weekend of discomfort or pain and on-again-off-again rain, I may have been counterproductively demonstrating that it is better to stick close to home, to the stereo and television, and to the parties and bars of our university town. Angelique had taken my course because she didn't know much about nature, had not been outside much, and she wanted to know if she liked it. I worried that overcast April Saturday morning that she would always associate the natural world with sickness and middle-of-the-night rescues. This, however, is what she wrote in her journal when we returned:

Despite my medical emergency and all of my complaining, I look back on the trip as a great experience—and yes, a fun one. I got to know some really interesting people, and I felt their support in every way. We all looked out for each other and that's what made it a learning experience. I learned that I could hike more than 15 miles in less than two days; that I had friends I never knew about before; that I could do something I thought I never could, and want to do it again. In fact, I would do it all over again—without the kidney stone, though—especially if I could do it with these people. . . .

As the saying goes, that which does not kill us makes us stronger. I may not be stronger physically, but I feel I have strengthened my self-confidence, and that is why I look back on the hike as a positive experience. So who's going to be around this summer? Wanna go for a hike?

Notes

1. I would like to thank the students in my spring 1998 English 487W course, Senior Seminar in Wilderness Literature, The Penn State Wilderness Literature Field Institute in the summer of 2000, and my spring 2001 English 487W course, Senior Seminar in the Literature and Culture of the Appalachian Trail. My special thanks to Angelique Flynn, David Jarecki, and Ryan Peterson for allowing me to quote from their journals.

2. The essays I am thinking of are those by Wilcove and Eisner (2000), Lopez (2001), Pyle (2001), Thomashow (2001), and Fleischner (1999, 2001–2002).

3. Orr is referring to Gray's *Re-thinking American Education* (1984, 34).

4. Pyle's essay, along with those of Lopez and Thomashow, is part of a recent issue of *Orion* dedicated to the question "Why Natural History?"

References

Abbey, Edward. (1968) 1971. *Desert solitaire: A season in the wilderness.* New York: Ballantine Books.

Bowers, C. A. 1997. *The culture of denial: Why the environmental movement needs a strategy for reforming universities and public schools.* Albany: State University of New York Press.

Bryson, Bill. 1998. *A walk in the woods: Rediscovering America on the Appalachian Trail.* New York: Broadway Books.

Dillard, Annie. (1974) 1998. *Pilgrim at Tinker Creek*. New York: Perennial Classics.

Elder, John. *See* In pursuit of a bioregional curriculum: An interview with John Elder.

Emblidge, David, ed. 1996. *The Appalachian Trail reader*. New York: Oxford University Press.

Emerson, Ralph Waldo. 1957. *Selections from Ralph Waldo Emerson: An organic anthology*. Edited by Stephen E. Whicher. Boston: Houghton Mifflin.

Fleischner, Thomas Lowe. 1999. Revitalizing natural history. *Wild Earth* 9 (2): 81–89.

———. 2001–2002. Natural history and the spiral offering. *Wild Earth* 11 (3/4): 10–13.

Gordon, Greg. 1999. Wilderness U. *Orion Afield* 3 (2): 10–14.

Gray, J. Glenn. 1984. *Re-thinking American education: A philosophy of teaching and learning*. Middletown: Wesleyan University Press.

In pursuit of a bioregional curriculum: An interview with John Elder. *Orion Afield* 3 (2) (1999): 26–28.

King, Stephen. 2000. *The girl who loved Tom Gordon: A novel*. New York: Pocket Books.

LaBastille, Anne. (1978) 1991. *Woodswoman: Living alone in the Adirondack wilderness*. New York: Penguin.

Leopold, Aldo. (1949) 1970. *A Sand County almanac*. New York: Ballantine Books.

Lopez, Barry. 2001. The naturalist. *Orion* 20 (4): 38–43.

McKibben, Bill. 1989. *The end of nature*. New York: Random House.

Nash, Roderick. 1982. *Wilderness and the American mind*. Third Edition. New Haven: Yale University Press.

Orr, David W. 1992. *Ecological literacy: Education and the transition to a postmodern world*. Albany: State University of New York Press.

Pyle, Robert Michael. 2001. The rise and fall of natural history: How a science grew that eclipsed direct experience. *Orion* 20 (4): 16–23.

Rothenberg, David, ed. 1995. *Wild ideas*. Minneapolis: University of Minnesota Press.

Rubin, Robert Alden. 2000. *On the beaten path: An Appalachian pilgrimage*. New York: Lyons Press.

Shepard, Paul. 1998. *Nature and madness*. Athens: University of Georgia Press. Original edition, San Francisco: Sierra Club Books, 1982.

Tallmadge, John. 2000. Toward a natural history of reading. *ISLE: Interdisciplinary Studies in Literature and the Environment* 7 (1): 33–45.

Thomashow, Mitchell. 2001. A biospheric natural history. *Orion* 20 (4): 24–37.

Thoreau, Henry David. *Walden*. 1973. Edited by J. Lyndon Shanley. Princeton: Princeton University Press.

———. 1988. *The Maine Woods*. New York: Penguin.

Walls, Laura Dassow. 1995. *Seeing new worlds: Henry David Thoreau and nineteenth-century science*. Madison: University of Wisconsin Press.

Wilcove, David S., and Thomas Eisner. 2000. The impending extinction of natural history. *The Chronicle of Higher Education* 15 (September): B24.

Wilson, Edward O. 1998. *Consilience: The unity of knowledge*. New York: Alfred A. Knopf.

❋ CHARLES MITCHELL

Teaching the Desert

The Literature of Landscape in and out of Place

In the fall of 1985 I more or less found myself teaching high-school English in Honolulu. This venture was not the culmination of some lifelong dream of living in paradise. Pigmentationally challenged from birth, I have never been able to muster much enthusiasm for sun, sand, and surf. Beach days during my childhood on Long Island filled me with fear and loathing, and I found the process of covering myself with sickeningly sweet-smelling grease to be absurd. What I loved, what I learned to love, were the shady summers of New England where I attended college, the crisp falls, the soft, snowy winters, the uncertain springs. So my move to the island of Oahu had nothing to do with climate. Indeed, I had barely considered the fact that my new home was going to present a different landscape from the one I was leaving behind. Mostly, I thought my friends would think I was cool for living in such a place and would be more likely to visit me than if I were living in, say, New Jersey.

Of course, the main reason I moved to Hawaii was because I had a job there. As I prepared my eleventh-grade course in American literature, I delighted in scheduling specific readings at what I thought were smartly appropriate times on the calendar. All of those New England fireside poets with their hymns to the beauty and pathos of fall fell right in line in October, and I was able to squeeze in some Robert Frost in late November. Yet as the weather remained essentially unchanged—at least to my mainlander's senses—and as the leaves on the trees simply refused to transform themselves into bold new patterns of color, I began to experience a kind of cognitive dissonance.

When we came to the fall and winter of Robert Frost, that dissonance turned to dismay. While two or three of my students had been skiing with their parents, and a few had once lived in northern climes, most of them were blissfully ignorant of the four-season landscape that loomed in the background of the anthologized canon of American literature. In Hawaii, the birch tree was an invasive species, and if my students ever swung from a banyan tree, it was a different experience altogether. The perplexed, almost scornful looks with which they greeted one of my touchy-feely discussion-starting questions—"What does the first snow smell like?"—finally woke me to the harsh reality that Hawaii was not New England.

After "Stopping by Woods on a Snowy Evening" bombed in Honolulu, I began to think more deliberately about the relationship between literature and the landscape that informed it. The anthology we were using—the umpteenth edition of a New Criticism classic—treated landscape as peripheral. The Mississippi River in *Adventures of Huckleberry Finn,* the New England of Frost's poetry, the California of Robinson Jeffers: these details of geography were no more than backdrop, at most part of an extended metaphor in which the river was really a road, and that road could be anywhere. This was made clear to the students in the introductory material that began each chapter, and it was made clear to me in the instructor's manual: real literature transcends such worldly details; an appreciation of Frost does not require an awareness of his landscape. In case we missed that point, there were two sections on "regional writers" and "local colorists" for whom the introductory material provided extended descriptions of the relevant landscapes. The message here was equally clear: to the extent that the specifics of landscape matter, artistry is diminished. Sarah Orne Jewett is marginalized because Maine is not a metaphor.

My understanding of these mysteries deepened after I moved on to graduate school in California and began to study the history of literary criticism. If the stodgy New Critics found a vibrant landscape to be an unholy intrusion upon the sacred world of art, the hip post-modernists whose debunking of the New Critics I relished treated landscape as a cipher. For those who deigned to address the subject at all, landscape was a construct, a conceit manufactured through the interaction of reader and writer. It could not inform anything. To hold that the meaning of a text was shaped by the landscape in which it was set, and that an appreciation of the text might be enhanced by an understanding of that landscape, was to engage in a form of misreading that verged on blasphemy. To insist that the actual sea mattered to Melville, or the plains to Willa Cather, was to invite the scorn of those critics who resented the notion that an annoying concept like place could make any sort of claim on them. All that is solid must be melted into solipsism.

While I did encounter critical perspectives that acknowledged the significance of place, I still struggled to understand the relationship between landscape and meaning. On one level, this struggle was personal. Eager to prove my seriousness as a scholar-in-training, I believed it necessary to separate my "pleasure reading" from my research and teaching interests. While on the clock, I dutifully devoted myself to keeping up with my field. But once the bell rang, I indulged in the work of David James Duncan, Terry Tempest Williams, and Edward Abbey. I would lose myself in landscapes I had never seen, regions that insisted upon their uniqueness with their own booksellers' associations and literary festivals: the Pacific Northwest, the Rocky Mountain North, the Southwest. I wondered whether I was missing something important if the only experience I had of these places was through the Sierra Club and Audubon Society calendars that helped me track the progress of the semester. Does a reader who knows a particular landscape "get more out of" a text than one who does not?

My struggle was also professional. As an apprentice cultural historian, I needed to be thinking about canons and curriculum. If one motif of the dominant cultural narrative was to render place invisible, then it seemed that a serious consideration of the diversity of American places was another way of challenging the relentless logic of that narrative. Place would thus join race, class, and gender as instruments through which the many voices of American culture were inflected. But how much does place really matter? And how does a teacher use this relationship in the classroom, where the peculiarities of place are accessible only through the mediated representations of print, pigment, and pixel?

These questions migrated with me when I moved on to what has been a ten-year run at a small college in upstate New York. Fate delivered into my hands sole proprietorship of a "department" of American Studies, the curriculum of which I have been free to shape within the most flexible of parameters. My institution also follows a unique academic calendar, with a six-week mini term in the spring coming after two twelve-week pseudo-semesters. This term offers an ideal opportunity for field courses of all kinds, and I have exploited that opportunity with relish. For the balance of this essay I will trace two strands of my exploration of the literature of landscape, in particular the literature of the desert Southwest: first, my use of the desert as metaphor, analogy, and case study in the core courses of the American Studies major, drawing on selections from Mary Austin, Edward Abbey, Leslie Marmon Silko, and Everett Ruess; second, a field course built around a more intensive study of some of those texts that includes three weeks of travel in New Mexico and Utah.

BRINGING THE DESERT TO THE FINGER LAKES

Few of the students who enroll at my small, upstate New York liberal arts college have had any experience with the landscape of the Southwest. Until very recently, neither had I. The desert oasis that I began to construct on the outskirts of New York's Leatherstocking region was thus, from the beginning, more conceptual than real. I have used the literature of the southwestern landscape to explore several broad questions: How has the desert—as a geographical feature and a cultural construct—challenged the traditional American Dream of abundance, progress, and unlimited growth? How has this landscape, with its mythical and spiritual richness, served as a stage for the playing out of the conflict between Americans' communal impulses and their devotion to an ethos of rugged individualism, the desire to be left alone and the fear of the loner? And what of the desert as a cultural laboratory? What spiritual, philosophical, social, and political nuances are nurtured by such a landscape?

The master narrative of the "American Dream" portrays the American experience as an irresistible, manifestly destined march into a future of progress and abundance. Not only is this vision immune to quantitative limits—there can always be more and more will always be better—but it is essentially unaffected by geography. By its very nature it can be carried to any place, and thus place itself, the particularities of landscape, becomes irrelevant. William Carlos Williams's *In the American Grain* contains one of the more delightful critiques of the way in which European immigrants transformed the North American landscape into something both homogenous and alien. The American Dream, as a kind of cultural economy, replicates itself in a way that is indifferent to features of topography, climate, and local culture. It is the conceit of this Dream that it shapes, rather than is shaped by, the landscape upon which it is played out.

Kathleen Norris, though writing about the Great Plains, poses a kind of conceptual desert against this homogenized vision of strip-mall America. The landscape of western Dakota offers a brand of desert wisdom, "a reminder of human limits." To live in such a place is to enroll in a "school for humility" where we are constantly reminded that we are powerless over circumstances (1993, 9). Of course, this notion of powerlessness, of limits on human endeavor, does not enjoy a prominent place in the discourse of the American Dream. From Alexander Hamilton's vision of ever-expanding domestic production, through Thomas Hart Benton's discovery of manifest destiny, through all the prophets of perpetual progress from Andrew Carnegie to Bill Gates, limits are to be transcended rather than respected; powerlessness is an illness to be cured. It is this attitude that mainstream American culture brings to the landscape, and it is the desert landscape that offers the biggest challenge to the triumph of this attitude.

In one of the courses I teach, "Perspectives on the American Dream," we devote half of the term to sketching a cumulative portrait of America's cultural self-image: what is this country about? Why all the fuss? What are the values and principles that underlie our sense of importance? We begin with the various theorizers of the American experience: Winthrop, Jefferson, Crevecoeur, Franklin, Hamilton, Thoreau, Frederick Douglass, Elizabeth Cady Stanton. In the latter part of the term we explore how these often contrary visions are reflected, resisted, or refuted in particular lived experiences. Richard Wright's *Black Boy,* William Finnegan's *Cold New World,* and Betty Friedan's "The Problem without a Name" are typical avenues leading us into this discussion. We also consider the desert.

Our first stop is the "making the desert bloom" school where we explore the development of southern California, Nevada, and Arizona, study the actions of the delightfully named Bureau of Reclamation and the creative way in which Floyd B. Dominy employed Jeffersonian rhetoric, and we look at how Boulder Dam was presented as the ultimate triumph of American ingenuity over the increasingly feeble forces of nature. We then consider the cracks in that triumph: the environmental consequences and violations of native treaty rights; the problems associated with sprawl; and the always amusing absurdities of painted lawns in Los Angeles and the proposal to dye Lake Mead purple in order to retard evaporation. We then turn to selections from Mary Austin and Edward Abbey, who deflate the pompous pretensions of the desert bloomers while also asserting the essential integrity of the landscape.

Austin opens *The Land of Little Rain* with a terse description. This is a place where "not the law but the land sets the limit," where the air is dry, the soil villainous, and the vegetation marked by neither beauty nor freshness. Most notable, for Austin, are the "desert floras" that "shame us with their cheerful adaptations to the seasonal limitations" (1997, 1–2). Here is a land that does not itself adapt but, as a matter of discipline, forces all that would live upon it to acknowledge limits and do some cheerful adapting of their own. Cattle, that vanguard of civilization in the American West, quickly become fodder for the carrion crow and other scavengers, a scene Austin describes with admiration. Where William Bradford's stark depiction of the starving time during the first winter of Plimoth Plantation stands as a prelude to the Pilgrims' inevitable triumph over the elements, the squalid tragedy that Austin details emerges as a lesson in limits, the result of the very nature of this place, a landscape that will not yield.

The story of the Pocket Hunter also stands as a cautionary tale for those who might too easily assume the pliability of this landscape. Engaged in the time-honored quest of forcing the land to yield its riches, the Pocket Hunter instead finds himself yielding to that land's transformative powers: he takes on the protective colors of his surroundings, becomes saturated with the elements, and gradually surrenders himself to a form of harmless madness. Rather than employing the resources of this land to assert a kind of cultural hegemony, he allows the land itself to become his destiny. The Pocket Hunter is the man Crevecoeur worried about in his *Letters from an American Farmer.* Sent off to the frontier to tame the wilderness by transplanting the institutions of Western civilization, the Pocket Hunter more nearly reverts to the conditions which that wilderness demands. Implicitly, at least, he accedes to the limits of that land. His encounter with the desert yields no visions of country-club subdivisions with swimming pools and lush fairways.

If Austin presents the desert as a landscape that can pretty much speak for itself, Abbey's desert demands to be both articulated and defended. In selections from *The Monkey Wrench Gang* and *Desert Solitaire,* Abbey defines this landscape as a natural and necessary counterweight to the soulless vision of middle America, the engineer's dream that would pave, straighten, and level the surface of the planet in pursuit of efficiency. His joyful skewering of the advocates of development and progress, those dangerously earnest heirs of Hamilton, Franklin, and George Babbitt, is rooted less in a notion that the desert will inevitably resist their efforts than in a conviction that their vision and values are destructive, that they represent not the advance of civilization but the corrosive force of a particularly virulent form of culture. The Pocket Hunter has been replaced by the industrial tourist, the Chamber of Commerce, and the water and mining interests, who, if left unchecked, will prove more than a match for the actual vultures soaring overhead.

Abbey invests his landscape with a set of values that, he insists, ought to define the culture of those who would live upon it. He argues that such a culture and any dreams that might cohere around it need to exist in an organic relationship with the particularities of place if they are to endure. To transform the desert into a cultural replica of Cleveland does violence to more than the integrity of the landscape. It also promotes the erosion of the values preserved within that landscape, the freedom and vital self-reliance that will be reduced to the lonely sound of one horn honking. In short, Abbey's desert becomes a battleground for the soul of the American Dream. Not only is it a place to come to in order to live differently, it is a place where one might learn how to live differently elsewhere. Like Norris's Great Plains, Abbey's desert serves as a laboratory for cultivating a kind of counter-cultural wisdom, an alternative to the homogenizing "just do it" ethics of the modern market.

The desert landscape also plays a key role in my course on the promises and perils of individualism. Assuming that the territory to which Huckleberry Finn set out is somewhere in the Four Corners area, and that Ralph Waldo Emerson provided the map, I lead my students through a meandering survey of the history of self-reliance as a psychological, political, and economic principle. Like Huck, we conclude our journey in the territories, in the company of Abbey (again), Leslie Marmon Silko, and Everett Ruess. Ruess serves as an intriguing companion for Huck, an older but in many ways more innocent fellow traveler. His wandering in Utah and Arizona, while lacking the social texture of Huck's trek down the river with Jim, produces the same mixture of exhilaration and loneliness that Huck experiences on those occasions when he is by himself. My students find Ruess's aversion to human society to be a bit precious, especially in comparison to Huck's more necessary flight from corruption and abuse. They are also sensitive to the paradox that a landscape that permits seemingly unlimited opportunities for self-exploration also holds unlimited potential for self-destruction. Ruess loses himself in the desert much as Edna Pontellier surrenders herself to the Gulf of Mexico in Kate Chopin's *The Awakening*, suggesting just how thin the line is that separates discovery from dissolution.

Abbey's contribution to such a discussion is obvious. "The Moon-Eyed Horse" from *Desert Solitaire* serves as a kind of parable, bringing Huck Finn, Everett Ruess, and Abbey himself face to face with the sublime seductiveness of desert solitude. The horse, a gregarious beast, seeks refuge from a life of harsh labor and abuse; in finding freedom, it has, perhaps, crossed the line into madness. Like Huck, my students feel, Moon-Eye was justified in running away, but they struggle to come to terms with the consequences of that action. The desert offers an enticing possibility of escape, a chance to "live free," but the terms of survival are so precarious that the "or die" half of the equation looms far more ominously than it does in New Hampshire.

Abbey also presents the desert as a laboratory for the politics of individualism and self-reliance. *The Monkey Wrench Gang* probably frustrates my students more than any other book I teach, in part because they have only second-hand knowledge of the landscape that the gang has pledged itself to defend. This makes it difficult to embrace the notion that a landscape can embody a set of values and principles worth defending. And though they grudgingly admire the gang's determination to defend its home, they are appalled by the tactics thus employed. They see in George Hayduke a character who embodies the heights and depths of rugged individualism, its undeniable claim to righteousness, integrity, and romantic appeal coupled with a futile, destructive quest for solitary perfectionism. Hayduke's rage seems, ultimately, out of character with the landscape he intends to protect; his restlessness keeps him from ever being at home there.

Leslie Marmon Silko's *Ceremony* engages Abbey at precisely this level. Both Hayduke and the Moon-Eyed Horse look to the desert as a place of refuge, a means of isolating themselves from and defending themselves against the incursions of civilization. Tayo finds in the landscape a means of saving "the people" from a crudely individualistic strain of evil. As he learns from Old Betonie, a kind of multi-cultural healer, preserving the self is a meaningless and futile gesture because the self does not exist in isolation. The posture of rugged individualism is in fact part of the problem, part of a culture that would deny the essential character of the landscape upon which it is trying to impose itself. Like Austin's desert, Silko's land of mesas and mountains imposes limits on those who would live within it. Tayo's recognition of this, his awareness of that "something larger" of which he was but a part, and his sense of the practical obsolescence of the unencumbered, solitary self, give him the strength to transcend the witchery that seeks to destroy the world. Where George Hayduke emerges from the landscape as resurrected Lone Ranger, Tayo submerges, or perhaps re-submerges himself within his landscape and the cultural traditions it has nourished. Silko's desert becomes a laboratory for re-imagining human community.

TEACHING THE DESERT IN PLACE

After several years of teaching the desert Southwest as a disembodied metaphor, I decided it was time to see how things looked from the near view. I have taught my travel course twice, with a total of twenty-three students. Twelve of them had taken one of the courses outlined above; only one had ever seen the area through which we would be traveling. Though I made some changes for the second offering of the course, the basic structure remained essentially the same, and I will discuss the two experiences as if they were one.

The course has several broad objectives. First, we consider the West as a state of mind, that "other place" that serves as an antidote to the over-developed world of the two coasts. Here, of course, we dip into the "new" western history, discussing the relationship between mythology and experience and the consequences, for both people and the places they live, of being part of a cultural myth. This leads directly into a consideration of tourism, the way in which the expectations of tourists are shaped and how those expectations in turn transform the tourist destination. Our sources for these first two units include Hal Rothman, Timothy Egan, Patricia Nelson Limerick, and Walker Percy's "The Loss of the Creature." We then focus this discussion on the interior Southwest, specifically New Mexico and Utah, as an illustration of the ideas we have been discussing. In addition to considering the political, economic, and social issues that characterize these two regions, we turn our attention to the role of the landscape in shaping the regions' cultural identity. We read Leslie Marmon Silko's "Landscape, History, and the Pueblo Imagination," William deBuys's *Enchantment and Exploitation,* Abbey's *Desert Solitaire,* and Terry Tempest Williams's *Desert Quartet.*

It should be apparent that I have chosen breadth over depth in this class, for reasons that are both pedagogical—this is perhaps the only exposure my students will have to this material, and sowing many different seeds may bear more fruit than planting one deeply—and practical: having taught a similar course in the Adirondacks, I discovered that staying in one place for more than a week produces a rather intense restlessness among twenty-year-olds. We complete most of our background reading during the first two weeks of the term, and then fly to Albuquerque to begin three weeks of travel. We explore Santa Fe, Taos, and Chaco Canyon, with a stop at Mesa Verde before crossing over into Utah. For the final week we are based in Moab, from which we can explore at ease the desert landscape of Abbey and Williams.

Studying tourism while simultaneously engaging in it provided the most intriguing experience of the course. Back in the classroom, our discussions of tourism had been, well, academic. Several of my students live in areas—Maine, the Adirondacks, the Catskills—that experience an influx of seasonal residents, and they helped us as a group to develop a broad sympathy with the plight of those being toured upon. The stress put on local services, the dislocation of long-time residents, the uncertainties of a service-based economy, and the resentment at being invaded by outsiders with quaint and condescending attitudes toward locals: these were problems that we analyzed in the laboratory, problems at which we shook our heads with confidence that we were not complicit.

And yet, every one of my students had at least one "I want to move here" moment as we traveled from one stunningly picturesque landscape to the next. Despite all we had read about the hardships that accompany the scenery, the environmental impact of sprawling development, and the ultimately self-defeating logic of moving to a place because so few people have moved there, we each imagined scenarios that would allow us to relocate to Taos, Santa Fe, Durango, or Moab. As we broke these moments down in discussion, we discovered that we were engaging in precisely the kind of thinking that boosters and developers count on: I am just one person. My little house up against the national forest will hardly be noticed, my water usage and sewage discharge won't make a difference. In short, the real problems will be caused by those who come later.

A similar phenomenon characterized the way we conducted ourselves as visitors. The detachment of the classroom had made it easy for us to ridicule the more obvious quirks of tourists: their naïve assumptions about authenticity, their sense of the world as a theme park, their willingness to be manipulated, their abrasive clothing and manners. We began our trip keenly aware of our own behavior and expectations, believing that since we were self-consciously studying tourism, we could resist the traps. The result was a good deal of awkwardness and hesitation. After visiting the pueblos at Acoma and Taos, several students confessed to feeling as if they were visiting Colonial Williamsburg or Plimoth Plantation, except they knew that these were "real people." They struggled with the sense that they were engaging in a form of voyeurism, even though they recognized that they were being invited to do so. Being aware of their own complicated mix of motives enabled them to think more critically about the way the tourist experience happens and the way in which the anti-tourist pose itself becomes another brand of tourism.

The primary focus of our self-consciousness was the camera. However attentive we might have been to the ways in which the camera shapes our experience, the fact was that my students were visiting places that all but one of them had never seen before. They wanted pictures, and after an initial period where they felt obliged to justify each shot, they surrendered themselves to the tyranny of the viewfinder. They took pictures of everything: buildings, people, scenery, signs. Despite the (possibly contrived) aura of intrusion, we purchased several camera permits at Taos Pueblo. Ironically, this flurry of picture-taking climaxed during our first day at

Arches National Park, where we came face to face with Edward Abbey and his merciless attack on industrial tourism.

We had finished *Desert Solitaire* before leaving New Mexico and received Abbey's warnings with a manner of solemnity usually reserved for scripture. Indeed, his "word of caution" served as an ethic by which we hoped to be judged:

> Do not jump into your automobile next June and rush out to the canyon country hoping to see some of that which I have attempted to evoke in these pages. In the first place you can't see *anything* from a car; you've got to get out of the goddamned contraption and walk, better yet crawl, on hands and knees, over the sandstone and through the thornbush and cactus. When traces of blood begin to mark your trail you'll see something, maybe. (1990, xiv)

Of course, we were all aware that we were heading off to canyon country precisely because of Abbey's book, but we believed that our manner of visiting would keep us on the side of the angels. After all, he had our interests in mind:

> Industrial Tourism is a threat to the national parks. But the chief victims of the system are the motorized tourists. They are being robbed and robbing themselves. So long as they are unwilling to crawl out of their cars they will not discover the treasures of the national parks and will never escape the stress and turmoil of the urban-suburban complexes which they had hoped, presumably, to leave behind for a while. (1990, 51)

Like good students, we filed this away as a lesson learned, and accepted the following as a kind of greatest-of-all commandment:

> Look here, I want to say, for godsake folks get out of them there machines take off those fucking sunglasses and unpeel both eyeballs, look around; throw away those goddamned idiotic cameras! (1990, 233)

The only problem is that there is no way to see Arches without engaging in industrial tourism. Even with those words ringing in our ears, we entered the park wrapped cozily and safely in our metal machines, wearing sunglasses, and each carrying an idiotic camera. We drove from viewing point to viewing point, got out of the van, walked out to an arch, took a picture, and walked back. Gradually, the students started admitting that we were doing precisely what Abbey insisted we not do. Despite our mutual scorn for industrial tourists, we wanted to see the arches, and we wanted pictures. By midafternoon a kind of fatigue set in that was part physical weariness, part psychic strain from watching ourselves fall help-lessly into a pattern that we had so much wanted to avoid.

In unpacking this experience the following day, our disappointment in ourselves gradually evolved into a conviction that some of Abbey's stan-dards were unreasonable. That, in turn, evolved into a more general dis-cussion of the effectiveness of Abbey's depiction of the region as a place under siege (this included a discussion of *The Monkey Wrench Gang* among those students who had read it). To be sure, the encroachments of industrial tourism were obvious, from the tacky-trendy offerings of Moab to the design of the park as a series of drive-up destinations. But for most of my students this was still modest compared to what they were familiar with "back home." Even with paved roads and pit toilets, Arches was far from a theme park. And while we appreciated the virtue of bloody knees as an emblem of having earned our desert experience, the rugged self-re-liance that Abbey urged upon his readers appeared, close-up, to be a form of self-serving elitism. Inwardly, I raged against this turn in the discussion, wanting to insist that my students were allowing themselves to be co-opted by the machine that defined complacency as democracy. But they had a point. While they were not exactly lethargic, only a few of them could be considered rugged outdoor types. The authentic desert experi-ence that Abbey sought to define was exclusive. It was meant to keep peo-ple out, people like them.

Another casualty of our travels through canyon country was Abbey's notion that the desert offered a last stand for freedom, a place uniquely suited to preserving the ideals and values that were everywhere else under attack. While such a claim worked very well in the abstract setting of the classroom, allowing us to discuss the ideas while taking for granted their relationship to the landscape, our actual encounter with the desert dimin-ished its ideological power. For students whose appreciation of American ideals had been shaped by visits to Boston, Gettysburg, Williamsburg, and Fort Ticonderoga, canyon country promised not freedom but anarchy. Such a laboratory could nurture only a Moon-Eye or a Hayduke, de-tached individuals who posed a danger to self and others. Even those stu-dents inclined to humor my suggestion that the values Abbey identified with this landscape were not inherently destructive found his urgency overwrought. As we explored the area, looking out over the Needles, the Maze, Cedar Mesa, and Comb Ridge, the sheer expanse of emptiness dwarfed Abbey's complaints. There was, it appeared, still ample space in which George Hayduke's descendants could make their last stand. How much of a threat did a little bit of neon in Moab really pose?

Abbey fared better when we shifted from a discussion of the desert as a field for polemic and ideology to a consideration of its aesthetic and philosophical aspects. And in this case, the effect of moving from the classroom to the field was reversed. If Abbey's politics made more sense in the abstract than they did when viewed against the concrete context of their primordial landscape, his emotional and psychological response to the desert became more accessible the more we explored the world he described. Indeed, he had anticipated this phenomenon rather explicitly, confessing the impossibility of putting the desert into a book. Of course, despite this impossibility, it is precisely the essence of the desert that Abbey strives to evoke in his prose: its silence and austerity, its paradoxical combination of bare-bones realism and brutal mysticism, its difference from mountain, forest, and sea. He insists that his subject is not landscape as metaphor but landscape as bedrock reality, that these qualities inhere in the landscape rather than being suggested by it. And yet, after several pages of trying to pin this quality down, he can only conclude: "There is *something* about the desert . . ." (1990, 243).

This something is entirely alien to my students, and it is not surprising that our classroom discussions pass over this part of the book rather quickly. We have a similar experience with Terry Tempest Williams's *Desert Quartet*. I find this to be a beautiful, evocative little book, yet the erotic imagery that Williams draws upon, the sensuality of her embrace of the landscape, is difficult to plumb in the abstract. Several of my students remarked that Williams's meditations were "like poetry," which meant that they didn't really have to understand them, just appreciate the effort. Indeed, teaching this book for the first time reminded me, uncomfortably, of my attempt at teaching Frost in Hawaii: "What does the desert feel like?" In the classroom, with no experience of the desert to draw upon, such material evokes a perfunctory admiration tinged with a regret that we do not have the ability to truly "get it." Potholes, slickrock, pourovers, fins, the very nature of the canyons themselves were mysteries we could only pretend to comprehend.

In the field, that poetry became much more accessible. After our initial trip through Arches, I organized a series of relatively unstructured explorations of Fiery Furnace, Devil's Garden (both within Arches), Grandview Point, and Neck Spring (both within the Island in the Sky district of Canyonlands National Park). We broke down into groups of two to three in order to provide some opportunity for solitude, and I asked the students to reflect in their journals on specific passages from Abbey and Williams. Each night, we would discuss the landscape we had explored and our reactions to it. The result was my most rewarding instructional experience of the course.

One student likened her stroll through Fiery Furnace to a kind of archaeological autopsy, a meander through the skeleton of the planet. This led into discussions of the way the exposed layers of rock invited reflections on time, on the place of human beings in the geological scheme, on what Abbey called bedrock reality. In comparing the desert to the mud and foliage world from which we had come—the rounded hills, the ecology of soil, shrub, and shade tree—we spoke in terms of hard versus soft, raw versus refined, harsh versus inviting. The forests of the Northeast promised a kind of protection, a structure to our ramblings; they seemed, one student said, to "reserve a place for us." By contrast, the desert left us vulnerable, exposed us to the unrelenting demands of sun, wind, and space; it made us feel distinctly out of place. In a striking entry, another student wrote about how the layers of topsoil and vegetation in the temperate zone suggested the mellowing accretions of civilization and culture, while the bare bones of the desert suggested something that was simultaneously dead and unformed. A discussion that had been cliché-bound and vague in the classroom was now characterized by an earnest quest to specify how this landscape worked upon us. The peculiar mix of fear and passion that characterized Abbey's and Williams's reflections on the desert was made palpable and compelling. And this was more than a series of "Oh, now I get it" moments. It was a product of feeling more than of thinking.

We also came to appreciate Williams's vision of the erotic landscape. Though the discussion here was predictably more awkward, we each spoke about the feel of skin on sandstone, the appeal of the intricately curved and intertwining rock formations through which we moved. The very language we used to describe our experiences emphasized the sensual over the intellectual. Several students drew sketches after the manner of the illustrations by Mary Frank that accompany Williams's prose. And as this discussion gradually opened up, as we became slightly more comfortable speaking of such things, several of us described the sense we had that in entering a canyon we were in some way entering another body and leaving our own behind. Few of my students had ever observed themselves reacting to a landscape. They knew of important places, special places, places for which they felt a kind of reverence, but these were places apart from themselves, places whose significance could be explained in rational terms. To respond to a landscape with love and desire, to experience a physical and emotional connection to a place, had not been part of their vocabulary. Perhaps the clearest measure of the difference between the classroom and the field was their response to the following passage from *Desert Quartet:*

> The silence that lives in these sacred hallways presses against me. I relax. I surrender. I close my eyes. The arousal of my breath rises in me like music, like love, as the possessive muscles between my legs tighten and release. I come to the rock in a moment of stillness, giving and receiving, where there is no partition between my body and the body of earth. (1995, 10)

In the classroom, this evoked a respectful embarrassment: I suppose it is art, but don't expect me to like it. After a few days' exploring some of these sacred hallways, my students were much more willing to interrogate this passage. While they might not have been able, or eager, to replicate her experience, they were willing to engage Williams on her terms, and in the process to engage the desert on its.

My students have been well prepared by their education to deal with abstract ideas and feelings—grief, loss, freedom, individualism, community. They are less well-prepared to engage the immediate, material contexts that give some of those ideas shape and resonance. Indeed, as David Orr has observed, the very project of modern education favors the abstract over the particular, the universal over the local. The landscape is a prop, a backdrop that is more virtual than real. It is subordinated to the ideas it suggests: we don't have to get it to get them. While it was beyond the scope of my course to address this systemic problem—and I agree with Orr that it is a significant one—we were able to consider in a modest way the relationship between a particular landscape and the culture it has nurtured. The shift from classroom to field, from metaphor to bedrock, highlights the different ways students respond to a literature that is infused with the flavor of place. If the functional irrelevance of landscape is one of the goals of the reigning cartel of multi-national post-modernists, then an encounter with the desert Southwest might be a way of sneaking a little sand into the crankcase. There is, after all, a *there* there, and that there both demands and rewards consideration.

References

Abbey, Edward. 1975. *The monkey wrench gang.* New York: Harper Collins.

———. (1968) 1990. *Desert solitaire: A season in the wilderness.* New York: Touchstone.

Austin, Mary. (1903) 1997. *The land of little rain.* New York: Penguin.

Chopin, Kate. (1899) 1994. *The awakening.* New York: Norton.

Crevecouer, J. Hector St. John de. (1782) 1981. *Letters from an American farmer and sketches of eighteenth-century America.* New York: Penguin.

deBuys, William. 1985. *Enchantment and exploitation.* Albuquerque: University of New Mexico Press.

Egan, Timothy. 1999. *Lasso the wind: Away to the new west.* New York: Vintage.

Finnegan, William. 1998. *Cold new world.* New York: Random House.

Friedan, Betty. (1963) 1997. The problem without a name. Chap. 1 in *The feminine mystique.* New York: Norton.

Limerick, Patricia Nelson. 1985. *Desert passages.* Albuquerque: University of New Mexico Press.

———. 1997. The shadows of heaven itself. In *Atlas of the new west,* edited by William E. Riebsame. New York: Norton.

———. 1999. Seeing and being seen: Tourism in the American west. In *Over the edge: Remapping the American west,* edited by Valerie Matsumoto and Blake Allmendinger. Berkeley: University of California Press.

Norris, Kathleen. 1993. *Dakota: A spiritual geography.* New York: Houghton Mifflin.

Orr, David. 1992. *Ecological literacy: Education and the transition to a postmodern world.* Albany: State University of New York Press.

Percy, Walker. 1976. The loss of the creature. In *The message in the bottle.* New York: Noonday.

Rothman, Hal. 1998. *Devil's bargains: Tourism in the twentieth- century American west.* Lawrence: University Press of Kansas.

Rusho, W. L. 1983. *Everett Ruess: A vagabond for beauty.* Salt Lake City: Gibbs Smith.

Silko, Leslie Marmon. 1977. *Ceremony.* New York: Penguin.

———. 1986. Landscape, history, and the Pueblo imagination. *Antaeus* 57 (Autumn): 83–94.

Williams, Terry Tempest, and Mary Frank. 1995. *Desert quartet.* New York: Pantheon.

Williams, William Carlos. (1925) 1956. *In the American grain.* New York: New Directions.

Wright, Richard. (1945 and 1977) 1993. *Black boy.* Restored Text edition, New York: Harper Perennial.

❋ R. EDWARD GRUMBINE

Going to Bashō's Pine

Wilderness Education for the Twenty-first Century

The great seventeenth-century Japanese haiku poet Matsuo Bashō, when asked by a student to describe the source of inspiration, is said to have replied, "If you want to know the pine, go to the pine." There are many ways to follow Master Bashō with a group of university students in the wilderness classroom.

Say the particular pine is ponderosa pine, the classroom is the high plateau of backcountry Zion National Park in late May, the course is *Natural History of the Colorado Plateau*, and there are twelve learners who are nearing the end of an eight-week field program.

First, there is the taxonomy describing the tree. Over the spring we have come to know other members of the Pinaceae, but we have not encountered ponderosa before: *Pinus ponderosa*, long needle leaves in threes, ruddy puzzlebark, cones with prickles on the scales, grows mostly above 1,600 meters in Utah in open stands, the most widespread pine in western North America. These forests provide habitat for birds and mammals new to us—songs from the olive-sided flycatcher and Swainsons thrush float down from the canopy. There are human uses of ponderosa pine to discover. The tree is cut and milled for construction lumber, and the needles make a resinous tea high in vitamin C, "like drinking the forest," remarks a student.

Then (science aside) there are various cultural constructions of ponderosa pine. The entire pine family is shot through with mythos, and "pine" conjures up many images in our group. We talk about what they mean, sharing a bit of our personal history with trees as we connect with a larger cultural story.

This forest near Sawmill Spring was cut heavily some seventy years ago and today the millsite is a green meadow and a pond with a springbox. We find giant stumps in the nearby woods, which butt against our concepts of national parks as pristine nature. This partially logged forest in a nature reserve is a place where human and natural histories intertwine.

Still, we return to the pine. The afternoon assignment is to go off into the forest, find a spot to sit, observe avian activity and make a field-journal entry, and then sit with the trees for a time and reflect on the day's activities. In this wild classroom, before science, history, and culture, the ponderosa pine is always present as a being-in-place, like us, alive and growing.

CHARACTERISTICS OF WILDERNESS EDUCATION

Wilderness education, as a new kind of environmental education, blossomed in the 1970s as the burgeoning public awareness of ecology combined with college student demands for alternative education.[1] Almost immediately, this movement differentiated into two parallel streams. Adventure education programs (Outward Bound, the National Outdoor Leadership School, and a host of nonprofits serving special-needs groups) focused on the noncredit teaching of outdoor skills, leadership, and personal growth through wilderness experience. Though college-age students made up the majority of adventure education participants up to the 1980s, today's programs are increasingly geared toward corporate professionals.

The second stream, academic wilderness education, offering credit toward undergraduate degrees, may be more radical in philosophy, goals, and methods. Wilderness education seeks to educate the whole person through, as Jonathan Fairbanks suggests, "a blend of reading, study, and experience that creates a sense that learning is part of a greater whole, that academic experiences contribute to life rather than merely serving as a formal prelude to it" (1980, 22). There are many ways, of course, to accomplish such learning, but academic wilderness education is unique because the field classroom is alive, a fundamental ally in learning. Living places from vacant lots to wild mountains and deserts are essential for wilderness education whether the length of study is an afternoon, a week, or a semester.

Along with dependence on living classrooms, academic wilderness education blends experiential learning (learning by doing) with the traditional transmission model of higher education (learning by information assimilation). The transmission model represents students as passive, empty vessels waiting to be filled with expert knowledge through lectures by professors. Though much empirical educational research shows the ineffectiveness of this transmission approach, the model and practice persist.[2] (It is difficult to describe precisely why universities do not often support academic wilderness education. Reasons include liability concerns, perceived loss of oversight due to off-campus locations, and a lack of institutional support for education theories and practices that deviate from the status quo.)

Beyond these two shared traits there are many variations between academic wilderness education programs. The Audubon Expedition Institute, for example, places a premium on environmental studies with attention to group process. Audubon students spend significant amounts of class time building community through shared decision-making. Since the program is bus-based, much field time is spent car camping and visiting regional and local experts throughout the country. Wildlands Studies is oriented toward research projects. These programs focus on a specific bioregion's environmental issues or work to collect data on species or ecosystems at risk. The wilderness and civilization program at the University of Montana explores the nature/culture boundary with a humanities emphasis.[3] In this program, students begin the semester with a two-week backpack and then return to campus to pursue group studies in literature, history, and philosophy with wilderness themes.

I taught my first wilderness education program in the southern Appalachians in 1975 for Antioch College and have worked in the wild classroom for several universities. Since 1982 I have directed the Sierra Institute wilderness studies program at the University of California Extension in Santa Cruz. Founded in 1974, the Sierra Institute (SI) offers three-, five-, and eight-week-long undergraduate environmental studies programs taught in backcountry areas throughout western North America, Belize, and Chile. It has been over a decade since I last surveyed the field ("The University of the Wilderness"), and it is time for a reevaluation. For the balance of this paper, I will use SI to portray specific wilderness education methods (especially those with an emphasis on using literature) before spotlighting future issues that will challenge all outdoor classroom programs into the next century.

PRACTICE IN THE WILD

We were camping in Grand Gulch, a sixty-mile-long gash eroded out of the southern edge of Cedar Mesa in southern Utah. The group was at that stage in a long hike where, if you are lucky, you feel the weight of industrial civilization lift off your shoulders and your perception sharpens. The Zen-bell song of the canyon wren. Tinkle of water over sandstone slabs. Angle of morning light. Day's work ahead: present an outline of Anasazi cultural stages and how we define them, hike a few miles in search of the ruin, and give an in-class writing assignment that ties the day's learning together.

My lecture is straightforward, though I emphasize the material-culture field marks of dwelling sites and rock art panels that allow one to estimate when and how the place was inhabited. We pack for the day hike and set off.

The ancestral Pueblo (Anasazi) people lived densely in Grand Gulch and their sign is everywhere. Students are fascinated by the Anasazi for two main reasons. First, contact with any prehistoric native people feeds the inclination to romanticize Indians. Second, most people just cannot conceive of how any humans could flourish in this dry desert place.

After a bit of searching against the eastern cliff we discover the ruin, remarkably intact. The Anasazi left seven hundred years ago, but we find a yucca fiber sandal, a very large potsherd among hundreds, numerous corncobs, red-painted figures on rock walls, a small intact kiva, and more. The place is magical, mythical, prehistoric, and also in the present, here and now.

Later, we draw together below the ruin. The Anasazi left no written accounts, but two nights ago we read and discussed Leslie Marmon Silko's essay "Landscape, History, and the Pueblo Imagination." Referring to the Old Ones, Silko begins "You see that after a thing is dead, it dries up . . . the spirit remains close by. They do not leave us" (1986, 83). We have just spent an hour inhaling the dust of this ruin. I give out the assignment: Pick an age (child, teen, adult, elder) you want to be. Pretend you are an Anasazi who lives here and describe what you did around home today, using what you know about ancestral Pueblo culture, what you have discovered here, and your imagination.

We are to meet back at camp in a few hours.

What might happen when a student mixes academic learning and knowledge of "the facts" with the living place where facts are born? How might a learner mix into this educational crucible his/her own creative impulse, along with the experiences of peers who are engaged with the same place and the same problems? Just as the body can be connected to the mind by a backpack full of books, wilderness education works best when relationships are developed beyond the simple act of holding class in the great outdoors.

❀

To educate the whole person, wild teaching is concerned primarily with connecting across boundaries in four key relationships:

- place/learning
- doing/knowing
- individual/group
- reflection/action

Place and Learning

David Orr has written that "place has no standing in contemporary education" (1992, 126), but in academic wilderness education place is paramount. The wild classroom provides a wholeness that allows for profound learning. Sierra Institute instructor Leslie Ryan calls this wholeness "physical integrity . . . often, for the first time in their lives, students' days are not split into bits. On the trail, in general, people experience an unprecedented freedom from distraction" (letter to author, January 5, 1999).

In Grand Gulch, the search for and discovery of the Anasazi site, the feel of knobby corncobs, tangy odor of ruin pack-rat urine, the sheer presence of the place, all drew us into deep learning. Stories were being created long before I gave the assignment.

Epiphanies are common in the wilderness classroom. Three springs ago in the Eel River country of the California Coast Range, Gina, a student on a field ecology program, was engaged in a difficult assignment: observe a single species for an entire day and record its behavior in your field journal. This work can be exciting but often, like much of field biology, it is incredibly boring. Gina watched a clump of budding wild onion and nothing happened for six and a half hours. Packing to leave and feeling that the day was wasted, Gina glanced down at the plant—and one flower soundlessly popped open. Then, one after another, in rapid succession, all five buds blossomed in the evening air. And then, tiny flies appeared to feast on ripe pollen . . .

I have taught ecology and natural history in the field and in campus classrooms and there is no substitute for observing species in the context of habitat. Like Gina, I have not observed flowers opening or pollinators at work in the lab . . . such behaviors have been selected against by the act of collecting a mere slice of life for display indoors.

Literature, however, is not dysfunctional indoors and it may be that reading Ed Abbey in the canyon country does not confer any special benefit to students. But there is more to literature than style and substance. In addition, there is the need to grasp what claim the canyons had on Abbey in the creation of *Desert Solitaire*. After teaching Abbey both indoors and out I believe that this cannot be understood without some familiarity with the canyons where the book was born. And further: when the study of literature includes exploration of one's own creativity, one's own response to the land, wild classrooms offer endless amounts of inspiration. Thoreau could not have written *The Maine Woods* if he had not journeyed beyond Walden Pond. The Great Salt Lake could offer refuge to Terry Tempest Williams only if she first had intimate contact with its birds and waters.

Doing and Knowing

"Aren't they just backpacking for credit out there?" Well, no. These are college classes taught outdoors, where learning by doing is married with assimilating information. Though universities certainly prefer abstract knowledge to learning by doing, wilderness teachers do not privilege experience. Outdoors, both kinds of learning are intended to give students the opportunity to test assumptions about native peoples and plant phenology with their own direct encounters.[4]

The anthropological construction of Anasazi culture periods helped students make sense of the ruin we visited, but it could never capture fully those people or their place. And maybe the framework was invalid—what direct evidence of its legitimacy could we find at the site?

In the field classroom, teachers are learners, too. Educator Alison King believes that instructors must play active roles in the joining of theory with practice. She suggests that teachers act as "guides on the side" instead of "sages on stage" (1994, 17). I have learned that the more I model active learning, the easier it is for students to become engaged with their own educational process.

Each autumn on the Colorado Plateau, Leslie Ryan and Alec Cargile teach a Sierra Institute program with coursework in literature and ethics that beautifully integrates doing and knowing. Though reading and writing play a significant role in their program, Leslie and Alec begin by teaching tracking and orienteering: "We consider tracking a form of reading and orienteering an analogy to ethical questioning" (letter to author, January 5, 1999). While students develop these skills, they also read and discuss David Abram's *The Spell of the Sensuous,* plumbing the diverse character of language and varieties of reciprocity.

By the third week (of eight), students begin to work on a draft of what will become their major project. They start to engage in an intensive revision process, which Leslie describes as

> analogous to learning about a place, or falling in love. . . .
> A conversation is about to take place between the story and the student. The student re-reads: the story speaks while the student listens. The student revises: the student speaks while the story remains quiet. A raven cries in the distance, a rock falls, a shadow crosses a knee: the landscape enters the conversation; the student and the story listen.

On the final hike of the program, Leslie and Alec spend an average of four hours with each student, attending to the final stages of this revision process. As Leslie states, "as the process goes on, the human teacher is able to stand farther and farther back, as the student gains trust and confidence in his or her direct communications with these other beings, the great friends, inspirations, and teachers who have, at least for the moment, all the time in the world."

Group and Individual

My students have been out alone gathering stories and now it's time to welcome them home.

After supper, we are cradled in darkness and firelight. Everyone takes turns reading aloud from his or her Anasazi story. One by one, the students are transformed: a child in a cradleboard watches ravens play in a blue desert sky; an old man with a feeble leg dreams back to the time he hunted desert bighorn above the canyon rim; a sister and brother out gathering rice grass get lost and together solve the puzzle of where home lies; a hunter paints a wall and prays for vision. Some of the details of the students' tales don't fit ancestral Pueblo reality, but these can be discussed later through my written feedback. The point is that the stories resonate, spring from a ruin in a real canyon inhabited by oaks, lizards, spirits, and a group of young explorers willing to share.

Every Sierra Institute instructor has favorite ways to knit individuals into community. Many use journal sharing and various read-aloud techniques to encourage group voice. These methods work well whether the class is on natural history or nature writing. Greg Gordon, who teaches literature and environmental issues in the northern Rockies, assigns an eco-autobiography where students write and share a nutshell version of how their relationship with nature evolved. Later, these stories are passed around the group and can also be developed further into an individual's final project.

Backcountry community life is far richer than what passes for the same on campus. Teachers and students share a journey—you backpack and camp together. Students may find that though the instructor knows all the plants or is a scholar of contemporary American nature writing, that same teacher is a weak hiker who tends to miss trail junctions. The footing is more equal in the backcountry around the mundane tasks of daily living. Beyond common ground, participants have common educational interests and goals. Students all take the same classes, so study groups form naturally. Individuals with particular strengths share expertise. Community support encourages individual safety in backcountry living and creativity in learning. For most participants, the result is a great expansion of sense of self, a deep sense of membership in an intimate human group, and a definition of community that includes the wild.

Reflection and Action

A young man spins a story about his first backpack with his dad. A woman takes the revision of her paper down to a hidden pool, washes her face, and sits against a juniper to watch the sun dip below a rock rim. Another woman crouches by an unopened flower all day and nothing happens until . . .

Many theorists agree with educators Pat Hutchings and Allen Wutzdorff that "reflection transforms experience into learning" (1988, 15). Students, however, are less and less capable of doing reflective learning because modern life and large lecture halls do not often allow for it. The outdoor classroom is built around active learning but reflection must also be accommodated, and at many scales. In class, I sometimes like to work with what educator M. B. Rowe (1974) calls "wait time," where ample space is allowed for thinking between questions and responses. Mountains at evening are excellent facilitators of "wait time" and reflection. In the high country an hour before dark, each group member goes off (with journal and headlamp) to find a place, sit quietly, watch the world, and not return to camp till darkness is complete. Over my twenty-five years of teaching, I have found that being still with the world is an experience that only a handful of students have ever had. But what better way is there to begin to learn, in the words of ethnobotanist Gary Nabhan, "to live well with the 'others' around you" (1997, 63)?

FUTURE ISSUES

Academic wilderness education, despite its strengths, is not in a strong position at the dawn of the new millennium. Since I surveyed the field in 1987 ("The University of the Wilderness"), most of the problems I described then have become worse. Here is a short list of what is of most concern to me.

Loss of Habitat

The biodiversity crisis that biologists warn about continues un-abated.[5] Yes, there were more acres of protected land in the United States in 1999 than there were in 1970, but wildernesses are increasingly frag-mented biologically from unprotected roadless lands. Though wilderness education does not depend on *legal* wilderness, it does require a certain amount of relatively "wild" habitat. And habitat degradation, combined with an increasingly urban population, makes it more difficult to access places that retain a semblance of ecological integrity. What writer Bob Pyle describes as "the extinction of experience" (1993, 104) goes hand in hand with the extinction of species.

Dominance of Technocratic Society

Life in the United States continues to become more technological, specialized, and rapid-paced. And so do the schools that serve American society. This does not bode well for kinds of learning that require com-mitments of time and reflection. The use of computers, for example, al-most defines membership in today's university communities, but users forget that such technologies amplify some forms of knowledge (explicit, context-free, digitizable) while reducing other forms (tacit, contextual, memory-based). Support for technical education (business, engineering, computer science), as measured by budget dollars and numbers of student majors, is increasing dramatically. At the University of California Santa Cruz, students have less flexibility to take elective credits outside major re-quirements. They are encouraged to "stay on track" and not stray beyond campus boundaries.

Fifteen years ago, author Wendell Berry wondered about how univer-sities could train "responsible heirs and members of human culture" in the face of such forces (1987, 77). Recently, Berry has been joined by a host of voices trumpeting alarm at the growing influence of technocracy on learning.[6] Yet Berry's standard is left unmet as teachers and students increasingly "become makers of *parts* of things" (1987, 77).

Decreasing University Support

At the University of California Santa Cruz, the environmental studies department has been forced recently to reduce by 50 per cent its support for its only intensive field program. Field biologists nationwide bemoan the loss of such courses.[7] With fewer field courses to participate in, students have less access to the wild classroom. Enrollments at Sierra Institute and other programs appear to be holding steady, but most report that they are spending more money and staff time to maintain the status quo.

Finally, even after thirty years there is still a paucity of empirical research on wilderness education methods and results. Does it really work better than the campus classroom? If so, how? No studies have elucidated what the optimal trip length or intensity might be or even what instructor qualities or specific activities might contribute to greater learning. The few recent studies (which are very narrow in design) report only that results are inconclusive and more research is needed.[8]

What Is "Wilderness"?

In a recent essay, "The Trouble with Wilderness," historian William Cronon suggested that "The time has come to rethink wilderness" (1995, 67). Cronon's view reveals changing attitudes toward wild nature in the United States—in fact, distinctions between people and nature are under reevaluation by many intellectuals, if not by the general public. What this debate holds for academic wilderness education is unclear. I believe that because many of those engaged in wilderness education ground their work in traditional definitions of wilderness, in the short run the field may experience less support from individuals and institutions that adopt Cronon's ideas. Current trends favor cultural constructions of "wilderness," but these same trends obscure the reality of wildness. Yet I also sense that those who cling to strict dichotomies between nature/culture, wild/tame, raw/cooked will find these views less useful as the new century unfolds. After all, it matters little whether a sacred mountain, population of native onions, Anasazi ruin, or city lot are labeled as natural or cultural artifacts. What is important, according to education philosopher Thomas Colwell, is "the particular ways in which and degrees to which they are interconnected" (1997, 8) and how much these relationships elicit compassionate behavior from us.

GOING TO BASHŌ'S PINE

Two thousand feet above the Pacific in California, just south of the canyon where Big Creek spills fresh water into the salty deep, there is a place of singular beauty and ecological significance. The beauty is easy to grasp—you face due west in open grassland on a dome at the end of one ridge among many ridges north and south, all diving steeply into endless blue waters. Close behind, giant trees speckle the grassland, waving their thick arms toward the ocean. These are ponderosa pines, far isolated from their nearest kin to the east, the westernmost population of the species in North America. How did they come to live here?

I brought my students to camp in this place in 1984, to sleep under a silver moon, to listen to night tides, and to puzzle over the pines. We watched the moon rise late, slept away from land's edge, and over several days examined and discussed the trees while counting seedlings. There were very few. The population appeared to be winking out.

In 1987, the Rat Creek fire torched sixty thousand acres of Big Sur, burning the mature ponderosas into dull black snags. The seedlings never had a chance.

Twelve seasons from the first visit and eight years after the fire, I returned to the pines with students. I shared the 1984 data, told the fire's story. We hiked to the old snags and, though many had toppled, several still threw out their branches to the wind. And in dense patches here and there under the snags, young green trees stood two to three feet high. We surveyed hundreds.

Pinus ponderosa prefers a hot burn. Fire incinerates thick grass, exposes mineral soil. Cones open to the heat and seeds disperse in the sea breeze.

"If you want to know the pine, go to the pine."

You can't count seedlings in a classroom. More important, you can't sense directly that culture, like fire-prone pines, is dependent on larger processes, deeper relationships that are ongoing and wild.

If our task is to grow a new culture in the New World, "a civilization that can live fully and creatively together with wildness," as Gary Snyder suggests (1990, 6), then a first step is to go to Bashō's pine to discover that the tree is whole and in relation, whether young or old, green or black, censused or left alone.

The learning is in the tree.

The tree endures.

Notes

1. A number of papers describing wilderness education were published early on, including Alan Drengson's "Wilderness Travel as an Art and as a Paradigm for Outdoor Education," Roderick Nash's "Wilderness Education Principles and Practices," Gene Rumrill's "Academic Horizons in Wilderness," John Miles's "Wilderness as a Learning Place," and my "The University of the Wilderness." Together, these papers defined the field and are valuable reference points.

2. See examples and literature cited in Clyde Herreid's paper "Why Isn't Cooperative Learning Used to Teach Science?" and Alison King's work, especially "Inquiry as a Tool in Critical Thinking."

3. The wilderness and civilization program has been reviewed recently in a paper by Laurie Yung and her co-authors, "Wilderness and Civilization."

4. A fine book on experiential classroom and field activities is *Knowing and Doing: Learning Through Experience*, edited by Hutchings and Wutzdorff.

5. For accessible overviews of the biodiversity crisis see Meffe and Carroll's textbook *Principles of Conservation Biology*, Noss and Cooperrider's fine book *Saving Nature's Legacy*, or my own account *Ghost Bears: Exploring the Biodiversity Crisis*.

6. For a sample of these critiques see C. A. Bowers, *The Culture of Denial*, Hayden Mattingly's "Seeking Balance in Higher Education," and David Orr's "Speed."

7. There is a sobering discussion of this trend in Reed Noss's "The Naturalists Are Dying Off."

8. This paucity of research is a measure of the lack of interest (and funding) in higher education for academic wilderness education. For examples of recent studies see Glenda Hanna, "Wilderness-related Environmental Outcomes of Adventure and Ecological Education Programming," D. P. Gillet et al., "The Effects of Wilderness Camping and Hiking on the Self-concepts and Environmental Attitudes and Knowledge of 12th Graders," and John Miles, "Teaching in Wilderness."

References

Abram, David. 1996. *The spell of the sensuous.* New York: Pantheon.
Berry, Wendell. 1987. The loss of the university. In *Home economics.* San Francisco: North Point Press.

Bowers, C. A. 1997. *The culture of denial: Why the environmental move-ment needs a strategy for reforming universities and public schools.* Al-bany: State University of New York Press.

Colwell, Thomas. 1997. The nature-culture distinction and the future of environmental education. *Journal of Environmental Education* 28.4 (Fall): 4–8.

Cronon, William. 1995. The trouble with wilderness, or, getting back to the wrong nature. In *Uncommon ground: Toward reinventing nature,* edited by Willam Cronon, 69–90. New York: W. W. Norton, 1995.

Drengson, Alan. 1980. Wilderness travel as an art and as a paradigm for outdoor education. *Quest* 32.1 (Winter): 110–20.

Fairbanks, Jonathan. 1980. The elastic classroom. *Journal of Environ-mental Education* 11.3 (Spring): 22–24.

Gillet, D. P., G. P. Thomas, R. L. Skok, and T. F. McLaughlin. 1991. The effects of wilderness camping and hiking on the self-concepts and envi-ronmental attitudes and knowledge of 12th graders. *Journal of Envi-ronmental Education* 22.3 (Summer): 33–44.

Grumbine, R. Edward. 1987. The university of the wilderness. *Journal of Environmental Education* 19.4 (Fall): 3–7.

———. 1992. *Ghost bears: Exploring the biodiversity crisis.* Washington, D.C.: Island Press.

Hanna, Glenda. 1995. Wilderness-related environmental outcomes of ad-venture and ecological education programming. *Journal of Environ-mental Education* 27.1 (Fall): 21–32.

Herreid, Clyde F. 1998. Why isn't cooperative learning used to teach sci-ence? *BioScience* 48.8 (July): 553–59.

Hutchings, Pat, and Allen Wutzdorff, eds. 1988. *Knowing and doing: Learning through experience.* San Francisco: Jossey-Bass.

King, Alison. 1994. Inquiry as a tool in critical thinking. In *Changing col-lege classrooms,* edited by D. F. Halpem and associates, 13–38. San Francisco: Jossey-Bass Publishers.

Mattingly, Hayden F. 1997. Seeking balance in higher education. *Conser-vation Biology* 11.5 (October): 1049–52.

Meffe, Gary, and Ronald Carroll, eds. 1997. *Principles of conservation bi-ology.* Sunderland, Mass.: Sinauer Associates.

Miles, John. 1986–87. Wilderness as a learning place. *Journal of Environ-mental Education* 18.2 (Winter): 33–40.

———. 1991. Teaching in wilderness. *Journal of Environmental Educa-tion* 22.4 (Summer): 5–9.

Nabhan, Gary P. 1997. *Cultures of habitat.* Washington, D.C.: Counterpoint.

Nash, Roderick. 1980. Wilderness education principles and practices. *Journal of Environmental Education* 11.3 (Summer): 2–3.

Noss, Reed. 1996. The naturalists are dying off. *Conservation Biology* 10.1 (February): 1–3.

Noss, Reed, and Allen Cooperrider. 1994. *Saving nature's legacy.* Washington, D.C.: Island Press.

Orr, David. 1992. *Ecological literacy.* Albany: State University of New York Press.

Orr, David. 1998. Speed. *Conservation Biology* 12.1 (February): 4–7.

Pyle, Robert Michael. 1993. *The thundertree.* Boston: Houghton Mifflin.

Rowe, M. B. 1974. Wait time and rewards as instructional variables, their influence on language, logic, and fate control, part I: Wait time. *Journal of Research in Science Teaching* 11: 81–94.

Rumrill, Gene. 1980. Academic horizons in wilderness. *Journal of Environmental Education* 11.3 (Summer): 4–6.

Silko, Leslie Marmon. 1986. Landscape, history, and the pueblo imagination. *Antaeus* 57 (Autumn): 83–94.

Snyder, Gary. 1990. *The practice of the wild.* San Francisco: North Point Press.

Yung, Laurie, Bob Yetter, Wayne A. Friemund, and Perry J. Brown. 1998. Wilderness and civilization: Two decades of wilderness higher education at the University of Montana. *International Journal of Wilderness* 4.2 (July): 17–20.

※ ALAN BREW

Where Passions Intertwine

Teaching, Literature, and the Outdoors

> It would be well perhaps if we were to spend more of our days
> and nights without any obstruction between us and the celes-
> tial bodies, if the poet did not speak so much from under a
> roof, or the saint dwell there so long.
>
> —Henry David Thoreau, *Walden*[1]

Last night, January twenty-ninth, I celebrated Edward Abbey's birthday with six of my students. Renée arrived early, and we worked together in the kitchen, washing lettuce for a salad and chopping olives,
mushrooms, and leeks for the pizza crusts I had prepared. We talked
about the recent restoration work my wife and I had been doing in the
house and about Renée's research for a capstone thesis she would write in
the fall. John joined us at six, bearing a paper grocery bag with his favorite
pizza toppings and two pints of Ben & Jerry's ice cream. As he rearranged
items in our freezer to make room for the ice cream, the three of us ex-
changed knowing glances. The Ben & Jerry's had a history.

The previous May, John and Renée had been students in my May-term
course Edward Abbey in the Southwest, and for twenty-five days we had
traveled together in Utah and Arizona, reading novels and essays by Edward Abbey and exploring the canyons and deserts that inspired them.
One night after a hot and hectic day of running errands in Tucson, I suggested that we buy Ben & Jerry's for dinner. The students gave me a few
briefly incredulous looks but readily agreed. We have continued to gather
for meals since the course ended, and pints of Ben & Jerry's always appear
before the end of the evening, perhaps as a good-natured reminder of my
lapse in professorial responsibility.

Shortly after John's arrival, the others—Wendy, Craig, Stacy, and Emily
(Ryan, our eighth companion in May, has recently moved)—arrive and

join us in the kitchen, sautéing onions, blending pesto, grating cheese, and spreading sauces on the crusts. Their banter fills the room, and as Emily guides the creation of the first pizza, Craig moves from crust to crust, surreptitiously adding slices of fresh mango to each one. When Emily's pizza comes off the stone in the oven, we form a circle on our recently refinished maple floors, plates on our laps. The banter continues as we take turns monitoring pizzas in the oven, and it isn't until all of them have been consumed that we move into the living room where I have started a fire.

We sit in front of the fireplace, and on a black trunk in the center of our circle, we place John's ice cream, seven spoons, and copies of Abbey's legacies—*Desert Solitaire; The Journey Home; Beyond the Wall; One Life at a Time, Please; A Voice Crying in the Wilderness; The Fool's Progress.* To commemorate Abbey's birthday, we've all selected favorite passages to read aloud, and I begin with a paired reading: Abbey's somewhat embellished description of Henry Holyoak Lightcap's birth from the second chapter of his semi-autobiographical novel *The Fool's Progress* and an authentic, though significantly more prosaic, description of Abbey's birth from James Cahalan's biography. When I finish, the others begin to share their passages. Some are from books we read together in May, but many are not. Stacy also reads from *The Fool's Progress*, Wendy from *One Life At a Time, Please,* and John from *A Voice Crying in the Wilderness.* Watching the students thumbing through their books and listening to them read, I realize that their personal libraries have grown since our trip and that their reading of Abbey is now following the course of their individual interests. This realization leads me to reflect on the catalyst for our shared passion— an academic course devoted to the study of stories in the outdoors.

If we go back far enough, we find that our earliest stories were created, shared, learned, and preserved in the outdoors, that well before the advent of colleges and universities with their ivy-covered walls and sloped-floor lecture halls, we gathered outdoors in small groups, often around fires, to share our stories. The majority of our stories, though, have been moved indoors, preserved on leaves bound between leather, cloth, and paper, or as electromagnetic pulses, and understandably the study of these stories, of literature, is associated now with indoor spaces, with comfortable chairs, with classrooms, with the stacks and recesses of library catacombs.

Given this shift in our culture, it is not unreasonable to ask what is to be gained by going out, by carrying books and the stories they contain from our classrooms and libraries into canyons and forests, mountains and swamps. Intuitively, and well before I began taking students outdoors, I knew that there was much to be gained, but it is only recently, in this age of assessment and academic accountability, that I have been challenged to articulate why teaching outdoors is, for me, pedagogically effective. My rationale, as I now understand it, is twofold. First, books and spending time outdoors are the two passions that most define who I am and the life I live. When I teach literature outdoors, I teach fully and vulnerably from the heart. Second, when the subject of the course is the words and images authors have used to capture their experiences and understandings of the natural world, then traveling and living with students in the outdoors provides vital opportunities for personal experiences that can inform and inspire vigorous engagement with the literature.

As a child, my first experiences with stories were indoors, sitting with my brother on a couch as our father read to us or prowling the aisles of my elementary school library. In my bedroom, I had a raised platform built in a corner under a stairway. Surrounded on three sides by walls and a built-in bookcase, I spent hours nestled in a beanbag chair, reading. The stories that I read, however, were seldom about being indoors.

One of my earliest literary discoveries was Jim Kjelgaard's novel *Big Red*. First published in 1945, *Big Red* tells the story of Danny Pickett, a seventeen-year-old who lives with his father in the Allegheny Mountains. Danny and his father eke out a subsistence living by trapping, varmint hunting, berry gathering, and honey collecting, but much of the novel is about Danny's adventures with Red, a champion Irish Setter whom Danny has been hired to care for. The climax of the novel occurs when Red and Danny track and eventually kill an unusually large black bear named Old Majesty.

The life Kjelgaard created for Danny was one I both related to and aspired to. Although I had never faced a renegade black bear, I could relate to Danny because geographically his world did not seem so different from mine. I lived in the Minnesota River Valley within walking distance of the river and its bottomlands, and I regularly visited my grandparents' cabin on the shore of a small lake in northern Wisconsin. I was familiar with deer and black bears; I had been blueberry picking with my grandma. Fishing and camping with my family, I aspired to a mastery of the woodcraft I saw displayed by Danny Pickett and my father.

As I grew older, my reading expanded, introducing me to outdoor places and experiences I could only imagine from my midwestern home.

Robin Lee Graham's account of his solo circumnavigation of the globe in *Dove* introduced me to sea travel and tropical ports; Mary O'Hara's trilogy about the McLaughlin family to ranching and the green grass expanses of Wyoming; and Roy J. Snell's *The Ski Patrol* to the snowy, mountainous world of Finland. Recognizing the path of my interests, young professors at the college where my father taught offered themselves as mentors, sharing stories of their own adventures in the Tetons and Cascades and introducing me to more mature reading about the outdoors: The Mountaineers' classic *The Freedom of the Hills*, Colin Fletcher's wonderfully wry *The Complete Walker*, and his accounts of long-distance hiking adventures in California and the Grand Canyon.

This reading led me to form new ideals for my outdoor experiences, and, as I delivered papers to customers of the *Mankato Free Press*, trudging through the snow in genuine, Vibram-soled hiking boots purchased with my earnings, my mind was often elsewhere, turning icy porch steps into mountain slopes. These new ideals were fueled further when my family traveled to the western United States, but it was not until my senior year of high school that I realized some of the ideals I had created from the pages I consumed in my cozy nook.

It was Christmas break, and I was in Washington, visiting one of the professors who had nurtured my interests in books and the outdoors. He had recently moved back to Seattle, his childhood home, and had offered to take me hiking in the mountains. We rose early on the morning I had been anticipating for months, and carefully filled our rucksacks with items necessary for a day in the mountains: extra sweaters and mittens, matches, first-aid kit, compass, food for a summit lunch, and a thermos of tea—just like the mountaineers I had been reading about. At the trailhead for Mt. Si, dressed in long underwear, wool pants, blue stocking hats, and mountain parkas, Luke showed me how to fasten gaiters over my hiking boots, and we were off, ice axes in hand.

The trail started as a thin muddy line winding its way through large pines, but as we moved upward, the mud turned to snow, and we began to catch glimpses of the peaks—hints of the summit view that awaited us. By early afternoon, we had reached tree line, and we took turns breaking a path through waist-deep snow to a sheltered area near the summit. After stamping out a place to sit, we settled down to a lunch of sandwiches, potato chips, and tea. The sun was warm, and as I shared bits of my sandwich with a jay who landed confidently on my bent knee, I realized a dream.

In retrospect, I can see that this trip marked a significant turning point for an interest that was soon to develop into a defining passion for my life. The summer after my freshman year in college, I had my first overnight backpacking experience in the Boundary Waters Canoe Area Wilderness, and then the outdoor experiences began to accumulate quickly. Now, I live outdoors for two months or more each year, and shorter excursions are an integral part of my daily rhythm.

It was also in college that my interest in reading broadened beyond books about the outdoors and began to develop into a passion for the formal study of literature. During my junior year in particular, while I was living in Exeter, England, I became enthralled by the literary analysis of William Shakespeare's dramas and Charles Dickens's novels. Their stories fascinated me, but what really captured me were two professors who had so immersed themselves in the worlds created by Shakespeare and Dickens that it was difficult, some days, not to confuse them with characters in the literary works they were teaching me to appreciate and love.

As I made my way through graduate school, I came to recognize that, although I shared my British professors' passion for literary study, I did not share their passions for the Renaissance world of Shakespeare or the nineteenth-century world of Dickens. Steadily, my work as an apprentice teacher and scholar turned toward my roots, and as it did my interests began to intertwine in increasingly complex and determinative ways. Now in my third year of full-time teaching, my twin passions have become inextricably meshed. Students in my College Writing course read *Walden*, my introductory literature course focuses on the interplay of humanity and nature in works ranging from Shakespeare's *As You Like It* to James Welch's *Fools Crow*, and every year I spend one month teaching literature in the outdoors, traveling with my students to the canoe country of northern Minnesota or to the canyon country of southern Utah. When I teach these courses, and especially when I am teaching outdoors, I am, like my favorite teachers in Exeter, teaching my passions, sharing with students those experiences that have most significantly determined my path through life—reading books and traveling, living, being outdoors.

Educational theorists, unfortunately, have been slow to recognize and validate the essential role that passion plays in the art of teaching, but without it, as students have always recognized, even the most fascinating subjects of study become cold and disconnected, meaningless. With it, as Parker J. Palmer observes in *The Courage to Teach: Exploring the Inner Landscape of a Teacher's Life*, teachers are able "to weave a complex web of connections among themselves, their subjects, and their students so that students can learn to weave a world for themselves."[2] These connections, as Palmer goes on to explain, "are held not in [the teachers'] methods but in their hearts—meaning *heart* in its ancient sense, as the place where intellect and emotion and spirit and will converge in the human self."[3] In *Meeting the Tree of Life: A Teacher's Path*, John Tallmadge makes much the same point, when he writes, "this was true teaching at last: the act of bearing witness, to own a truth you have lived beyond all pretense."[4] I hesitate, as most teachers do, to claim too much, but when I observe students reading *extra* novels and essays of literary criticism after all formal assignments have been completed, or read in a student's final course evaluation that she feels "Abbeyfied," or gather with students in a circle on the floor of my living room to celebrate an author's birthday months after final essays and grades have been submitted, I know that a valuable web of connections has been woven.

Of course, the nature and significance of these connections are not always readily apparent. But, as my experiences with teaching literature outdoors accumulate and as my own struggles with the convergence of intellect and emotion and spirit continue, I can see that vigorous connections between individuals and literary expressions of the human condition depend vitally on genuine personal experience.

For me, the catalyst for this realization was C. L. Rawlins's book *Sky's Witness: A Year in the Wind River Range*. Ostensibly a narrative account of Rawlins's experiences as a backcountry hydrologist, *Sky's Witness* is also an exploration of Rawlins's struggles with predecessors in the genre of nature writing, and particularly with that icon of the genre, Henry David Thoreau. Throughout the book, Thoreau appears as a doll, "strolling the inner woods"[5] of Rawlins's head. His first appearance is an antagonistic one: "The mountains in winter," Rawlins writes,

> have an austere beauty; words like *purity* and *dignity* leap up in response. Yet we seem, in our little tribe, to revel in the opposite. Marty makes jokes about toilets and listens to Iggy Pop on his Walkman, John tells me of white-trash adventures overseas, and I come up with bondage scenarios involving foresters, clerks, and Doberman pinschers. It all seems right at the time.[6]

But then, his Thoreau doll appears. They argue, and Thoreau tells Rawlins what he should leave out of his nature tale.

Over the course of *Sky's Witness*, Thoreau continues to appear at key moments, trying to temper Rawlins's account of his experiences in the Wind Rivers; ultimately, the crux of their struggle becomes clear. Rawlins has read many nature tales, tales by authors such as Emerson, Jeffers, and Han Shan, and when he was younger they influenced his behavior: "Years ago," he writes, "I had visions of staying out, away, apart,"[7] and in fact Rawlins did retreat to the high Salt River Range for two months. Looking for lessons in the woods, he filled notebooks with metaphors, haiku, and parables.[8] As he matured, however, and as his own experiences in nature multiplied, Rawlins found that the words and ideals of these nature tales were insufficient: two months in the Salt River Range left him lonely;[9] the superlatives, epiphanies, and *Götterdämmerung* sunsets left him longing for "an honest thump or a stumble."[10]

Disillusioned with the literary cornerstones of our cultural attitudes toward nature, Rawlins struggles with what he labels "the poet's burden." This burden, which he defines in an essay printed in *High Country News* two years after the publication of *Sky's Witness*, has at its root a struggle with how we see, think of, and speak of the earth; it is, as he further explains, "a struggle with words and images, and with the history of words and images, the shifting currents of mind."[11] In other words, Rawlins's squabbles with Thoreau are manifestations of the poet's burden, of his struggle with the words, images, and currents of mind that have influenced how we see, think of, and speak of the earth and our relationship to it.

As I pieced together the import of Rawlins's squabble with the nature writing tradition, I recognized that the poet's burden is also one that I carry. Steeped, as I am, in the words and images of nature tales, I find myself pursuing a realization of their ideals in my own experiences. Living as a teenager in the Midwest, I turned icy steps on my newspaper route into mountains. Living in the Piedmont of North Carolina, I chased snowstorms in the mountains of Virginia because briefly, on grazed-over balds, I was able to experience the blustery, alpine conditions that I had come to associate with *true* wilderness. When I fail in my pursuit of these ideals, I often am left confused, discontented, wrought with unresolved tensions between my actual experiences and those I've been led to anticipate by the words and images of others. Often it's hard for me, as Rawlins observes, "to tell what part of my feelings come from books and legends . . . to say what I know of [a] place itself. . . ."[12] Only by immersing ourselves in both, I am coming to understand, can we fully bear the burden, moving ever closer to an understanding of our place in the world.

In *Democracy and Education*, John Dewey, a philosopher and educator, articulates the significance of this realization for educational practices. "Much of our experience is indirect," Dewey writes; "it is dependent upon signs which intervene between the things and ourselves, signs which stand for or represent the former."[13] In many respects, Dewey explains, our ability to have indirect experiences mediated by signs is a positive trait because in general "the scope of personal, vitally direct experience is very limited."[14] Rawlins makes a similar point when he observes that "our love for myth may be biological convenience. . . . patterns that work are passed on not just in the genes, but in the language, as songs, dances, and stories. A child hearing that first tale is suddenly a half-million years old."[15]

On the other hand, "there is always a danger," Dewey continues, "that symbols will not be truly representative; danger that instead of really calling up the absent and remote in a way to make it enter a present experience, the linguistic media of representation will become an end in themselves."[16] This danger is one that Ralph Waldo Emerson, that bookish nineteenth-century graduate of Harvard, acknowledged when he asserted that "meek young men grow up in libraries" and critiqued the "book-learned class" for valuing books "not as related to nature and the human constitution, but as making a sort of Third Estate with the world and the soul."[17] "Books," Emerson proclaimed, "are the best things, well used; abused, among the worst."[18] For teachers, and especially for literature teachers, the temptation to make the linguistic media of representation an end in themselves, to make books a Third Estate, is ever present, and we also face the danger of assuming, as Dewey observes, "that pupils have a foundation of direct realization of situations sufficient for the superstructure of representative experiences erected by formulated school studies."[19] "Before teaching can safely enter upon conveying facts and ideas through the media of signs," Dewey concludes, "schooling must provide genuine situations in which personal participation brings home the import of the material and the problems which it conveys."[20]

When the "material" for a course is the linguistic representations of human experiences in the outdoors, as it is in many of my courses, I am convinced that taking students outdoors to live and travel together is one of the most effective strategies for providing genuine situations that will bring home the import of the course's material. To illustrate, I turn to the experiences of two students who participated in my northern Minnesota canoe course, "Pens & Paddles in the North Woods."

In this course, students read literary accounts of North Woods canoe journeys while we planned and then completed a ten-day journey in the Boundary Waters Canoe Area Wilderness. Paddling, as we were, in a wilderness area of over one million acres and reading from works that ranged from Henry David Thoreau's "Ktaadn" to James West Davidson and John Rugge's *The Complete Wilderness Paddler*, the students had ample opportunity to compare their experiences to those of their literary predecessors.

A common theme in much of the literature that we read was the contrast between travel in the wilderness and travel in cities. In *Canoe Country*, for instance, Florence Page Jaques writes, "What a way to travel—no trains to catch, no traffic to annoy us, no towns to reach by evening, no appointments to remember! . . . We are finding more than peace here. This is an authentic and profound release from modern intricacies."[21] Reading this passage in the midst of modern intricacies, where such passages are often read, it is seductive and persuasive, but, as one of my students discovered, the release that Jaques describes is not always so easy to realize—even while paddling the same lakes that Jaques paddled. Here's what Abe wrote in his final essay for Pens & Paddles:

> When one journeys through the maze of lakes and forests that make up this wilderness one becomes involved in a dual relationship. With factory-made canoes, tents, clothing, and stoves and mass-produced food, fuel, and bug dope, most corners of the globe are represented. These conveniences are designed to help make the wilderness experience more familiar, more like home. What they truly accomplish is defining a separation between the wilderness and ourselves. But this same separation is what draws most of us out of the cities and into the woods. So as I paddle across this lake in my canoe made in Maine with materials and chemicals from across the globe, wearing my pants that were purchased in Minneapolis but made in Malaysia, how do I draw an intimate connection with the wilderness around me? How am I to become intimately involved with my surroundings while I am protected, covered, and transported by things that themselves have no connection to this area?

Another student from Pens & Paddles who brought to the course very clear expectations for the experience she wanted to have in nature was surprised to find that she was transformed not so much by nature but instead by the experience of traveling with others in the outdoors. Tonya's final essay began with these observations:

> Tying a knot in the bungee cord which crisscrossed to form a storage space under the canoe seat, I suddenly realized that everyone in the boat shed would be on the trip with me. . . . Until that moment . . ., I [had] pictured myself having an individual experience in the BWCAW; it never really occurred to me that I would be sharing the experience with seven others. Even after this initial realization, I pictured myself having an individual ex-

perience within the group. I expected to travel along with my class, but saw myself separated from the others. . . . I imagined that I would have a different state of mind and attitude that would automatically exclude me from the others. Not that I wouldn't enjoy spending time with my classmates, but it simply wouldn't be the proper place to do so. I am serious when outside. I am in awe and look reverentially upon everything with silence. Nature changes my thoughts and my spirit. Being with others during this time seemed highly inappropriate, . . . like having visitors over on your wedding night.

From here she goes on to explain the traumatic childhood experiences that led her to conceive of nature in this way and how her experiences in Pens & Paddles led her to a new appreciation for human nature—as well as a deeply personal appreciation for the words of two authors that we read in the class. She concludes,

Having had many sad occurrences in my life, I sought nature as an escape to the most basic form of life, hoping to forget the pain of the world behind me. I never wanted people along. . . . But now I was laughing, more than I had in a very long time, and at the same time I felt the rhythms of nature, though not focusing on them exclusively, they were still working in me. I no longer felt alienated from my surroundings because of my companions. In a different way than usual, I felt closer to my environment because of them. . . . And then I realized that my problems were separating me from nature more than I had thought, because they constantly brought me back to the unnatural world in little ways, more than the company of any person could. . . . When an eagle is pointed out and we all look at it together, when we talk together and laugh, we have unification with the natural world. And I thought, "This is what it was like when all men were primitive and living within the scope of their environment. In my continual aloneness in nature, I have missed something fundamental and basic— humanity." Douglas Wood acknowledges this as he discusses the significance of a circle of people surrounding a campfire: "The image of the circle is especially strong in evoking the dimensions of life, whether the human circle of community [. . .] or the cave, the hunting party, the council ring. It involves not anonymity, but knowing, and being known: it involves sharing, trust and interdependence"[22] . . . My outdoor experience was now influenced by human nature, which I had previously not acknowledged as an important part of the natural world. As Sigurd Olson says, "The bush is a complex of many joys," and the first one he lists is "companionship on the trail."[23] . . . There were times when a couple of us stood on a rock gazing at a sunset, and nothing was said. Nor did anything need to be verbalized—the presence of companions was still there, and it was a positive feeling to know their nearness without hearing them.

For both of these students, travel in the Boundary Waters provided a genuine situation in which their personal participation brought home the significance of the representative experiences described and discussed in the literature of the course. Abe found there were things he needed to acknowledge about his experience of the Boundary Waters that were missing or suppressed in the writing of others. Tonya, whose preconceptions about experiences in nature reflect the pervasive influence of Thoreau's *Walden* sojourn, Abbey's desert solitaire, and Dillard's Tinker Creek pilgrimage, found first contradictions and then affirmation as her personal experiences of the Boundary Waters led her to connections with Wood and Olson. Would the full import of our complex "dual relationship" have been recognized by Abe if he had not read Jaques *and* paddled in her path? Would Tonya have understood the import of Wood's circle or Olson's complex joys if she had not stood on a rock at dusk in the silent presence of companions whom she had come to know through muddy portages, wind-whipped crossings, shared meals, and much laughter? Or, perhaps more importantly, would Tonya have recognized the import of what Thoreau, Abbey, Dillard, and others have left out—the connections they have chosen not to write about in their nature tales?

As I complete this essay, I am distracted by a book on the corner of my desk. It is hand-bound with white yarn, a piece of corrugated cardboard folded over irregular, cream-colored sheets of richly textured paper. Pasted to the cover at odd, overlapping angles are a number of brief statements, each with a caption: "You don't understand! There's geology everywhere, okay!"—*Craig gets a crazy, evil look in his eyes.* Centered on the cover is a four-by-six color photo of seven students in shorts, t-shirts, and sandals leaning against a large sign that reads "Hite: Glen Canyon National Recreation Area." A slip of paper pasted across the upper-left corner of the photo boldly proclaims, "The Wild Bunch." This book is a gift from the students in my Edward Abbey course, prepared by them in the midst of their busy academic schedules and presented to me at one of our regular reunions. I can think of no better remembrance for our time together.

But, it is also a gift that I am hesitant, even a bit embarrassed, to share with others. Would others be offended by the vulgarity of some of the quotations on the cover? Quotations that read, "Renee's sucking, Stacy's wetting herself, and Craig and Ryan won't put out!" Would they understand why all of the students in the photo have their middle fingers raised, profaning a National Recreation Area? To quote Rawlins, the vulgarity, the irreverent actions all seemed right at the time. They were part of our common experience, and despite the fact that we were traveling and living in some of the most magnificent and awe-inspiring natural areas preserved in our country, our thoughts were not all pure, certainly not all dignified. Would others understand?

I worry because looking at this single artifact from our shared experience, people will not see other artifacts. They will miss, for instance, the beautifully poetic reflections captured in Emily's final essay, where she wrote,

> Sun-warmed reddish brown, my hands have soaked in the color of the desert. Even after the last bit of Utah dirt has washed down the drain I can still see smooth sandstone, lined and layered, in my scarred, creased skin. Each crevice, each canyon, each scar has a story. Every wrinkle records a bit of history. Each hangnail—fragile, thinly layered cells, flaking back from the thicker, tougher nail—expresses series of drought, flood, and abrasion.
>
> * * *
>
> The human scars on the desert distress me, and I am grateful for Abbey's part in preserving what's left mostly untouched. Now, what can I do? I wonder. How can my hands, burned the hue of sun-warmed sandstone, heal current scars and prevent future ones? They could grow strong enough to swing a sledgehammer, demolishing dams and bridges. They could shake hands with politicians, breaking down barriers with compromise. Or they could write stories, drawing people into the land. Yes, stories, I like that. I think I'll tell stories.

Stories. Scars. Dirt. Hands. Hands clasping. Arms hugging. Passions intertwining. These are what the casual reader of my hand-bound book might miss.

Notes

1. Henry David Thoreau, *Walden* (Princeton: Princeton University Press, 1971), 28.
2. Parker J. Palmer, *The Courage to Teach: Exploring the Inner Landscape of a Teacher's Life* (San Francisco: Jossey-Bass Publishers, 1998), 11.
3. Ibid.

4. John Tallmadge, *Meeting the Tree of Life: A Teacher's Path* (Salt Lake City: University of Utah Press, 1997), 200.

5. C. L. Rawlins, *Sky's Witness: A Year in the Wind River Range* (New York: Henry Holt and Company, 1993), 35.

6. Ibid.

7. Ibid., 123.

8. Ibid., 309.

9. Ibid., 123.

10. Ibid., 17.

11. C. L. Rawlins, "My Kingdom is a Horse," *High Country News,* 7 August 1995.

12. Rawlins, *Sky's Witness,* 275.

13. John Dewey, *Democracy and Education: An Introduction to the Philosophy of Education* (New York: The Free Press, 1966), 232.

14. Ibid.

15. Rawlins, *Sky's Witness,* 122.

16. Dewey, 232.

17. Ralph Waldo Emerson, "The American Scholar," in *The Portable Emerson,* ed. Carl Bode (New York: Penguin Books, 1981), 56.

18. Ibid.

19. Dewey, 233.

20. Ibid.

21. Florence Page Jaques, *Canoe Country* (St. Paul: Minnesota Historical Society Press, 1989), 21.

22. Douglas Wood, "In a Smaller World." In *North Writers: A Strong Woods Collection,* ed. John Henricksson (Minneapolis: University of Minnesota Press, 1991), 278–80.

23. Sigurd F. Olson, "Beyond the Ranges," *Open Horizons* (Minneapolis: University of Minnesota Press, 1998), 108.

References

Abbey, Edward. 1987. *One life at a time, please.* New York: Henry Holt and Company.

———. 1988. *The fool's progress: An honest novel.* New York: Henry Holt and Company.

———. 1990. *A voice crying in the wilderness* (Vox Clamantis Deserto). New York: St. Martin's Press.

Dewey, John. (1916) 1966. *Democracy and education: An introduction to the philosophy of education.* New York: The Free Press.

Emerson, Ralph Waldo. 1981. The American scholar. In *The Portable Emerson,* edited by Carl Bode, 51–71. New York: Penguin Books.

Fletcher, Colin. 1964. *The thousand-mile summer in desert and high sierra.* Berkeley: Howell-North Books.

———. 1968. *The man who walked through time.* New York: Alfred A. Knopf.

———. 1969. *The complete walker: The joys and techniques of hiking and backpacking.* New York: Alfred A. Knopf.

Graham, Robin Lee. 1972. *Dove.* New York: Harper & Row.

Jaques, Florence Page. (1938) 1989. *Canoe country.* St. Paul: Minnesota Historical Society Press.

Kjelgaard, Jim. (1945) 1992. *Big Red.* New York: Bantam Books.

Mountaineering: The freedom of the hills. 1960. 5th ed., 1991. Seattle: The Mountaineers.

O'Hara, Mary. 1946. *The green grass of Wyoming.* Philadelphia: J. B. Lippincott Company.

Olson, Sigurd. 1969. Beyond the ranges. In *Open Horizons.* Minneapolis: University of Minnesota Press.

Palmer, Parker J. 1998. *The courage to teach: Exploring the inner landscape of a teacher's life.* San Francisco: Jossey-Bass Publishers.

Rawlins, C. L. 1993. *Sky's witness: A year in the Wind River Range.* New York: Henry Holt and Company.

———. 1995. My kingdom is a horse. *High Country News* 7 (August).

Snell, Roy J. 1940. *The ski patrol.* Chicago: The Goldsmith Publishing Company.

Tallmadge, John. 1997. *Meeting the tree of life: A teacher's path.* Salt Lake City: University of Utah Press.

Thoreau, Henry David. (1854) 1971. *Walden.* Princeton: Princeton University Press.

Wood, Douglas. 1991. In a smaller world. *Canoe* (July 1989). In *North Writers: A Strong Woods Collection,* edited by John Henricksson. Minneapolis: University of Minnesota Press.

❋ BRENT CUTHBERTSON
JANET DYMENT
LESLEY P. CURTHOYS
TOM G. POTTER
TIM O'CONNELL

Engaging Nature

A Canadian Case Study of Learning in the Outdoors

INTRODUCTION

The idea that being in the outdoors contributes to people's wellness is not a new one. From the physical benefits of gardening to the therapeutic potential of wilderness trips, the healing and stabilizing power of nature has been documented (see Altman and Wohlwill 1983; Kaplan and Kaplan 1992). With respect to social paradigms, the writings of John Muir, Henry David Thoreau, Aldo Leopold, Grey Owl, Rachel Carson, Annie Dillard, and many others have helped alter the place of nature in the Euro–North American psyche during the past century. In concrete terms, a variety of institutions and organizations have emerged in the past few decades offering programs catering to diverse populations that situate natural settings squarely at the centre of the experience. The demand for nature-based "youth-at-risk" programs as well as other therapeutic and inclusive outdoor recreation programs in Canada routinely outpaces supply (Potter and Cuthbertson 2002). Even the anecdotal evidence of watching others, especially children, interacting outdoors is enough to convince many of us that the blessings of connecting with nature are indeed numerous and profound (Nabhan and Trimble 1994).

A rich literature has developed examining and extolling the virtues of incorporating nature into formal and informal educational settings. A number of researchers have investigated the importance of nature and place attachment in the lives of young children (Chawla 1992; Cobb

1977; Nabhan and Trimble 1994; Sobel 1993). Many others have explored the important role that natural spaces can play in creating effective learning environments in primary and secondary schools (Bell 2001; Horwood 1994; Lieberman and Hoody 1998; Ryan 1991; Thomson and Arlidge 2000). Despite recent political moves in Canada toward a more conservative approach to education, the research to date is overwhelmingly clear about the advantages of teaching and learning in close association with natural settings.

However, in spite of the knowledge about the advantages of incorporating nature into primary and secondary school curricula, much less is understood about the role natural settings could play in achieving the educational objectives of post-secondary institutions such as universities and colleges. Most learning in these institutions tends to happen inside large, but often cramped and windowless, rooms. In discussing building design at universities, Orr speaks to a fundamental flaw in how and where post-secondary education takes place:

> It is paradoxical that buildings on college and university campuses, places of intellect, characteristically show so little thought, imagination, sense of place, ecological awareness, and relation to any larger pedagogical intent. . . . Buildings have their own hidden curriculum that teaches as effectively as any course taught. (1994, 112–13)

Such architecture has helped to leave the dubious legacy that serious study and the "distraction" of the outdoors are not compatible. Although it is unlikely that people's connection to nature wanes with the onset of adulthood, the socialization alluded to by Orr has no doubt had an impact on how higher education is structured in North American society.

A variety of issues and questions could be raised that make modern educational practices at the university level problematic, but a particularly cogent one might focus on pedagogical possibilities instead of just criticism. In other words, some reflection on courses and programs that are consciously designed to incorporate nature into their curricula in a direct and meaningful way could help to shed some light on the relationship between theory and practice of post-secondary education in nature. What if teaching at universities didn't happen inside all the time? What if faculty taught some of their classes outside, drawing on the motivational power of direct contact with nature? What if nature was conceptualized as teacher instead of merely a backdrop for activity, or if entire courses occurred outside? And what if the theoretical groundings of these experiences were intentional and designed to be pedagogically coherent with course goals and objectives? This chapter explores a program that claims some degree of consistency in that regard. We begin with a brief description of the program as a whole, after which four courses are explored as illustrative examples of the different ways that nature is engaged in the program.

THE PROGRAM

The School of Outdoor Recreation, Parks and Tourism (ORPT) at Lakehead University is unique in Canada, offering students opportunities to study recreation in natural environments. Lakehead University is located in Thunder Bay, Ontario, on the northwestern shore of Lake Superior. Somewhat isolated from other large urban centres, the area is rich in cultural heritage and surrounded by numerous protected areas, vast tracts of crown (publicly owned) land, and an abundance of lakes, rivers, and picturesque natural features.

The relatively pristine and sharply contoured landscape that surrounds Thunder Bay provides a superb opportunity for the integration of theoretical and applied perspectives found in ORPT's four-year honours degree. The program offers a variety of social science and professional preparation courses that emphasize the study of recreational activities and leisure pursuits related to and dependent upon the natural environment. The out-of-doors serves as a critical medium for the teaching, learning, and application of theories, knowledge, and skills. Most courses in the program support one or more of three academic streams: outdoor leadership, nature-based tourism, and protected areas. In addition, students may pursue one of several four-year double-degree options that combine the Honours Bachelor Outdoor Recreation Degree with a degree in Geography, History, Natural Science, or Women's Studies.

The program's goals include providing a venue for ensuring the integration of conceptual and applied knowledge; facilitating relationships with practitioners; enabling an understanding of scientific approaches in ORPT fields; fostering a positive and responsible interaction with human and natural environments; and encouraging active involvement in and contributions to quality of life linked to the natural environment. ORPT promotes shared responsibility for learning and places an emphasis on the application of knowledge in the wider community. Furthermore, the program prides itself on graduating proficient and ethically responsible practitioners who serve the community and have the ability to think critically, to solve problems, and to undertake research.

TABLE 1: Engaging Nature in ORPT Courses

FIRST YEAR:		THIRD YEAR (cont.)	
Group Dynamics in ORPT	X	Commercial Recreation and Tourism	X
Introduction to ORPT	X	Nature-Based Tourism	X
Organization and Management in ORPT	X	Topics in Parks and Protected Areas	A
Environmental Issues in ORPT	B		
Theory and Practice of Leadership	X	FOURTH YEAR	
		Honours Project II	X
SECOND YEAR:		Experiential Education in Outdoor Recreation	V
Programming and Evaluation	X	Private Stewardship	A
Forest Recreation Management	X	Deep Ecological Perspectives in Nature-Based Recreation	A
Outdoor Skills and Theory I	C		
Outdoor Skills and Theory II	C	Advanced Outdoor Adventure Leadership	C
Inquiry and Analysis in ORPT	X		
Theory and Practice of Tourism	X	Outdoor Centre Management	B
Theory and Practice of Parks and Protected Areas	X	Field Explorations II	D
		Advanced Concepts in Group Dynamics	A
THIRD YEAR		Advanced Studies in Heritage Interpretation	B
Honours Project I	X		
Outdoor Education Practices	X	Advanced GIS and Remote Sensing	X
Ecological Literacy	B	Polar Tourism	C
Expedition Management	X	Therapeutic Recreation and Adventure Therapy	B
Outdoor Adventure Leadership	C		
Topics in Leadership	V	Tourism Analysis	X
Field Explorations I	D	Issues in Sustainable Tourism	V
Heritage Interpretation	B	Park Planning and Management	X
Geographic Information Systems	X	Areas and Facilities Planning	B
Advanced Inquiry and Analysis	X	Coastal and Marine Recreation	X
Topics in Tourism	X	Wilderness Issues	X
Inclusive and Special Recreation in Outdoor Environments	X	Directed Studies	V

KEY:

X) classroom-based courses that do not use the outdoors

V) courses in which the use of outdoors varies with the instructor

A) classroom-based courses that occasionally use the outdoors

B) classroom-based courses that have significant portions devoted to outdoor study

C) courses that split classroom and field components and spend more time in the field than inside

D) field-based courses for which the vast majority of the content is covered in, and geared toward, the outdoors

Table 1 lists all courses currently in ORPT and the degree to which the outdoors is a direct part of the course delivery. It is clear that not all courses directly engage the outdoors as part of the pedagogy or course content. In fact, of the forty-six courses offered over the four years of the program, twenty-one (46 percent) involve some degree of direct experiences in the outdoors. Aside from the constraints inherent in university settings for supporting such alternative approaches, this also constitutes a recognition that not all subject matter is ideally suited to the outdoors. Nonetheless, those courses that are conducted wholly indoors support those that are outdoor-oriented by other means, such as concept development. That said, we now turn to an examination of four courses that respectively exemplify the categories A through D in Table 1. These courses are Environmental Issues (Type A); Ecological Literacy (Type B); Outdoor Skills and Theory I and II (Type C); and Field Trip I (Type D). In addition to representing varying degrees of outdoor class time, these courses also illustrate four types of engagement with nature: nature as motivator, teacher, classroom, and home. It is important to note, however, that these pedagogical roles of nature operate at varying degrees in all ORPT courses that embrace learning outdoors.

TYPE A ENGAGEMENT: ENVIRONMENTAL ISSUES

Environmental Issues, a required first-year course in ORPT, in some ways sets the tone for contact with nature and the outdoors for students. This course is designed to introduce students to environmental issues in outdoor recreation and to assist in the development of an environmental perspective that encompasses a concern for the natural environment from local to global levels. Topics covered usually include a variety of perspectives in environmental thought, social and political structures of environmental policy and decision making in Canada, relevant scientific principles, and current environmental issues of significance to outdoor leadership, protected areas, and nature-based tourism. At approximately the halfway point in the course, one of the two weekly-lecture time slots gives way to a facilitated seminar in which students explore issues and concepts through guided discussion and experiential pedagogy. It is during these seminar classes that outdoor areas around campus are incorporated into the course. Two specific examples of how this is done will help to illustrate the role of outdoor and natural settings in providing motivation for students' connections beyond the classroom walls.

Nature as Motivator

An axiom of environmental education is that educators need to facilitate affective connections to nature as part of the learning. In making the assumption that caring *about* something or someone will contribute to a caring *for* that something or someone, educators have tapped into the concept of motivation. Despite our lack of a deep understanding about motivational pathways (Russell 1999), it is generally accepted that triggering the keys of motivation in students is caught up with the goal of encouraging people to take up active roles in support of nature. Employing the motivational potential of nature, then, is one of the elements embodied in this first illustrative course, Environmental Issues.

In the first of two examples, students are to prepare for a discussion on individual and collective ecological impacts of Western lifestyles by arriving at their seminar class with a calculation of their personal ecological footprint. The ecological footprint, an applied concept developed by Wackernagel and Rees (1996), is a calculation of a general area of land (in either acres or hectares) needed to sustain human activities. Upon convening in a large open area on campus, students are asked to measure out the average ecological footprint of seminar members and mark the boundaries with corner flags. For many the impact is immediate. In debriefing the students, it becomes clear that the numerical representation of the space needed to sustain their lifestyles remains an abstract concept for them until they witness how that number translates to the land in front of them. Especially powerful for some is the realization that it takes very few of the class members to require a section of land bigger than the university campus. In this case, it seems undeniable that as a motivational tool for personal change, similar results could not be achieved by merely making the calculations in a classroom.

While the intellectual and emotional impact of the exercise described above may be motivational for some, it is undoubtedly a negative message regarding human relationships with the rest of nature. A conscious effort is thus needed to offset what could manifest defeatist or even anti-human sentiments if such messages constituted the only staple diet of motivational input. Other sessions provide the counterbalance to these potentially dangerous trends. In another seminar, for example, the question for discussion centres on the ethics of human recreation in nature. On one hand, it could be argued that the perceived need to "play" in nature does not justify the ecological impacts of people's activities in those natural areas. Indeed, many students struggle with this and view their recreational forays as inconsistent with their overall beliefs. However, while irresponsible outdoor recreation is not defensible by any ecologically sensitive ethic, its seemingly logical antithesis—leaving all natural areas free from human visitation—is not only unlikely, but also potentially damaging, because it contains within it a human/nature separation.

In order to address this dilemma, students gather in a meadow encircled by a larger treed area adjacent to the built-up portion of campus. Seminar members are asked to close their eyes while a natural and cultural history, written in poetic prose, is read about the very meadow in which they are sitting. Responses to the reading and their new connection to the meadow are solicited in the discussion that follows and their reactions are woven into the ethical question of being in nature. At some point, the position that nature and humans are part of each other and that any attempt at separation may create a false dichotomy is raised. The implications of this position for outdoor recreation ethics are then explored.

This second seminar exercise is inspired by Leopold's artful weaving of culture and nature in *A Sand County Almanac* and by a variety of ethicists who decry the separation of humans from the rest of nature. The theoretical relevance of such a seminar topic is not merely to rationalize the use of "wilderness" or nature but rather to encourage stronger connections to the rest of nature for students in ORPT, to inject an element of moral consideration into their interactions with the rest of nature, and to motivate them to recognize nature's need for humans to understand it. In the words of Reed and Rothenberg:

> It is not enough to agree that we should love our place; we have to really love it if our declarations are to have any practical consequences. This, of course, means knowing our place, and that means getting out into it. (1993, 155)

TYPE B ENGAGEMENT: ECOLOGICAL LITERACY

A recent addition to the ORPT curriculum is a third-year required course on ecological literacy. This course examines the process of coming to know about, care for, and act on behalf of the cultural and ecological integrity of place—whether place is one's home, the location of a nature-based tourism excursion, an outdoor recreational setting, or a protected area initiative. Links between ecological literacy and a sustainability ethic are discussed. For example, students deliberate their responsibility and role as ORPT practitioners in the development of sustainable communities where what is sustained "is not economic growth, development, and market share, or competitive advantage, but the entire web of life on which our long-term survival depends" (Capra 1999, 1). Gateways, barriers, and pathways to ecological literacy are explored through literature (such as Capra 1999; Carson 1956/1984; Golley 1998; Orr 1992; Van Matre 1990), and importantly through outdoor experiential learning.

Drawing upon the pedagogical philosophy that it is not enough to learn about nature, rather we must learn both in and with nature, the ecological literacy course devotes a significant amount of class time to outdoor study. Weekly field trips (both on and off campus within a twenty-minute drive) increase students' familiarity with the natural and cultural interplay of local landscapes. Through a combination of field trips, self-directed outside activities, nature journaling, and storytelling, this course aims to encourage a personal connection with the local bioregion and the desire to continue to actively engage in reading and writing landscapes long after the course's completion. Importantly, the ecological literacy course seeks to elevate the role of nature from some "thing" to observe, to the role of nature as teacher.

Nature as Teacher

The course examines the current debate on what it means to be ecologically literate. While some definitions focus primarily on the acquisition of cognitive skills (RELATE 2001), Stables and Bishop (2001) caution against narrow conceptualizations of ecological literacy that imply only the ability to read and write *about* the earth. A more holistic, attentive approach involves accepting the landscape *as text* where the learner is actively engaged in *reading* (directly comprehending) and *writing* (acting upon) the landscape itself. This broader form of ecological literacy is what Stables (1998) terms critical ecological literacy. The term is adapted from Williams's and Snipper's (1990) tripartite distinctions (functional-cultural-critical) of language literacy where print is replaced by place. In other words, critical ecological literacy is the ability to make meaning of place to self and others through active engagement with that place. According to Stables and Bishop (2001), ecologically responsible citizenship requires critical ecological literacy, which in turn is dependent upon functional ecological literacy (comprehension of ecology) and cultural ecological literacy (comprehension of human dimensions of landscapes such as land use patterns and cultural icons). Furthermore, bioregionalists suggest that ecological action is most powerful if the *text* that one is able to comprehend functionally, culturally, and critically is one's *home-place* (Aberley 1993; Andruss, Plant, Plant, and Wright 1990; Snyder 1990).

Critical ecological literacy requires active engagement with place. Lutts (1985, 39) commented that personal participation with place "helps to develop a sense of continuity of self and surroundings." Landscapes shape our thoughts, language, movement, architecture, and artistic expressions, and we in turn influence landscapes. And so through dialogue with place it is possible to come to learn more about ourselves in and as nature. In sum, ecological literacy education requires—in part—first-hand experiences that cultivate personally meaningful relationships with specific places (Abram 1996; Golley 1998; Orr 1994; Snyder 1990). Thus, it is in close conjunction with landscapes and waterscapes that a course on ecological literacy must take place.

The shift from nature as object to nature as teacher becomes apparent through a major course assignment called "The Storied Landscape." The storied-landscape assignment invites students to spend an extended amount of time (the assignment spans eight weeks) in less human-dominated areas on campus to discover nature as teacher. The exercise encourages students to co-create meaning of a specific place, to discover a story, through first-hand involvement. The aims of the assignment are threefold. First, the assignment is an attempt to move away from the human-centered learning to a more ecocentric position where the animate landscape and its often marginalized voices are acknowledged as a valid and enriching source of knowledge. While the importance of direct experience in education is certainly not something new, what is perhaps more novel, especially in higher education, is the idea that the landscape has just as much, if not more, to offer the learner as do print and electronic media. Conservative education, even environmental education, favours abstract scientific knowledge and print-based learning over the practice of natural history (Bell 1997). This reliance upon book learning is sometimes reflected in the students' initial reactions of disbelief, confusion, and apprehension when asked to replace the library with the landscape as the *primary* source of information and inspiration for the storied-landscape assignment. Thus, leading up to this major assignment, is a series of self-directed "learning from the landscape" activities that are aimed at helping students develop the attitude and aptitude to learn directly from nature. Interestingly, one of the most commonly mentioned obstacles to learning directly from nature was making time to be outside.

Second, the assignment aims at moving away from the abstract (learning *about* squirrels) to the specific bioregional knowledge (learning from *that* squirrel). Lutts noted that environmental education

> . . . has traditionally been very effective at teaching about *generalized* eco-
> logical processes and environmental hazards. Out of *particularized* experi-
> ence and understanding of our own unique places, however, grow personally
> meaningful relationships with personally significant environments. [Environ-
> mental education] that combines both is likely to be especially effective in
> promoting environmental understanding, values, and action. (1985, 38)

Finally, this student-directed learning experience is designed to blend nature study with creative oral expression. Students are not asked to submit a written paper about the story, but rather to share *their* (landscape-student) stories orally with peers at the places of the stories' origins, thus inviting the class to participate in the meaning of place as well. Students have responded with a variety of styles including simple narratives, songs, dramatizations, and poetry. Their stories blend ecological (and sometimes cultural) knowledge with interpretations of particularized experiences. The act of story creation and the art of storytelling may lead to new ways of relating to and celebrating the animate world. On the importance of stories, place, and relationship, Abram commented,

> The telling of stories, like singing and praying, would seem to be an almost
> ceremonial act, an ancient and necessary mode of speech that tends the
> earthly rootedness of human language. For narrated events . . . always hap-
> pen *somewhere*. And for an oral culture, that locus is never merely inciden-
> tal to those occurrences. The events belong, as it were, belong to the place,
> and to tell the story of those events is to let the place speak through the
> telling. (1996, 163)

Ecological literacy has no endpoint. Rather it is an active engagement with place, an ongoing dialogue with place, and it is nurtured through celebration of place. Thus to teach about ecological literacy and to develop ecological literacy, we need to heed Wordsworth's beckoning: *Come forth into the light of things. Let Nature be your teacher.*

TYPE C ENGAGEMENT: OUTDOOR SKILLS AND THEORY I AND II

Outdoor Skills and Theory (OSAT) I and II, two required second-year courses, provide an experiential and theoretical basis for a wide variety of outdoor pursuits. The format of these two courses is the same;

students participate in a weekly two-hour lecture, as well as field exercises throughout the semester. The field components consist of day outings, two-day workshops, and three-day overnight experiences that complement and build on material presented in the lecture sessions. These outings occur at a number of locations in the Thunder Bay region. Some are relatively remote and pristine, while others are within the city limits. Although the lecture component of these courses plays an important role in the curricula, the field activities allow for both the theoretical and practical application of knowledge critical to those using the outdoors as a classroom.

Nature as Classroom

OSAT I and II utilize experiential learning techniques both in the classroom and in the field. The Association for Experiential Education (AEE) defines experiential education as ". . . a process through which a learner constructs knowledge, skill, and value from direct experience" (2002). Further, Priest and Gass (1997) have identified eight principles that are associated with experiential education. These include direct and purposeful experience; appropriate level of challenge; natural consequences; participant-based change; present and future relevance; synthesis and reflection; participant responsibility for learning; and active engagement. These fundamental aspects of experiential education are inherent components of the outdoors, especially when the outdoors is used as a classroom. Immediate and real feedback is received in the outdoor environment. Students are able to grapple with the ramifications of their actions, be personally affected by them, and through planned lessons and debriefing sessions transfer these experiences to their current state and future being. This pedagogical approach, and use of the outdoors as a classroom in both OSAT I and II, form the foundation for student learning in these courses.

OSAT I, which takes place during the fall semester, is set in the context of three broad skill areas: rock climbing, canoeing, and backcountry travel. Students are exposed to basic rock climbing skills and may choose to participate in a supplementary session that stresses advanced rock climbing practices. Theoretical facets of rock climbing such as the physics of belay systems and fundamental climbing techniques are taught. Students also participate in both whitewater and flat-water canoeing over a three-day weekend. Here, they are able to link physical skills such as paddle strokes and body positioning with river hydrology and "reading the water." Additionally, they are introduced to minimum-impact camping through the tenets of the Leave No Trace program, an internationally recognized curriculum. The backcountry travel component of OSAT I encourages students to develop a proficiency in hiking and camping skills. Further, students are encouraged to utilize theoretical knowledge gained from a first-year course entitled Group Dynamics throughout the duration of OSAT I as they explore fundamental group processing techniques, examine group development, and experience group management and teaching methods. This framework allows students to not only practice technical skills, but, more importantly, make the critical link to theory and professional practice in outdoor settings.

OSAT II occurs during the following semester and uses activities such as skiing, winter camping, snowshoeing, ice climbing, river travel, and dogsledding to promote skill development and theoretical knowledge for living and travelling safely and comfortably in winter environments. Students enrolled in OSAT II are exposed to several skiing genres; classic and skate Nordic technique, telemark, and backcountry styles are all included as one-day introductory lessons. The winter-camping field component includes such skills as shelter construction, dressing for and sleeping in cold-weather conditions, menu planning, and equipment selection and use. The snowshoeing section includes use of both contemporary and traditional snowshoes. Students learn differences in designs and styles of snowshoes as well as how to tie their own bindings using lampwick, a traditional material used for this purpose. Theoretical aspects of winter outdoor recreation such as snow studies, thermal dynamics, ski waxing, and dressing using the layering system encourage students to make the link to practice during the field sessions. OSAT II strives to strike a balance between traditional theory and technique and modern advances in outdoor equipment.

Portions of OSAT I and II are devoted to the development of technical outdoor skills that enable students to live comfortably and travel safely in the outdoors in a range of environmental conditions, and it may appear that this is the main intent. However, through the use of the outdoors, the primary endeavour of OSAT I and II is to develop the students' ability to connect these skills to theoretical knowledge and to apply these skills and knowledge to future experiences. To assist in and encourage this transfer, there is a wide range of theoretical components that complement these basic outdoor skills. These include the historic development of outdoor activities, risk management, physiology, sociology, and psychology of outdoor recreationists, and the underlying philosophies of outdoor techniques.

The historical development of outdoor activities provides a realization of how the outdoors has been used as a place to educate and recreate. This is essential, as students discover that many parallels exist in today's world. Additionally, this complements the inclusion of traditional outdoor skills and techniques in OSAT I and II. Many time-honoured methods form the foundation for modern applications, which allow for a richer understanding of one's relationship with the natural world. For example, students learn to light fires with flint and steel, often cook over open fires, and learn to construct shelters using natural materials. The instructors for OSAT I and II believe that in the rush to embrace modern technological innovation, personal growth, learning, and connection to the natural world may be compromised. OSAT I and II challenge students to reconsider these advances with more traditional outdoor equipment and wilderness living methods, while at the same time keeping the Leave No Trace philosophy and minimum-impact ethic in mind. The practice of traditional methods alongside contemporary practices encourages a richer understanding of the outdoors and of human existence in the natural environment.

An understanding of the sociology and psychology of people in the outdoors is a vital part of the OSAT I and II curriculum. The study of how and why people use the outdoors as a place for education and recreation enables students to firmly understand the motivations, behaviours, and feelings of others in an outdoor context. More importantly, perhaps, it encourages students to clarify the understanding of their own experiences in the outdoors and transfer this understanding to other courses and everyday life.

OSAT I and II both present the underlying concepts of skills needed to successfully flourish in the outdoors. The inclusion of such concepts as dressing using a layering system, the physiology of hypothermia, pros and cons of water treatment systems, physics of forces on rock-climbing anchors, movement of water over and around river features, and how cross-country ski wax functions provide for a richer understanding of subject matter. Students are granted the tools to not only physically perform a skill but to understand why a skill is performed in a particular manner. This learning is enhanced through practice in outdoor settings.

An important teaching technique used in both OSAT I and II is a reflective journal. Students are expected to log their experiences from both an objective and subjective perspective. The reflective journal allows for the integration of skills and theory, serving as well as a lasting record of skills and accomplishments. Students are encouraged to explore the connections between the classroom experience and outdoor activities. Recording their thoughts, experiences, and perceptions helps students to transfer what they have learned to future experiences. Reflection has been noted as a key aspect of the experiential learning process and is particularly powerful when used in conjunction with outdoor experiences (Knapp 1992).

OSAT I and II utilize both the traditional classroom and the outdoors to make the critical link between theory and technical skills. In the context of the outdoors, the use of experiential education techniques enhances student learning experiences. Additionally, OSAT I and II place knowledge and skills in the context of professional and personal development. As these courses lay the theoretical and practical foundation for future School of ORPT courses with field components, engaging nature as a classroom is a key factor in the success of these endeavours.

TYPE D ENGAGEMENT: FIELD TRIP I

Field Trip I is a required third-year course that has traditionally provided students with an intensive experience in one of northwestern Ontario's natural areas. Examples of field trips include a two-week wilderness tandem canoe expedition, a Canadian heritage voyageur canoe trip, a Lake Superior sea-kayaking expedition, and a dogsledding trip. Drawing upon the theories and skills gained in Environmental Issues, Ecological Literacy, and OSAT I and II, as well as a variety of other theoretical and applied courses, students are provided with an opportunity to apply and enhance a variety of skills related to pre-trip planning, leadership, risk management, backcountry living skills, heritage interpretation, natural history, and group dynamics. Importantly, the extended time spent in the outdoors introduces the idea of nature as home.

Nature as Home

In Field Trip I, students are provided with the unique opportunity of journeying in a remote natural environment for an extended period of time. All of their necessary possessions are carried in a backpack, canoe pack, or dogsled. For most of our students, this two-week experience will be the longest time they have been away from the conveniences of electricity, phones, e-mail, and central heating. And for many students, this will also be the first time that such an extended, contiguous contact with free nature will give them the opportunity to feel "at home" in wild places.

In order to help students feel at home in nature, an important focus of Field Trip I is to help students to feel safe, comfortable, and familiar living in a natural setting. In achieving this focus, some remarkable experiences occur on the trip for individuals and groups. Often students will attribute the intensity, beauty, and splendour to the fact that the trip has happened so far away from the clutter and confines of the city and university environment. And indeed many choose to look at this experience—at least initially—from this escapist perspective. This cognitive separation of city and nature is evident in the often repeated sentiment that "this never could have happened at home in the city."

However, another essential part of Field Trip I is helping students understand that nature *is* home, just as the city *is* home, and the university *is* home. A significant element of the course thus involves revisiting the concepts they have learned in the Environmental Issues and Ecological Literacy courses, and encouraging students to resolve the false dichotomy that exists between the perceptions of home in the city and home in nature. Snyder recognizes the need to minimize this constructed duality between perceived human and more-than-human realms. In exploring the relationship between humans and the rest of nature, he writes:

> It has always been part of basic human experience to live in a culture of wilderness. There has been no wilderness without some kind of human presence for several hundred years. Nature is not a place to visit, it is *home*— and within that home territory, there are more familiar and less familiar places. (Snyder 1990, 7)

With a view to understanding that humans are an important part of the landscape's story (both currently and historically), students on Field Trip I courses are encouraged to appreciate and respect Canada's rich heritages by exploring the historic context of landscape-human interaction in the area. For example, students learn how the routes they are travelling on were once important "highways" connecting eastern and western Canada. They also learn how Aboriginal people lived sustainably in the region for the last ten thousand years. A standard practice on these trips is to engage students through journal-entry readings of early European explorers and story telling from First Nations oral traditions. Contemporary political issues confronting these areas are also woven into the discussions on trips. These course elements are designed to facilitate students' connections to the landscape through understanding the place beyond just their own experiences there.

When people are able to see "nature as home," much can be learned about human interactions and community development. Capra notes the importance of creating sustainable communities and suggests that nature can provide us with guidance in achieving this: "In our attempts to build and nurture sustainable communities, we can learn valuable lessons from ecosystems, which are sustainable communities of plants, animals, and microorganisms" (Capra 1994, 1). By understanding the ecological principles of interdependence, recycling, partnership, flexibility, and diversity, Capra asserts that humans can create social and cultural environments that will meet present and future needs.

An important part of Field Trip I is encouraging students to develop healthy learning communities. This is possible, in part, due to the small size of the faculty and the interdisciplinary style of ORPT that allows many faculty to get to know students on a personal level before they participate in Field Trip I. As such, an extremely rewarding aspect of the work is watching students learn, grow, and change throughout their four-year tenure in the program. Nowhere is this growth and change more obvious than on Field Trip I, where students are given opportunities to demonstrate old, and to gain new, intrapersonal and interpersonal skills.

In Field Trip I, students are placed in relatively unfamiliar environments (e.g., remote natural settings such as Lake Superior, Wabakimi Provincial Park) and are travelling via relatively unfamiliar media (i.e., sea kayak, dogsled, whitewater canoe, voyageur canoe). Such combinations are valuable because they present a stark contrast to the students' familiar environments, allowing them to examine and explore their own intrapersonal and interpersonal qualities.

Another unique component of Field Trip I is that, unlike a typical classroom setting, it is conducted in groups of eight to twelve people. The small-group setting combined with an unfamiliar environment often serves as a critical factor for behavioural and attitudinal change. Properly orchestrated small-group interactions can exponentially increase task accomplishment at an individual and group level (Priest and Gass 1997). At an individual level, students on Field Trip I often demonstrate new confidence in themselves, increased willingness to take risks, improved self-concept, enhanced leadership skills, and greater reflective thinking skills. Within the group, it is very common to observe students demonstrating enhanced cooperation, more effective communication skills, greater trust in others, increased sharing of decision making, new ways to resolve conflicts, and enhanced leadership skills. While it is rewarding to observe intrapersonal and interpersonal growth throughout their time in the program, it especially rewarding to see these changes accelerated during Field Trip I.

It is important to note that the concept of community in Field Trip I extends beyond relationships between people to include relationships between people and the rest of nature. Students on these trips are encouraged to develop a strong sense of connectedness to the rest of nature. This inclusive relationship is facilitated through structured activities such as natural history lessons, hikes, required readings, and journaling. While these structured activities help to encourage a deepened connection to nature, we also believe that it is equally important to take advantage of the numerous unforeseen opportunities that emerge on field trips. Unplanned activities, such as watching the northern lights, seeing a moose and her calf, and seeking shelter from a lightning storm, certainly help to facilitate a sense of being part of the larger community of life.

While on expeditions, we encourage students to explore and understand the interconnections between their "home in the city" and their "home in nature." Central to facilitating this recognition is the concept of transference (Priest and Gass 1997). Faculty members working with these courses strive to help students understand the interconnections between their lives in the city, their lives at university, and their lives in nature.

One way transference occurs from "home in the city" to the "home in nature" is when faculty members revisit concepts taught in the university classrooms and demonstrate practical illustrations in the natural environment. The theories, lessons, and values taught in foundational courses in ORPT are revisited as faculty members encourage discussion about the sustainable management of the places travelled in. Students learn about the natural and cultural histories of the landscapes they are working with in order to have an understanding of issues related to the sustainable management of visitor numbers, visitor behaviours, endangered species, and natural disturbances. On some of the trips, students, staff, and faculty members establish formal relationships with parks managers and conduct research throughout their travels (e.g., campsite impact assessment) that will be useful in guiding management decisions for the protected area. In performing this research, they apply the concepts and theories acquired in the classroom. When students combine their "intellect with experience" (Orr 1992, 128), they are able to recognize the interrelationships between the subjects they have been studying and are able to understand how the leadership, parks, and tourism streams relate to each other and how they apply in nature.

Students are also encouraged to transfer their experiences from Field

Trip I back to their homes in the city. In order to help students do this, many of our faculty and staff encourage students to critically reflect upon their experiences in order to create deeper meaning, thus allowing them to see the interconnections between and among their homes. Indeed, facilitated reflection is explicitly taught and is practiced throughout students' tenure in ORPT. Critical reflection about one's relationship to self, others, and setting can be difficult for some, thus instructors craft reflective sessions to introduce the idea of nature as home to stimulate meaningful thought. Gathered around a fire, lying under a blanket of twinkling stars, sitting on a rocky outcrop overlooking a lake, chatting with a canoe partner while paddling across a lake, or watching the sun slip off the horizon while feeling the temperature plunge are all teachable moments. Experiences such as these, distanced from the physical and emotional clutter of everyday life's cultural artefacts, can lead students to profound realizations about their personal lives, their world views, and the people with whom they share their journey.

Through these reflective experiences, we explore how students can apply what they learned on Field Trip I to other places in their city homes (e.g., at school, on the job, or within their families). Some lessons are more easily and directly transferable between homes, such as the concept of simplicity in lifestyle. Other learning, however, requires more abstract thought and even paradigm shifts in their application. For example, the notion that city homes are also part of nature (albeit often an impoverished nature) may require a transformation in thinking that can, at least at first glance, run counter to students' reverence of what they consider to be natural. Nonetheless, the potential this concept holds to blur the lines between the dichotomies of wilderness/city and nature/human is considerable. It also contains possibilities with respect to how one might envision the reconstruction of "a natural city."

CONCLUSION

There are, of course, links and overlaps between and among the classes highlighted here. As previously mentioned, the portrayal of these courses in light of the four themes of *nature as motivator, nature as classroom, nature as teacher,* and *nature as home* was for illustrative purposes. Table 1 and its typology was developed as one way of explaining the variety of engagement and the duration of that engagement in the courses in ORPT. The discussion is not meant to indicate that the typologies are restricted to the sorts of courses with which they were associated in this chapter. It would not be difficult to demonstrate, for example, that seminars in the Environmental Issues course also fit well with the theme *nature as classroom* or that students would gain insights into *nature as home* and *nature as motivator* through the Ecological Literacy sessions and assignments. The interdependence of virtually all the courses in the program is recognized by faculty and staff. Third- and fourth-year courses tend to build not only on the concepts and content of earlier ones but also on the very discussions and assignments developed during those first two years.

The manner and method of introducing nature-based components into each of these four courses are at once similar and varied, but all have goals which tie them to the program as a whole. The authors believe that humans and the rest of nature do not exist in isolation from each other, despite the physical and social constructs that contribute to such a dualistic view. Whether teaching on campus or in wilderness, faculty members realize that the students' experience of nature may be equally powerful in either setting. While there is a recognition that students should be exposed to extended trips in relatively free nature, instructors acknowledge the problems of privileging wilderness as a way of connecting with the rest of nature (for a thoughtful critique of nature as wilderness, see Cronon 1995).

Freeing nature from the domination of the idea of wilderness does not, however, necessitate an acceptance of just any perception of nature. Viewing humans and nature as indistinguishable should not, say, open the door for relativistic orientations that might indicate that because humans are part of nature, all human activity is also natural and therefore acceptable. Such positions tend to neglect the role of moral connections. In ORPT, students are encouraged to reflect not only on their connections to wilderness nor solely on their urban lifestyles but on how these come together in an ethical orientation to all of nature.

Without wishing to downplay the serious problems in university education generally, and specifically in its relationship to nature, this chapter has focused on the positive, the pedagogical possibilities that exist for nature-based programs in Canada and North America. Our position is, quite simply, that any serious attempt to meld humanity, the rest of nature, and learning requires a program that operates on multiple levels of connections to nature—a nature that blurs the lines of city and wilderness, a nature that includes human citizens, a nature that contains the potential to demonstrate to our students that the very identity of all life is dependent on all other life.

96 ❋ Brent Cuthbertson et al.

References

Aberley, D., ed. 1993. *Boundaries of home: Mapping for local empowerment*. Gabriola Island: New Society Publishers.

Abram, D. 1996. *The spell of the sensuous*. New York: Vintage Books, Random House.

Altman, I., and J. Wohlwill, eds. 1983. *Behavior and the natural environment*. London: Plenum Press.

Andruss, V., C. Plant, J. Plant, and E. Wright. 1990. *Home: A bioregional reader*. Gabriola Island: New Society Publishers.

Association for Experiential Education. 2002. *Frequently asked questions: Experiential education*. Retrieved February 11, 2002, from http://www.aee.org/faq/nfaq.htm#ee.

Bell, A. C. 1997. Nature study from a learner's perspective. *Canadian Journal of Environmental Education* 2: 132–44.

———. 2001. Engaging spaces: On school-based habitat restoration. *Canadian Journal of Environmental Education* 6: 209–24.

Capra, F. 1994. Ecology and community. Retrieved August 30, 2001, from http://www.ecoliteracy.org/pages/publications.html.

———. 1999. *Ecoliteracy: The challenge for education in the next century*. Liverpool Schumacher Lectures. Berkeley: Center for Ecoliteracy.

Chawla, L. 1992. Childhood place attachments. *Place Attachments*, 63–86. New York: Plenum Press.

Carson, R. 1956/1984. *The sense of wonder*. New York: Harper and Row, Publishers.

Cobb, E. 1977. *The ecology of imagination in childhood*. New York: Columbia University Press.

Cronon, W. 1996. The trouble with wilderness; or, Getting back to the wrong nature. In *Uncommon Ground*, edited by W. Cronon, New York: W. W. Norton and Company.

Golley, F. 1998. *A primer for environmental literacy*. New Haven: Yale University Press.

Horwood, B. 1994. Integration and experience in the secondary curriculum. *McGill Journal of Education* 29 (1): 89–102.

Kaplan, R., and S. Kaplan. 1992. *The experience of nature: A psychological perspective*. Cambridge: Cambridge University Press.

Knapp, C. 1992. *Lasting lessons: A teacher's guide to reflection*. Charleston, W.Va: ERIC (Educational Resources Information Center).

Lieberman, G. A., and L. L. Hoody. 1998. *Closing the achievement gap: Using the environment as an integrated context for learning*. Ponway,

Calif.: Science Wizards.

Lutts, R. 1985. Place, home, and story in environmental education. *Journal of Environmental Education* 17 (1): 37–41.

Nabhan, G. P., and S. Trimble. 1994. *The geography of childhood: Why children need wild spaces.* Boston, Mass.: Beacon Press.

Orr, D. W. 1992. *Ecological literacy: Education and the transition to a postmodern world.* Albany: State University of New York.

Orr, D. W. 1994. *Earth in mind: On education, environment, and the human prospect.* Washington, D.C.: Island Press.

Potter, T., and B. Cuthbertson. 2002. Inclusive recreation in the outdoors: A Canadian perspective. *First Pacific Rim Conference on Leisure Education: Conference Proceedings,* 176–84. First Pacific Rim Leisure Education Conference, Hawaii, January 11–14, 2002.

Priest, S., and M. Gass. 1997. *Effective leadership in adventure programming.* Champaign, Ill.: Human Kinetics.

Reed, P., and D. Rothenberg. 1993. *Wisdom in the open air.* Minneapolis: University of Minnesota Press.

RELATE 2001. *Realizing environmental literacy through advanced technology and experimentation.* Retrieved June 2, 2001, from http://lpsl.coe.uga.edu/RELATE/text/define.html.

Russell, C. 1999. Problematizing nature experience in environmental education: The interrelationship of experience and story. *Journal of Experiential Education* 22 (3): 123–28.

Ryan, C. 1991. The effect of a conservation program on schoolchildren's attitudes toward the environment. *The Journal of Environmental Education* 22 (4): 30–35.

Snyder, G. 1990. *The practice of the wild.* San Francisco: North Point Press.

Sobel, D. 1993. *Children's special places: Exploring the role of forts, dens, and bush houses in middle childhood.* Tuscon, Ariz.: Zephyr Press.

Stables, A. 1998. Environmental literacy: Functional, cultural, critical. The case of the SCAA guidelines. *Environmental Education Research* 4 (2): 155–64.

Stables, A., and K. Bishop. 2001. Weak and strong conceptions of environmental literacy: Implications for environmental education. *Environmental Education Research* 7 (1): 89–97.

Thomson, G., and S. Arlidge. 2000. *Five-minute field trips: Teaching about nature in your schoolyard.* Calgary, Alberta: Global Environmental and Outdoor Education Council of the Alberta Teacher's Association and the Calgary Zoo.

Van Matre, S. 1990. *Earth education: A new beginning.* Greenville, W.Va.: The Institute for Earth Education.

Wackernagel, M., and W. Rees. 1996. *Our ecological footprint.* Gabriola Island, B.C., Canada: New Society Publishers.

Williams, J. D., and G. C. Snipper. 1990. *Literacy and bilingualism.* New York/London: Longman.

PART II: Strategies for Teaching

Introduction to Part II

The selections in Part II, "Strategies for Teaching," provide suggestions for field-based assignments, class sessions, and semester-length courses. The first essay, Katherine R. Chandler's "Can't See the Forest or the Trees: Finding Focus," explains how drawing, tree shrines, and walking can cut through distractions and help students focus on their writing during environmental-literature and composition-course field trips.

Focus is also a theme of Laird Christensen's "Writing the Watershed," an essay describing his success in designing a course that asks "students to become more familiar with their own bioregion," and then to share their knowledge with the local community. It describes how students gathered and published stories about a badly polluted local watershed in order to increase awareness and change attitudes. Instructors interested in service learning projects that combine writing with environmental issues will find this essay particularly illuminating.

The following essay also describes a project designed to raise awareness of environmental values, this time in the English Lake District. Poet Terry Gifford's "Teaching Environmental Values through Creative Writing with School Children" describes a program and specific techniques for engaging "with the mountain environment through a variety of forms of writing, leading to a debate about environmental issues" in the secluded Duddon Valley.

The next essay explains specifically how perceptions can be changed and how teaching outdoors can facilitate the three dimensions of transformative learning—ecological, cultural, and social. In "Going Out as a Way In: Social, Cultural, and Ecological Learning and the University Field Trip," Liz Newbery and Bob Henderson describe three separate field trips to "near nature," wilderness, and urban spaces to illustrate how achieving critical awareness can lead to meaningful personal and social change.

Fred Taylor's "'On the Path, Off the Trail': Teaching Nature Writing as a Practice of the Wild" provides suggestions specifically geared toward teaching nature writing. He explains four practices of writing—attentiveness, freedom to explore, receptivity, and openness to sharing—as central to teaching this genre.

Part II: "Strategies for Teaching" concludes with Andrew Wingfield's "Road Trip: Self-Directed Field Work as a Learning Journey." This final essay discusses a semester-length research and writing project in which students take a trip and then write about their experiences. This essay shows how traveling outside the classroom helps students develop a desire for lifelong learning and how it assists them in becoming independent thinkers, researchers, and writers.

※ KATHERINE R. CHANDLER

Can't See the Forest or the Trees

Finding Focus

"Dr. C?"

A student's voice snapped my concentration, but I could barely tear myself away. One more line, just one more line . . .

"It's 3:40. Weren't we supposed to regroup at 3:30?"

Three-forty? Ten minutes late? I don't do that! I stay aware of where we are within a class period and certainly do not ignore my students. Snatching journal and pencil, I hustled for the gazebo, our afternoon meeting place. What I saw confirmed my personal reluctance to end the trance. Bodies were still belly down in the weeds, students absorbed, intent with their pens. Clearly, many of them had also slipped out of time; even one of my most consistent clock-watchers was unwilling to relinquish the moment. One more line, their poses suggested, just one more line. What a contrast from the discouraging, disruptive outdoor classes I had previously attempted.

The material I teach in American environmental literature and my nature-focused composition course invites us to move outside for some portion of our learning. On the first day of environmental literature, I greet my students with Joseph Wood Krutch's counsel spread across the blackboard.

> "Up, up and quit your books" is not an adjuration commonly thought advisable in universities, but there are occasions—as for instance, when studying Wordsworth [or Thoreau]—when it might be worthwhile (Krutch 1967).

Knowing, of course, how Krutch also valued books, I embrace his dictum, yet my application of this principle has not been wholly successful.

I am not a biologist or a skilled natural historian; I am a literature

St. Mary's College of Maryland. St. Mary's River in foreground, Chesapeake Bay in background.

professor. My course objectives do not include providing students with detailed scientific information about our forests, bioregion, or watershed; I take students outside to engage them in a concrete way with the abstract notions they encounter in our reading and to encourage practices that help them to become more attuned to the natural world. Contemporary environmental writers emphasize the urgency of our need to become more discerning observers of the world of which we are a part, and to accomplish that, I do not need to take students hiking the Appalachian Trail, sailing the Chesapeake, or exploring Atlantic beaches. My goal is to aid students, and, I must confess, myself, to become conscious of our immediate surroundings, so the ecosystems in which we live are no longer merely backdrop but processes in which we recognize our participation and bioregions to which we commit our attention. What we read in class initiates this awareness, but that means little unless we also discover how the place we walk through on the way to class reveals volumes about who we are and how we are to live—if we learn to learn from it.

Our place, St. Mary's College of Maryland, curves around Horseshoe Bay, a widened turn in the St. Mary's River. Following the western shore of the Chesapeake straight south from Annapolis, St. Mary's is near the end of the peninsula created by the Chesapeake Bay and the Potomac River. The waterfront campus is only three miles west of the Chesapeake and eleven miles north of the St. Mary's egress into the Potomac. This is tidewater territory, defined by water—rivers, creeks, inlets, coves, ponds, marshes, and bogs. We live among oysters and blue crabs, ospreys and bald eagles. Loblolly pines, sweet gums, pin oaks, and tulip trees dominate our forests, with understories of dogwoods, azaleas, mountain laurels, and redbuds. American hollies are a distinctive feature of southern Maryland because of their height, some reaching forty feet. Our setting is lovely—a quality that students name as a reason for choosing St. Mary's—and varied enough that,

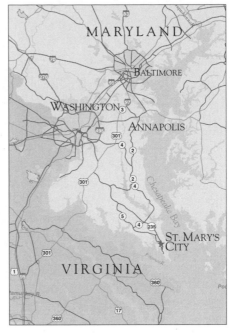

within walking distance, I am able to take us to different types of locations.

Too often, however, when I take students outside, attention wanders. In the past, outdoor classes have sometimes deteriorated into sessions of distraction. My efforts to bring students closer to the world of nature have been considered by some as occasions to vacate the world of learning. Passing friends on nearby paths tempted greetings, or someone's distant round of Frisbee golf proved far more intriguing than the essay of the day. Discussion at times became disjointed, or a planned activity floundered. Consequently, we rarely ventured out in a fully meaningful way.

Until, that is, 3:40 that April afternoon when I witnessed students lying on the grass too involved in their work to check the time. The difference?

Focus.

Focus had been missing in my early efforts to conduct class outside. The need to focus is obvious, and assuredly I had tried, but my choices of *how* to focus students in the out-of-doors were based on indoor pedagogical strategies. In the classroom, chalkboards, closer proximity, and visual or auditory focal points bind us in ways unavailable, even undesirable, outside. Plus, we have four walls to hold back outside stimuli. I had been thinking in terms of classroom format—training I had received was naturally in a classroom context. I am convinced that we have fostered a dichotomy: inside we learn; outside we play. Outside connotes freedom, even freedom from responsibility. This principle pervades our culture and holds true on multiple levels. What I had to learn was not to harness freedom but to direct attention and train senses.

Scientists and natural historians know that we learn from observing and experiencing nature; thus, complementing the classroom with the out-of-doors is pedagogically sound. Biologists at St. Mary's wade their students into the marshes to monitor dissolved nitrogen levels and boat them onto (and into) the river to monitor the abundance of submerged aquatic vegetation—river meadows, one professor calls them. Merging the study of literature with the outdoors can be a tougher stretch. I am discovering, though, how our surroundings provide perfect opportunities for learning foundational principles that help us develop as thoughtful members of our communities, cultural as well as natural. It took failures for me to understand how to corral the overwhelming rush of sensory input and create a narrow focus under a broad sky. What I will discuss are some of the activities I now employ, some I have abandoned (and why), and the process that I now take students through to move more effectively *into* the outside.

That April afternoon when my students and I stretched belly down in the weeds provided the occasion for my epiphany. When I noted that I was not the only one reluctant to leave my journal work—"one more line; just one more line"—I realized that we had just experienced an engrossing outdoor class. What particularly intrigued me was that, in our journals, we were not writing, we were drawing. That "one more line" was not another line of journal-entry prose; it was another stroke delineating the trumpet of a daffodil or the base of a sycamore. Pursuing an idea through writing was known to me; unearthing ideas by forming a shape on a page was new. I was not attempting to teach the skills of line drawing. Not an artist, I found the power of sketching as a means to focus illuminating. I learned that I cannot draw the leaf of a dandelion to capture its shape and size (if not its essence) without fully concentrating. Back and forth, from leaf to page, my eye follows a focused path. In this, I was not alone. Many of my students that day were reluctant to abandon their drawing. "Wait! I'm not done with the stem!"

The first four chapters in Annie Dillard's *Pilgrim at Tinker Creek* had been our reading, and the questions she raises in "Seeing" were what I wanted to emphasize. I designed this class period to demonstrate the value of juxtaposing different perspectives. Shifting between close-up and panorama seemed a memorable way to illustrate how multiple views enable fuller understanding, assisting us to reconsider not only what we see but how we look. Since varying perspective and alternating pace are valuable principles in thinking and writing as well as observing, we would be able to draw multiple conclusions from the experience. Of course, we could also make connections with ecological relationships, as some students did.

One source for this April *Pilgrim* class activity was Claire Walker Leslie's and Charles E. Roth's *Nature Journaling*, which includes in its introduction a page-length section titled "Focusing Through Drawing What You See" (1998, 11–12). Leslie and Roth recommend drawing from multiple perspectives, but to accomplish our activity within the time frame of the class period and demonstrate the concept, I selected two: ground observation and whole landscape (23–24). We commenced class on a bluff overlooking the St. Mary's River. No one stepped forward claiming to be an artist; in fact, a few muffled mutters of "I can't draw" sounded, but after assuring the group that I couldn't draw either and a brief explanation that we were attempting to record what we saw, not to achieve artistic excellence, we separated to select our spots.

During the first fifteen minutes, I periodically glanced about to register the students' level of engagement. They had settled in and become absorbed. What happened then even now amazes me. When teaching, I remain in that metacritical zone attuned to students, but on this afternoon I became so engrossed by the act of sketching a diminutive twig that I lost track. Miraculously, the lines on my paper actually began to resemble that twig.

Then, I looked out across the river, framed a panorama with my hands, and started to sketch. Not so good. Stick-figure quality. Back to close-up. The ground cover I was lying on captivated me once I noticed that thousands of individual plants created what had initially looked like a solid carpet. Then, only moments later, it seemed, my student called to me.

The significance of my absorption was slow to emerge. Even while we showed our sketches and discussed what we had experienced in the context of questions raised by Dillard, I did not fully realize what had transpired. The students' drawings and the insights in their comments corroborated that I was not the only one taken into deeper concentration. On the concrete level, some pointed out observations they had never made before: various color shades, height or diameter of plants five centimeters small, side as well as top views of organisms, infinitesimal fungi

on tree bark. The questions in journals accompanying their sketches ranged from the objective "What functions do these tendrils serve?" to the more philosophical "Have we touched each other at all?" (referring to a cedar tree). Exploring the distinctions between "looking" and "seeing," students probed more abstractly, remarking on the surprising complexity of what they saw. They offered perceptive speculations about differences Dillard suggests between seeing by analyzing and seeing by letting go (1999, 32–33), and reading students' subsequent journal entries confirmed my sense that I was on a worthwhile track. I discovered that, for the majority, this outdoor activity had generated a lasting, significant effect.

When my epiphany came, the impact of what had transpired hit with the force and permanence of a decision that instantly feels right. Focus. Since sensory energies from our surroundings engage and envelop us, why not employ them more purposefully as pedagogical tools and mnemonic devices? Not only were students focused during this outdoor activity, but they drew meaningful conclusions as well as meaningful shapes. Previously when outside, I had attempted to get students to concentrate through literary exercises; so what was different? Instead of limiting my vision by employing the outdoors as tangible versions of images or as aesthetically pleasing backdrop for reading poems aloud, I had had students examine something specific *in* their environment. Connections to literature and life could be provided by framing questions before or after the experience.

What I came to understand is that, in a very real and significant sense, when we employ appropriately designed outdoor activities, we are not only making a specific point within our discipline, we are training students to pay attention. With each year, I more fully comprehend how crucial that training is. Most of us today too frequently view our surroundings as just that, surroundings, background to the real action. One student expressed in his journal what I often feel in the press of daily obligations when he wrote that his "purpose of walking is solely to get from point A to point B," adding that he tries "to do this as quickly as possible."[1] One additional benefit of the environmental literature we read is the reminder that, regarding the external and the internal world, "we do not have the final forms, not all the answers, that we are still in process, chiggers, humans and the rest" (Hubbell 1986, 67) and that the "eyes of the future are looking back at us and they are praying for us to see beyond our own time" (Williams 2001, 215). Those reminders, however, rarely arrive with a set of pedagogical instructions.

As I began taking my students outdoors with the vague directive to observe, they often were perplexed about how to proceed. My instructions did not include instructions. Through my trials and errors, I learned that to retrain attention so that it became attuned to place, I had to be more specific. The process I developed and will delineate illustrates a means I have found that works to guide students toward productively interacting during outdoor classes. Initially, I accomplished this more instinctively than consciously, but with continual reassessment of each class, I realized that "training" my students is necessary, and it needs to be globally envisioned and thoughtfully constructed. While the incremental steps I describe are ones that can be replaced with a wide range of activities, the principles remain fundamental.

As a start, I have found it best to begin small. At first, I introduce the outdoors with a very brief experience outside or by focusing on only one natural object. This step as well as the next one helps students to pay close attention—a key skill that needs developing. Solo experiences provide a good second stage in the "training" process. These private experiences in their environment allow students the opportunity to witness their individual patterns of behavior and make changes on their own and of their own volition. Having students consistently reflect through writing is another key in this developmental process. As they "think through their pens," they practice moving beyond surface responses, another critical skill to foster. Once we move outdoors as a group for longer periods of time, I design activities that encourage students to focus on one sensory stimulus or interact with the natural world in a clearly specified way. Once I began taking students through this process, our outdoor classes have promoted more concentrated involvement and more significant learning.

When starting this "training," by small, I literally mean small. In composition, I take students outdoors much less than I do in environmental literature because the primary mission of the course remains focused on writing. In the case of a writing course, keeping outdoor exercises brief has actually been more effective than longer forays. When students are writing their first paper for the course, a narrative, I emphasize employing concrete, specific, sensory diction. As they reach the editing stage of their papers, I open one class by telling them we are headed outside—the element of surprise adds to the effectiveness. With only pen and notebook, all go outdoors for fifteen minutes and write a description of what they see. On our return to the classroom, I ask them to set that freewriting aside, then I teach a class about specific as opposed to general diction and employing the concrete as a way of designating the abstract. After soliciting examples from their readings, I ask students to return to the description they wrote at the beginning of class to circle vague nouns and lackluster verbs. Their task is to replace "bush" with "azalea covered in blossoms" and "is" with "leans" or "stretches." While I am fostering greater sensitivity to word choices, I can reinforce the value of paying closer attention to what we observe.

I believe that short outdoor experiences can effectively accentuate a principle and make it memorable. After reading Steinbeck's two-page anecdote in *The Grapes of Wrath* in which a tortoise manages to "plant" a wild oat head that had caught in his shell, we go outside to gather as many different kinds of seeds and pods as we can locate. The originating impulse of this foray outside was Steinbeck's first paragraph of that episode describing the variety of seeds' "appliances of dispersal": their "twisting darts and parachutes for the wind, little spears, and balls of tiny thorns, and all waiting for animals and for the wind, for a man's trouser cuff or the hem of a woman's skirt." In one context we are examining the seeds' "anlage of movement" (1976, 19–21); in another, we are gaining a glimpse of the wonders of word choice. As students compare the wide-spreading wings of maple keys (fruits) with the prickly burr-balls that fall from sweet gums, we become cognizant of objects we commonly step on or kick from the walkway. In fifteen minutes out of doors, students memorably experience the power of personal involvement along with the power of compelling description.

In Environmental Literature I feel more justified conducting entire classes outdoors than I do in Composition because our readings as well as the experiential goals of the course invite the fostering of observational skills. I have learned to take students through a preparatory process before we venture outdoors for a two-hour or longer class, and this "training" is critical. Initially, I began with the short outdoor forays, but I soon discovered that providing a more thorough foundational introduction prior to going outside helped to make longer field classes less distracted and more meaningful. I wanted students to develop a close connection with the natural world over a period of time, but asking them to do something like observe the sun rise every day for a week seemed too broad a starting point. Stanley S. Blair's article on teaching Thoreau to first-year students included an activity that sounded risky to me because I was not convinced that students would take it seriously (1996, 98), but, for students also struggling to connect with Thoreau's *Walden*, the idea seemed worth hazarding. I experimented.

As I describe the exercise, I will provide students' reactions as indicators of how well this worked. Having started small, in this instance focusing on one natural object, students were primed to engage with the natural world in a more thought-provoking manner when we subsequently moved outside. I brought in a wide range of objects collected during my morning walks and displayed them on a picnic cloth I spread out on the floor in the center of our circled classroom seats.

The predominantly dark cones, rocks, shells, and sticks stood out clearly against the blue cloth, and I asked students to look over the items thoughtfully with the intent to select one to live with for the next ten days. If required, they could get up and examine objects more closely, even heft them. When it came time for choosing, I requested that they do so considerately and quietly. I was impressed with how seriously they honored that request.

Immediately after they had made their selections, I had students describe in their journals what drew them to their particular objects. Responses reveal that even in those first few moments, focusing in this manner helped them to see more than their customary perspective. About that first encounter, one student wrote,

> What drew me to this little wisp that was once a living plant? I like its shape. It is fanciful, with tiny branches going every which way. There are tiny "flower"-like things (remains of grain seeds?) that dot it, making me think of lace. The plant looked so ephemeral as if it would disappear that I wanted to hold it, to catch something before it was gone.[2]

Another student's initial thoughts:

> As the throng of students crowded around the pale blue cloth slowly cleared out, and I was left standing amid the stragglers, I quickly glanced over the remains, the unwanted appendages of nature, the flesh and bones deemed too undesirable to take back to a seat. And there it was, lying on the cloth, its dark brown color intensified against the sky blue. What it was, exactly, I did not know. I was only sure of one thing: somehow this object of beauty, nature personified, had been overlooked.[3]

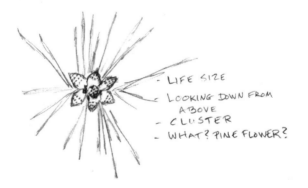

What heartened me was how students were already starting to merge thinking with looking, and for ten days at least, the practice became a part of their day. Their subsequent ten-minutes-a-day entries confirmed that something beyond the ordinary was under way. A few examples will demonstrate the wide range of directions in which the students ruminated.

> As I examine my plant, I can't help but realize the order within the chaos that exists. The individual fronds are in fairly evenly spaced circles as you

progress up the stem. Despite this sense of order, there is an overwhelming feeling of chaos because the fronds are so crazy. This order and chaos take me back to my Chemistry class this morning in which we discussed entropy.[4]

Or

What I like the best about my rock is its solidness. Although it feels deceptively light and has holes, tunnels, and little passages carved into and out of it because of time, weather, critters, etc., it is still extremely hard, and nothing I can ever do to it will make it change, other than smashing it, which I don't plan on doing. But in a time in my life when so much is changing (graduation, finding a job, moving into my apartment), I've found myself comforted in the past couple of days by holding the rock and knowing that it's not going to change.[5]

Or

When I crack you open, will a soul fly out and smack me in the face shouting, "You don't believe in me?!!? Well, *believe that!*"

I tell my friends that plants have souls (which is why I eat meat), but this seed seems hollow—sorrowful, soulless. Like a fallen hair or sloughed skin cell, it has been discarded from the body by the big G, gravity, who decided it was its time to go so plucked away its tenuous fingertip hold.

I bite you, nut.[6]

From tasting to identifying to smelling to naming to wondering what kind of noise the inanimate object made, to philosophizing about it, pondering its role in the ecosystem or relationship to what Thoreau was observing or what it suggested about the psyche of the chooser—most students ranged widely during their ten-day relationship. Some even lamented the close of the experiment. "I feel as though, through my writings, we have formed a bond that will be hard to break," one student wrote. Observational skills were accompanying reasoning and imagining skills—a project I felt served as a substantial starting point before heading outdoors.

Private experience provides an important and, I believe, necessary second stage in this training process. I have discovered that students often have the freedom to attempt more meaningful interactions with their environment if they first undertake them without the presence of their peers. When in a group, I have caught the conspiratorial rolling of the eyes when I ask students to try an outdoor activity beyond the realm of conventional, "acceptable" behavior. As we know, one reluctant participant can sour what might otherwise be a compelling encounter. Thus, before we go outside together as a class, I always assign to students at least a couple of solo outdoor activities. Alone, each individual can ignore potential embarrassment or scepticism and push beyond those social discomforts into a frame of mind that allows productive interaction with his or her surroundings.

One activity I now require is for students to adopt a tree as their "tree shrine." This term originates with Thoreau. About rambling through woods and groves he writes that "Instead of calling on some scholar, I paid many a visit to particular trees. . . . These were the shrines I visited both summer and winter" (1997, 181–82). For the whole semester, the tree each individual selects is the student's to watch burst into spring, to sit under when he or she wishes to read or relax or write, to climb when craving retreat. This is to be their living entity to know, like, love—a manageable fraction of the outdoors with which they can develop a relationship. Periodically, I ask students to write about their tree, and one journal entry will demonstrate why solitary experience can be so valuable. Being alone can help students to access connections or thoughts they might not ordinarily "see."

> So I have this tree, and like me, I believe that it enjoys thinking of itself as a nonconformist. You see, it prefers to bask languidly in the sun on a river-bank, lying on its side instead of standing tall. It would rather laugh with the newly sprouted pines inching from the moss than participate in the gossip of the canopy, which in winter would be listless and quiet if not for the stalwart cardinals and chickadees. Though I am down a gully by the river, I can see the road from here. I cannot decide if it is good, this intrusion of progress into this natural shrine that I have stumbled upon, but it does remind me that though I try to escape civilization in nature, nature itself will never escape civilization.[7]

In solitude, the student is able to move beyond inhibitions, to explore, create, and respond without fear of mocking eyes. I also see in these tree-shrine entries that students are, as Terry Tempest Williams frequently writes, "nurtured by solitude" (1992, 152). The combined forces of being alone and journal writing help to deepen the individual's experience.

Writing proves key in helping students move beyond inhibitions and surface reactions. For all early-stage contacts with the outdoors, I have students write. Fundamental principles underlying experiential education include reflection as an essential step to making any activity significant—we all have difficulty reaching deeply for those insights without concomitant reflection.[8] Senses send to our brains memorable messages; writing helps us to discern what those messages mean.

Early in the semester, while still reading *Walden*, I attempt to stretch observational skills further by sending students outside to try, as Thoreau suggests, to "saunter with the eye." I request that they go off by themselves, away from all others, and give sauntering a try. Meandering in this manner is not easy because, even if we concentrate on the external world, our tendency is to move toward some sight we actively choose. This sauntering is not like Thoreau walking home from the village at night so preoccupied with thought that he charges through the woods almost on autopilot (1997, 153). This is the Thoreau who, in the first part of his essay "Walking," declares that for "health and spirits" he requires each day at least four hours of sauntering (1976, 594).

I describe this practice to students explaining the Asian influences that led Thoreau to walk with an openness to all around him. John P. O'Grady calls this "a form of perception free of any irritable reaching of ego-mind after objects and facts, a way of 'seeing' that overcomes the mind-body dichotomy" (1993, 24–25). I request that students avoid searching for something specific and allow sensory stimuli to flow to them. Since this is, if there be such a thing, abstract practice, I launch them off on their own for thirty minutes with a quotation from Thoreau's journals, some of which I repeat here, as send-off inspiration. "I must let my senses wander as my thoughts, my eyes see without looking. . . . Go not to the object; let it come to you. . . . What I need is not to look at all, but a true sauntering of the eye."[9]

I confess that the first time I sent students sauntering in this manner, I had misgivings and sent them for only twenty minutes, envisioning their freedom from the classroom and the non-sauntering gaze of their professor as time to run about together or doze. Contrary to what I expected, I have been impressed. Students' performance and their reactions in journals have confirmed that, while alien, "sauntering with the eye" is a practice worth attempting. One student wrote, "This exercise provided wonderful insight into what I may be doing wrong, or rather what I'm missing out on," and another,

> I've realized that it is hard to distinguish between me calling to nature and nature calling to me. I call to the color green in all my doings, and I couldn't help but hear it out there. I tried to let my mind not actively seek it out and found it hard to not hear. I'd close my eyes, and I could feel it. I leaned on a tree with beautiful variations of moss greens, and it called to me. I put all nature out of my mind, but it always called me back.[10]

Not all students mastered the technique or fully understood what they were attempting, but I always find that most take it seriously. A note came to me via e-mail after the first time I sent students off on this experiment. This note has, over the years, served as my inspiration. A portion of the e-mail follows.

> Dr. Chandler,
> I thought you might like to read what I wrote in my journal today after "sauntering." It was definitely a worthwhile experience for me . . .
> February 2, 1998
> I was out walking today for the sole purpose of being outside and looking around. I walked places I had never been before. I have always stayed on the path, and I have always walked relatively quickly, only having time to notice the regular shape of the bricks that lead me from class to class or to a meal or to the post office. I am always in a rush to get somewhere without ever enjoying the journey as well. But today I got off that path. I walked to the edge of the woods; I looked over hills I had never looked over before; I saw streams that I had never seen before. The most interesting thing, though, was that when I was at the edge of the woods, and I looked back to where I came from—back to that path that I know so well—I could hardly recognize it. It was as if I were looking at a place I had never seen before. As I continued walking, I also started to wonder what this campus looked like before the buildings and the paths—before it was shaped and defined the way it is now. And I wonder how and if it will change later. There's an interesting parallel that can be drawn between my observations and my life—the way I'd been shaped, and the way I can change . . . and the path that I'm on.
> That's it. Thanks for giving me twenty minutes to discover something about myself.
> —Tanya[11]

Whatever it is that students learn from this activity, whether it be about themselves or something beyond themselves, students consistently report that the sauntering practice has helped them to see something different about how they live.

How *do* we live? I remind students that nature writers following in Thoreau's tradition repeatedly return to this, one of his central questions. Regarding outdoor classes, "how do we live" serves me as both an important motivation and an important justification. "Tell me, what is it you plan to do / with your one wild and precious life?" Mary Oliver asks at the end of "The Summer Day" (1992, 94). Oliver admits to not having answers to questions such as "Who made the world?" but she also asserts that she does "know how to pay attention." Paying attention is crucial, certainly one of the keys to living fully and thoughtfully. "A March morning," Aldo Leopold reminds us,

> is only as drab as he who walks in it without a glance skyward, ear cocked for geese. I once knew an educated lady, banded by Phi Beta Kappa, who told me that she had never heard or seen the geese that twice a year proclaim the revolving seasons to her well-insulated roof. Is education possibly a process of trading awareness for things of lesser worth? (1970, 20)

My goal is to provide both awarenesses. Teaching students the art of paying attention is as critical as is critical thinking in the contemporary business—busy-ness—of life.

Finally, when taking my classes outside as a group, I direct them to focus on one among the many sensory stimuli they are receiving. We have met at 5:30 in the morning with a member of the biology faculty, not for a bird walk but for a bird listen. During that outing, silence and focus on birdsong is critical. To reinforce principles we are discovering in Leopold's land ethic, we have conducted an eco-scavenger hunt with a list of questions that students created, including locating where the flood plain is low and prevents grass growth or finding a plant that has had its growth altered for the convenience of humans. When reading Edward Abbey, we have gone outside to look at the world lying flat on our stomachs, an idea that came from students inspired by Abbey's *Desert Solitaire* and his charge to get out of the car and "walk, better yet crawl, on hands and knees." His description of creeping forward on his belly watching two gopher snakes dance "from the snake's-eye level" also generated our activity (1971, xii, 23), one in which via language and picture we described à la scientific illustration what we saw, paying attention to textures and shapes as well as colors and sizes.

2/11   6:00 am
class

flowers - Say. kinds   purple, lavender, white, pink
Shapes - innumerable - beautiful
textures - disappear when the frost melts
      fuzz on leaves
      frost encased
frost adds a gleam/glitter that is beautiful
      but it outlines the detailed structure
      of each leaf, blade of grass
I wish I could draw - the
      detail is extensive, each fine line outlined by the frost

All dif. sizes, too - down to the leaves that
      are the size of a pin head

When we encounter Gary Snyder, with Asian beliefs influencing his philosophy, we have trekked to the woods along the campus border to participate in a meditative walk into the center of a nautilus-shaped structure that a philosophy student, as part of his year-long senior St. Mary's Project, had constructed. This open-to-the-sky contemplation hut, built from the physical plant's refuse heap of bamboo and twig trimmings, provided a focal point for metaphorical implications of circles and their significance in nature. We have tried ecological role playing, imagining ourselves to be a creature natural to our bioregion in an attempt to understand an "other's" perspective (Tallmadge 1999, 20). I have had students go outside to re-establish a connection with an element, then write about their earliest memory of either earth, water, or air (Hermsen 2000, 240). Jerome M. Segal's *Graceful Simplicity* motivated our joining with a philosophy class for one outing. We visited four campus locations that students designated as sacred and at each shared the deepest concepts and questions raised in our respective courses.

I have taken students on outings designed to mark special occasions—John Muir's birth date or our last day of class. In our final class, as one means of synthesizing our studies over the course of the semester, I created a dialogue using Terry Tempest Williams's "A Eulogy for Edward Abbey" and Edward Abbey's "Down the River with Henry Thoreau," which students chose to take to the Garden of Remembrance to read aloud overlooking the river. Several years ago, a class meeting fell on the officially designated Earth Day. I believed it important for students to connect with the earth that day on an individual and personal level, and each of us created our own way to commemorate the occasion. One student's choice was to sit by the edge of the river. She wrote,

> I just sat. I didn't think or listen. Just laid back, with my eyes shut and imagined myself melting into the ground. Every part of my body tingled as my cells became viscous liquid. I would like to say I was becoming the earth, but it was more like I was one with the earth. Then I began to listen . . . I listened to the waves lapping the shore. The gliding movement of the water molecules back and forth, back and forth. Thinking of how the motion breaks apart the molecules. Thinking how my melting cells could begin to erode away and mix with the moving H_2O molecules, back and forth, back and forth.[12]

This student was, by the end of the semester, able to focus on her own.

A focus, especially an interactive focus, is key to the success of any outdoor activity. Being "out there" has impact when field trips extend over days or weeks or months; "out there" does not necessarily work when coming directly from a classroom. Emerging from the fluorescents into the sunshine is altogether different. We need to help students make the shift in environments in ways that help them meaningfully access something specific in their surroundings and process it as significant.

Even the most sincere request to "observe what is around you," received with the most genuine effort to try, does not always work. Discussing a reading or a concept is not usually the most effective activity, either. I have had mixed results when asking students to focus on their books when we are outdoors; that pursuit is by its very nature disjunctive. One brutally hot afternoon we did read aloud Mary Austin's "The Woman at the Eighteen Mile." The heat in this non-arid, mid-Atlantic, eastern-seaboard setting evoked Austin's desert climate. It worked. The next time I tried the reading, on a cloudy, humid day, it did not.

The original tour of students' tree shrines, the tree-to-tree "pilgrim-age" I attempted while reading *Pilgrim at Tinker Creek*, also faltered. Instead of asking students to walk silently from tree to tree formulating a question related to their reading, I now ask them to walk silently from tree to tree paying close enough attention that they will be able to detect what they commonly ignore: ascertaining the give of the ground beneath their feet, noting different light refractions of variously greened leaves, identifying subtle estuarine scents they detect in the breeze. I have realized, along with doing something clearly related to what we are reading, *purposefully* interacting with the natural world is essential. Simply replicating outdoors what we conventionally do in a classroom does not work.

Anne Dillard
Pilgrim at Tinker Creek

My passion for environmental literature is driven by what motivates my belief in the value of outdoor experiences. "How do we live?" How can we learn to live in the world if we have no immediate experience with it? "Only by understanding where I live can I learn how to live," Scott Russell Sanders states (1993, xiv), and my way of helping students toward that understanding is to provide guided opportunities to gather sensory as well as intellectual experiences. I am not taking students out to play, although laughter and climbing trees have their place in my course, but the impetus behind each is serious. In relation to both our natural and human communities, I am, I hope, helping students to be, as one young woman insightfully phrased it, "a part, not apart."[13] When thought of in terms of this earth and our individual span on it, even our class is not a trial run. How I conduct the course exemplifies, in part, how I live and impacts, perhaps, how they live.

The epiphany instigated by the first time I took a class outside to draw has led me into the most significant teaching moments I have experienced. It is the combination of truth reflecting on our senses merging with ideas gathering in our minds that makes outdoor teaching situations so powerful. Nothing I do in the classroom has yet produced the impact of that combination. "I very much enjoyed drawing today," a student wrote after sketching among the weeds. I am pleased that she enjoyed it, but how she continues says even more to me.

> I've always been a self-proclaimed non-artist, so the experience was not really one of great expectations. But maybe it's my fairly humble attitude that allows me to truly enjoy trying to sketch—because then I'm not focused on the end product so much as the experience of observing my own little piece of nature. This type of activity requires a great deal of patience as well as an open mind and a willingness to make "mistakes." My drawings might appear to be mere sketches to others, but to me they are a personal reflection of precious time spent enjoying my surroundings and learning to focus on life other than my own.[14]

Humility. Patience. Open-mindedness. Personal reflection. Enjoyment. Learning to focus on life other than one's own. Could there be better reasons for merging education with the out-of-doors?

If there are, I will find them.

Notes

1. Journal entry for English 230, After Thoreau: American Environmental Literature, January 24, 2002, Jeffrey Peyton.

2. Journal entry for English 230, After Thoreau: American Environmental Literature, January 22, 2002, Debbie Lee.

3. Journal entry for English 230, After Thoreau: American Environmental Literature, January 22, 2002, Charlotte Shearin.

4. Journal entry for English 230, After Thoreau: American Environmental Literature, January 24, 2002, Lauren Webster.

5. Journal entry for English 230, After Thoreau: American Environmental Literature, January 23, 2002, Marcy Richardson.

6. Journal entry for English 230, After Thoreau: American Environmental Literature, February 10, 2000, Corita Jones.

7. Journal entry for English 230, After Thoreau: American Environmental Literature, February 2002, Shaun Griffin.

8. Any book on experiential education will include discussions of the necessary role of reflection. Two resources I have used are *The Theory of Experiential Education*, Karen Warren, Mitchell Sakofs, Jasper S. Hunt, Jr., editors (Association for Experiential Education, Dubuque, Iowa: Kendall Hunt Publishing Company, 1995), and *Experiential Learning in Schools and Higher Education*, Richard J. Kraft and James Kielsmeier, editors (Association for Experiential Education, Dubuque, Iowa: Kendall Hunt Publishing Company, 1995).

9. The excerpt from Thoreau's journal that I use is quoted by John P. O'Grady on page 25 in *Pilgrims to the Wild*.

10. Journal entries for English 230, After Thoreau: American Environmental Literature, January 24, 2002, Jeffrey Peyton, and January 24, 2002, Katharine Fritz.

11. Note written by Tanya Kuck.

12. Journal entry for English 230, After Thoreau: American Environmental Literature, April 20, 2000, Holly Zahner.

13. Journal entry for English 230, After Thoreau: American Environmental Literature, February 22, 2000, Kelly Barnes.

14. Journal entry for English 230, After Thoreau: American Environmental Literature, March 9, 2000, Rebecca Hassinger.

References

Abbey, Edward. 1971. *Desert solitaire: A season in the wilderness*. New York: Ballantine.

———. 1995. Down the river with Henry Thoreau. In *Words from the land: Encounters with natural history writing*, edited by Stephen Trimble. Expanded Edition. Reno: University of Nevada Press.

Austin, Mary. 1996. The woman at the eighteen-mile. In *A Mary Austin reader*, edited by Esther F. Lanigan, 100–107. Tucson: University of Arizona Press.

Blair, Stanley S. 1996. "What are you doing out there?": Teaching Thoreau to college freshmen. In *Approaches to teaching Thoreau's Walden and other works*, edited by Richard J. Schneider, 98. New York: Modern Language Association.

Dillard, Annie. 1999. *Pilgrim at Tinker Creek*. Perennial Classics Edition. New York: HarperPerennial.

Hermsen, Terry. 2000. Earth water air fire: An exercise in creative memory. In *The alphabet of the trees: A guide to nature writing*, edited by Christian McEwen and Mark Statman. New York: Teachers and Writers Collaborative.

Hubbell, Sue. 1986. *A country year: Living the questions*. New York: Random House.

Krutch, Joseph Wood. 1967. *Baja California and the geography of hope*. Edited by Kenneth Brower. San Francisco: Sierra Club.

Leopold, Aldo. 1970. *A Sand County almanac*. New York: Ballantine.

Leslie, Clare Walker, and Charles E. Roth. 1998. *Nature journaling: Learning to observe and connect with the world around you*. Pownal, Vt.: Storey Books.

O'Grady, John P. 1993. *Pilgrims to the wild: Everett Ruess, Henry David Thoreau, John Muir, Clarence King, Mary Austin*. Salt Lake City: University of Utah Press.

Oliver, Mary. 1992. *New and selected poems*. Boston: Beacon Press.

Sanders, Scott Russell. 1993. *Staying put, making à home in a restless world*. Boston: Beacon Press.

Segal, Jerome M. 1999. *Graceful simplicity: Toward a philosophy and politics of simple living*. New York: Henry Holt.

Steinbeck, John. 1976. *The grapes of wrath*. New York: Penguin Books.

Tallmadge, John. 1999. Writing as a window into nature. In *Into the field: A guide to locally focused teaching*. Nature Literacy Series Number 3. Great Barrington, Mass.: The Orion Society.

Thoreau, Henry David. 1976. Walking. In *The portable Thoreau*, edited by Carl Bode. New York: Viking Press.

———. 1997. *Walden*. Edited by Stephen Fender. Oxford: Oxford University Press.

Williams, Terry Tempest. 1994. A eulogy for Edward Abbey. In *An unspoken hunger, stories from the field*. New York: Random House.

———. 2001. *Red: Passion and patience in the desert*. New York: Pantheon Books.

———. 1992. *Refuge*. New York: Random House.

Writing the Watershed

I first heard it while breaking a path down to the Pine River from a low hill that holds the bodies of some two dozen Chippewa, mostly children. Dry snow, brushed into waves by a northwest wind, washed around my knees as I high-stepped toward the site of *Shing-wa-kaus-king*, the last Pine River village of the people who call themselves Anishnabeg. What I heard then, while slogging toward the curtain of bare trees that traced the river's path on a powder-blue sky, was the land beginning to speak. It was telling a story.

And it had plenty of tales to tell. But on this crisp February afternoon, I was not listening to the story of ice-mountains written on the low roll of moraines, or to the epic drama of those cone-laden pioneers who followed the soil north so many years ago. Still under the spell of the tiny graveyard that grew smaller with every step, I heard only stories of the Anishnabeg. I could almost make out the faint shrieks of their children at play, scampering and sliding in clouds of powder among the willows. Among the hardwoods that shadow the Pine through the snow-shouldered farms of central Michigan, I thought I glimpsed the backs of bear-robed figures dropping hot stones into birch-bark buckets, thickening maple sap to syrup. I even heard echoes of the old, old story about how maple syrup once dripped straight from the trunk—till Nanabozho watered it down so the people would not waste these short days beneath their taps, mouths agape.

At last I was beginning to see past the straight-edged fields of corn and beans that made up this quilt called Gratiot County and to discern something of the land's original features. Looking back, I suppose that this enhancement of perception was all along the real goal of a course I was teaching at nearby Alma College. But when I designed my Environmental

Narratives class, I was addressing an absence; I hadn't fully envisioned the presence that would replace it.

It was several years ago, while gathering college syllabi for the Association for the Study of Literature and Environment, that I first noticed how few courses ask students to become more familiar with their own bioregion and then to share this experience with the rest of the community. Among the dozens of excellent syllabi that Peter Blakemore and I collected, the majority that brought nature into the English classroom wished simply to introduce students to writers who see the world through ecologically informed eyes. Of course, such classes perform a valuable service, but I was most excited by those occasional courses that tried to teach students to understand their membership in *specific* ecosystems.

At the University of Nevada, Reno, for example, Cheryll Glotfelty designed her Composition II class so that students would develop their writing skills while collaborating on a book about a species native to the area. As her syllabus noted, along the way students would learn a number of skills essential to their success in college, including time management, research, interpretation, revision, documentation, and effective collaboration. Two days' drive north, at the University of Montana, Hank Harrington began his Natural History class with a weekend spent on an island in nearby Flathead Lake. He asked each student to choose a particular species growing on Wild Horse Island and to observe its characteristics and contexts before returning to campus to compare observations with those of earlier natural historians. Students were then to revise their findings into scripts that would be broadcast on a local radio program called *Field Notes*.[1] Examples like these inspired me to wonder about other ways in which college English classes might serve local communities by helping them better understand their home ecosystems.

I began to imagine a service-learning course in which students would gather and publish the stories of the local watershed, making them accessible to area residents. Because people are less likely to degrade an environment they care for, I hoped that such a publication might help local residents recover the sort of intimacy that Robert Finch had in mind when he explained, "ultimately we can only care for and connect with that which we have come to love. I think that only by storying the earth do we come to love it, does it become the place where imagination chooses to reside."[2]

Of course, stories have long encouraged an intimacy in people's relationships with their environments, especially in subsistence cultures where an efficient overlap of oral traditions and specific geographies could mean the difference between want and plenty.[3] But knowing the stories of the places we live takes on a different type of urgency in a post-industrial culture, where the means of our shelter and sustenance seldom appear connected to any specific community. When food is presumed to come from the grocery store rather than from a particular plot of agricultural land, what occurs on those acres—or in the streams that drain them—is of little concern to the consumer.

With both our economy and our popular culture encouraging this delusion of detachment from the ecological communities that sustain us, it was inevitable that the consequences of our actions would eventually become dire enough to inspire the series of reactions that we refer to as environmentalism. Within this context, recovering the stories of our local bioregions is a most radical act: once we learn again how to love the places we call home, business as usual is no longer acceptable. "Love is where attentiveness to nature starts," insists John Elder, "and responsibility to one's home landscape is where it leads."[4] Indeed, learning the stories of our bioregions, and recognizing our inescapable participation in locally specific ecological systems, has the potential to transform our patterns of behavior, according to Mitch Thomashow, Director of the Doctoral Program of Environmental Studies at Antioch New England Graduate School.[5] Thomashow adopts Richard Borden's concept of "ecological identity" as the title and theoretical foundation of his important 1995 study. According to Borden, learning to see ourselves as members of ecological communities "leads to changes of identity and psychological perspective, and can provide the foundations for an 'ecological identity' . . . which restructures values, reorganizes perceptions, and alters the individual's self-directed, social, and environmentally directed actions."[6]

Clearly, deepening our knowledge of local ecosystems—and understanding our membership in them—can bring about profound changes in the way we treat them. Whether or not the human residents of the Pine River watershed were ready to understand themselves as interdependent knots in a web of energy exchange, they at least deserved a glimpse of how their local bioregion functioned before it was forced into the service of industry and agriculture. And so, in the spring of 2000, fifteen students and I pieced together a sixty-page booklet called *Recovering Pine River*. By the grace of gifts and grants, hundreds of these bioregional biographies have since found their way from diners and general stores, schools and barbershops, into homes throughout the watershed, sharing forgotten stories of the Pine River. The success of this project leads me to offer an account of that process in the hope that it might inspire similar projects in other communities.

❈

It was Aldo Leopold, I suppose, who planted the seeds of *Recovering Pine River*, though it took them years to germinate. Each time I've read *A Sand County Almanac*, I've nodded along as Leopold argues the need to change the role of our species from conquerors to plain members of the land community; and as a teacher I've echoed his insistence that such a revision mandates "respect for [our] fellow members, and also respect for the community as such."[7] Attempts to apply Leopold's revolutionary theory to our daily lives lead quite directly to what Gary Snyder terms *watershed consciousness,* which encourages "the practice of profound citizenship in both the natural and social worlds."[8] Such dual citizenship lies at the heart of the bioregionalism—a perspective that encourages us to see ourselves as belonging more fundamentally to specific ecosystems than to artificial geopolitical units. But it seems unlikely that we will ever learn to function as productive citizens of local bioregions if we don't even know who our neighbors are. The first step, then, toward responsible membership in a land community is learning to recognize it, and this means peeling back the layers of human constructions that conceal our sustaining ecosystems.

Of course, it is easier to recognize the presence of an ecological community in places like the Bob Marshall Wilderness or even the Okefenokee Swamp, where the human role still seems peripheral, than to imagine a functioning ecosystem at work behind the man-made mask of Alma, Michigan. Many locals would define this Pine River community in terms of the grid of asphalt that links church to strip mall, refinery to home. If you asked people around Alma about the ecological community of the Pine River, those who didn't shrug and shake their heads would likely point you north of town, toward the third-growth pines of Lumberjack Park.

I understood, perhaps better than most, this inclination to look beyond the Alma town line in search of an ecological community, for I have spent my life in wilder places, whether growing up at the foot of Oregon's Cascade Range or working as a ranger in the resurgent forests of northern New England. When I arrived in central Michigan what I saw, at first, was flat, denuded land, where strips of homogeneous American commerce occasionally broke the monotony of industrial agriculture. But when Leopold spoke of the need to see ourselves as members of a land community, he recognized that we belong to such a community, inescapably, wherever we are.

Of course, some folks in and around Alma might rather not see themselves as part of the Pine River's particular ecological web, for it is a savagely degraded watershed. It's not just the industrial pesticides that soak the local farms, then drain through twigs and branches into the main trunk of the river—though low sweeps of crop-dusters frequently rattled my bedroom window and kept me from trusting my shallow well. No, worse pollution comes from the town's remaining oil refinery and even *worse* from the site of a chemical plant that flushed DDT and other toxins into the Pine for half a century. Less than five miles downstream, near the ghost of the old Anishnabe village, the Environmental Protection Agency has established a Superfund site in an attempt to lower concentrations of DDT to a level that is closer to acceptable. The legal limit, however, remains far beyond the reach of current technology.

Because river systems may be considered the hearts of their bioregions, the Pine River watershed is very sick indeed. But if Finch is right—that we care only for what we love—then telling the story of the Pine River is a necessary step toward its recovery.

The students have grown quiet here, clustered tightly as they look across the dirty snow to where the river pools in a slow, artificial curve. Across the water and behind the retaining wall, a low white mound is all that remains of Velsicol Chemical, which closed its doors in 1978. A crimson sign on the beach blazes a warning against swimming, and it is easy to imagine that the ghostly bather on the sign—arms flung high in panic, mouth and eyes agape—is not drowning but dissolving in a witch's brew of chemicals. Students recall their interviews with local residents who described "pike, four feet long, their eyes ate out with pus."[9] They have heard how water drawn from the Pine River ate a hole through the bottom of a galvanized bucket at the Department of Natural Resources.

These hardly seem the same students who, just an hour before and a dozen miles upriver, thrilled to find the etchings of beaver teeth in sharpened trunks of willows. They had scattered through bare forest there, sketching in their journals and studying the slow release of winter on the river. "The solid, smooth ice gives way to open water," wrote one, "and the flow of the river is constantly, patiently moving the melting point toward the shadier shore." Another compared the river's surface rippling in the breeze to "cellophane that didn't get stretched perfectly over a bowl."[10] They pointed, they laughed, they scribbled their impressions along faint blue lines. They asked the names of trees.

Here at the Superfund site, they are silent. It is not only the DDT that scares them, although they have learned that the sediment has contained up to six thousand times the "acceptable" level of contamination. No, right now most are thinking about PBBs, a carcinogenic flame retardant that was accidentally mixed into cattle feed supplement shortly before the plant closed. The contaminated feed was trucked to farms throughout the state, passing toxins through beef and dairy products into nearly every person on Michigan's lower peninsula—including the parents of many of these students. Geologist Murray Borrello, our guide for the afternoon, jokes that "any of you raised in Michigan don't ever have to worry about spontaneous combustion."[11]

The lessons we learn hit some students harder than others. "When I decided to go to Alma College, I didn't even know there was a river," recalls Anne Henningfeld, who soon found herself frequenting a peaceful stretch of the Pine. "I thought the river was beautiful and, having been raised on water, it brought me home." Now, hearing of the river's contamination, she feels betrayed, violated: "My body convulsed," she later explains. "I could feel the little bits of PBB floating in my bloodstream, sticking to the insides of my intestines, mingling with the cranial fluid at the base of my skull. The river I had never heard of was the site of an accident that now lives in my body."[12]

The differences between the forested river upstream and this toxic pool are dramatic and sobering. The few trees that shade the small park and playground on the riverbank seem a half-hearted attempt to breathe life back into this place. As we glance around the neighborhood, it is difficult not to recall stories of the clouds of caustic dust that frequently hid one neighbor's home from another's. The cofferdam that holds back the most toxic stretch of water, the low hill covering the capped-over site, the fences and the warning signs—these images tell the story of a disaster. But what we see here is only a small part of the Pine River's story. To look at the river and see only tragedy is as wrong as judging someone's entire life by how they looked during a recent illness.

There's more to this story than pollution.

Before the students began to record the stories of the watershed, they studied how other authors convey natural history to readers with little scientific background. If our work was to be effective, we knew we must make it interesting and accessible to the widest possible audience. We read Henry Thoreau and David Rains Wallace, John Muir and Annie Dillard, Loren Eiseley and Scott Russell Sanders, comparing styles and discovering what worked for us—and, just as important, what didn't. Following Thomas Lyon's lead, we weighed the balance of natural history, philosophy, and personal reflection in each reading.[13] It soon became clear that the students preferred pieces that emphasized personal reflection and, to a lesser extent, natural history. We paid special attention to three books devoted to specific bioregions: Thomas Sherman's *A Place on the Glacial Till*, an eloquent, loving natural history of Oberlin, Ohio (and the single best example of a bioregional biography I have found); John Hanson Mitchell's quirky history of his neighborhood near Westford, Massachusetts, entitled *Ceremonial Time: Fifteen Thousand Years on One Square Mile*; and Terry Tempest Williams's *Refuge*, a deeply personal ode to the Bear River Migratory Bird Refuge on the shore of Utah's Great Salt Lake.[14] We compared examples of authorial presence and narrative structure and studied how authors use figurative language to bring to life a landscape's geology and botany.

In addition to literary analysis, students were sharpening their skills at observing the bioregion and recording their impressions. I had adapted Lawrence Buell's "Environmental Imagination Project," which asks students to return to the same outdoor observation post each week and practice different modes of perception. They classified the spot's inhabitants, used senses other than sight to experience their place, and tried on a variety of nonhuman perspectives.[15] Students were also busy interviewing local residents, adding layers of human memory to the stories we were gathering. Although I was not aware of it at the time, our work embodied the four themes that John Elder claims are fundamental to environmental education: attentiveness to students' home landscapes, the convergence of natural sciences and the arts, time spent out of doors, and human connections.[16]

Once students determined which strategies bring natural history to life, they began their own work, starting with the region's geology. After learning the local history of sedimentation and glaciation, each student produced a creative rendition of the watershed's formation. We wrestled with problems like evoking geologic time or the massive size of glaciers. It would not be enough, we knew, simply to describe a glacier ten thousand feet thick, for numbers that large tend to remain abstract. We wanted people to *see* the glacier, and so we chose a trope that would be familiar to residents of central Michigan:

> Sometimes we have to dig our way through drifts that gather to four or five feet, and the compacted snow at the bottom is always the heaviest. Imagine, though, that the snow keeps falling until it has covered the land to the height of a two-story house—about twenty-five feet. The weight would be

crushing. Still, it keeps falling and freezing, falling and freezing. Eventually it accumulates to the height of *four* such houses—a hundred feet of snow. It is difficult to imagine so much weight.[17]

Once people can imagine what a hundred feet of snow might look like, they can more easily extrapolate from that. "Imagine 400 two-story houses stacked atop one another," we wrote, "and you will begin to understand the immensity of the glaciers that shaped the state of Michigan."[18]

The more we learned and scribbled, the more naturally our new knowledge began to evolve into *awareness.* Chasing the back roads north on weekly trips to Mt. Pleasant's food co-op, I found myself becoming excited by changes in elevation. No longer could I drive up an incline—not even those so subtle that you *feel* rather than see them—without imagining a landscape ruled by glaciers. How, I wondered, could I ever have mistaken this landscape for flat?

The same enhancement of perspective occurred as we learned about the slow return of plant life to the scoured landscape. Lichens came to seem utterly heroic, as did the grasses and stunted trees that followed. We learned how boggy the area had been before the land was drained for farming, and soon we were imagining mastodons browsing in tamarack swamps down behind the football field. Dick Roeper, a biologist at the college, pointed us in the direction of Conservation Park, and there we moved silently between the chalky pillars of 300-year-old beech trees, then passed along directions to our readers.

Learning about the original human inhabitants of the watershed was especially revealing, since it showed that it *is* possible for our species to find a working balance with the rest of the community. While studying Anishnabe oral traditions and hearing archeologist Scott Beld describe local sites, we began to understand native economic cycles and the culture that reinforced them. Not discounting their use of fire, we concluded that humans had achieved a fairly stable relationship with other members of the bioregion for more than eight thousand years. Within this context it became clear that the effects of European economic practices over the last three hundred years are a brief but ultimately tragic deviation from the norm of local human history.

Our lessons about the Anishnabeg were made vivid by a visit to the site of *Shing-wa-kaus-king* and the cemetery later established there by Lutheran missionaries. As students solemnly threaded the cluster of weathered headstones, most of which simply read "Indian Child," one stood out: Sara Mirk-i-we, described as "Mother of the Chippewa," died in 1859 at the age of 110. We imagined the changes she must have seen over that century. The Anishnabeg were at war with one or another European population, off and on, for the first sixty-four years of her life. Moreover, she was born into a time of loss. When she first opened her eyes to the green world called *Michi-gami*, all of it still belonged to the native people—in practice, if not on paper. By the time she closed them for the last time, the Anishnabeg held only one piece of land in all of Michigan, twenty miles north on the Chippewa River. Given the changes she must have witnessed—warfare, disease, alcoholism, poverty, and the inestimable loss of land and culture—it was easy to imagine that Sara Mirk-i-we greeted death with at least some small relief.

As we turned our attention to the last century and a half, it was with a lingering sense of melancholy. The stories of European settlers offered little romance after what we had learned of Anishnabe culture—and because we knew what would follow. We discovered that the Saginaw River drainage basin, which includes the Pine, was the most productive lumbering region of the state until it was cleared in the late nineteenth century. At one time this might have been a source of local pride. To my students, however, understanding the effects of industrial logging within a larger ecological history encouraged a more sober appraisal: "With the trees gone, the banks of the river sank and became mush," wrote one student, "savagely battered by thousands of logs hammering downstream." "Floating logs downriver may have made business sense," recognized another, "but it was an ecological disaster."[19]

If there was anything that lent a sense of hope to those final weeks, it was the interviews that students conducted with local residents, especially with the elders. Of course, many of their recollections vividly confirmed the sustained human abuse of the watershed. Some remember toilets draining directly into the river, while others recall local petroleum refineries discharging so much effluent that the high-water level was marked each spring by a line of oil on the trees.

Despite what their stories revealed about human abuses of the Pine, however, these voices added a necessary perspective. These are real people who have lived their lives as best they know how within a particular cultural and economic context. No one ever intended any harm. Students began to see that our society has conceived of rivers mainly as systems to serve the human population, whether as power for the mills, sources of drinking water and fish, or even sewage disposal. Understanding a watershed as an ecological community is a concept that has not yet occurred to most people, and talking with elders helped students balance the ecological perspective they learned in school with the economic and social realities beyond the classroom walls.

Once students had transcribed their interviews and revised their weekly creative renditions, they turned in anonymous versions of each. We then broke into editorial collectives, which were responsible for identifying passages from student writing that seemed especially vivid or informative. They also reviewed student photographs, determining where each belonged in the narrative. The use of editorial collectives kept the process fundamentally dialogic: that is, students worked together on all aspects of the project instead of dividing tasks between them.[20] This approach, combined with the knowledge that their decisions contributed to a potentially important public document, helped students avoid some of the more common problems of collaborative writing, such as uneven quality and inequitable distribution of work.

Then, suddenly, the term was over.

As the campus emptied out, I found myself left with pages and pages of highlighted passages. It was only then that I realized the amount of work required to stitch these pieces together. Moreover, because I had accepted a new job in Vermont, less than a month remained in which to produce a camera-ready document. The students deserved to play a much larger role in the final stages of preparing the manuscript, and I am presently encouraging this at Green Mountain College by stretching a similar class over two semesters. But with the students already gone for the summer, I found it necessary to impose my own narrative structure on the manuscript to a greater degree than I would have preferred. There were many passages from student writing that fit in nicely as they were, and tying those into the rest of the text was not difficult. However, substantial gaps remained at many points in the narrative, and the original passages that I composed to fill them made up more than half of the final text. Fortunately, Mary Rosalez, a local student and gifted writer, remained available to help out during the revision stages and distribute the finished product.

Once I had what seemed to be a complete narrative, Mary and I began editing with an ear to stylistic coherence—no easy task when you're dealing with sixteen authors. I soon discovered that the personal reflection students had found most engaging in their readings often resisted a collaborative approach. It might have been possible to preserve more of their individual impressions and experiences in a collage structure; I felt, however, that narrative coherence would make the text most accessible to a general audience. In the end, some student writing was eroded by an overriding narrative voice, but in a number of cases I kept their passages intact and introduced them within the text, quoting the authors.

The first printing has gone fast, and copies have found their way into the local schools. Before reading *Recovering Pine River*, many of the students in Mary Ann Leonard's sixth-grade class knew only that the river was polluted and that they should stay away from it. Granted, they seemed most impressed to discover that giant beavers once swam the river, or that bromide clouds from the chemical factory would eat the paint off cars and houses, but a number of them were amazed to learn that the Pine had ever been a healthy river. They were impressed to learn that people in their community are working to try to clean up the river. Several students even expressed their intention of helping.

Recovering Pine River ends by focusing on specific actions that people can take to help improve the health of the watershed, but the final page makes clear that, first and foremost, helping the river recover demands imagination. "Let us imagine," wrote one student, "what it would be like one day to bring home that fat trout we catch in the Pine and actually eat it without worrying about the poisons. Let us imagine a river that people look at not with pity, but with pride."[21] When we can imagine such a river, we will begin to desire such a river, and our actions will follow from that. If the stories in *Recovering Pine River* have led people to imagine—even for only a moment—what it would be like to live in a healthy, vibrant watershed, then it has already been a success.

Notes

1. Both syllabi appear in *The ASLE Collection of Syllabi in Literature and Environment*, edited by Laird Christensen and Peter Blakemore, 26 August 2002. (http://www.asle.umn.edu/pubs/collect/collect.html)

2. Finch's remarks are taken from a dialogue with Terry Tempest Williams, included in *Writing Natural History: Dialogues with Authors*, edited by Edward Lueders (Salt Lake City: University of Utah Press, 1989), 41.

3. See, for example, Keith Basso, *Wisdom Sits in Places: Landscape and Language Among the Western Apache* (Albuquerque: New Mexico University Press, 1996), and Leslie Marmon Silko, "Interior and Exterior Landscapes: The Pueblo Migration Stories" in *Yellow Woman and a Beauty of the Spirit: Essays on Native American Life Today* (New York: Simon and Schuster, 1996), 25–47.

4. John Elder, "Teaching at the Edge" in *Stories in the Land: A Place-Based Environmental Education Anthology,* Nature Literacy Series Number 2 (Great Barrington, Mass.: Orion Society, 1998), 11.

5. Mitchell Thomashow, *Ecological Identity: Becoming a Reflective Environmentalist* (Cambridge, Mass.: MIT Press, 1995), 2–4.

6. Borden is cited in Thomashow 1995, 4.

7. Aldo Leopold, *A Sand County Almanac, and Sketches Here and There* (New York: Oxford University Press, 1949), 204.

8. Gary Snyder, *A Place in Space: Ethics, Aesthetics, and Watersheds* (Washington, D.C.: Counterpoint Press, 1995), 235.

9. Watershed Writing Collective, *Recovering Pine River* (Alma, Mich.: WTW Publications, 2000), 47.

10. Watershed, 2.

11. Watershed, 53.

12. Watershed, 53.

13. Thomas J. Lyon, *This Incomperable Lande: A Book of American Nature Writing* (New York: Penguin, 1989), 3.

14. Thomas Fairchild Sherman, *A Place on the Glacial Till: Time, Land, and Nature within an American Town* (New York: Oxford University Press, 1997); John Hanson Mitchell, *Ceremonial Time: Fifteen Thousand Years on One Square Mile* (New York: Anchor Press, 1984); Terry Tempest Williams, *Refuge: An Unnatural History of Family and Place* (New York: Vintage, 1991).

15. Christensen and Blakemore.

16. Elder, 13–14.

17. Watershed, 4.

18. Watershed, 4.

19. Watershed, 34.

20. Andrea Lunsford and Lisa Ede, *Singular Texts/Plural Authors: Perspectives on Collaborative Writing* (Carbondale: Southern Illinois University Press, 1990), 133–34.

21. Watershed, 59.

References

Basso, Keith. 1996. *Wisdom sits in places: Landscape and language among the western Apache.* Albuquerque: New Mexico University Press.

Christensen, Laird, and Peter Blakemore, eds. 1999. The ASLE collection of syllabi in literature and environment. University of Minnesota. (http://www.asle.umn.edu/pubs/collect/collect.html), 14 February 2002.

Elder, John. 1998. Teaching at the edge. In *Stories in the land: A place-based environmental education anthology*, 1–15. Nature Literacy Series 2. Great Barrington, Mass.: Orion Society.

Leopold, Aldo. 1949. *A Sand County almanac, and sketches here and there*. New York: Oxford University Press.

Lueders, Edward, ed. 1989. *Writing natural history: Dialogues with authors*. Salt Lake City: University of Utah Press.

Lunsford, Andrea, and Lisa Ede. 1990. *Singular texts/plural authors: Perspectives on collaborative writing*. Carbondale: Southern Illinois University Press.

Lyon, Thomas J. 1989. *This incomperable lande: A book of American nature writing*. New York: Penguin.

Mitchell, John Hanson. 1984. *Ceremonial time: Fifteen thousand years on one square mile*. New York: Anchor Press.

Sherman, Thomas Fairchild. 1997. *A place on the glacial till: Time, land, and nature within an American town*. New York: Oxford University Press.

Silko, Leslie Marmon. 1996. Interior and exterior landscapes: The Pueblo migration stories. In *Yellow woman and a beauty of the spirit: Essays on native American life today*, 25–47. New York: Simon and Schuster.

Snyder, Gary. 1995. *A place in space: Ethics, aesthetics, and watersheds*. Washington, D.C.: Counterpoint Press.

Thomashow, Mitchell. 1995. *Ecological identity: Becoming a reflective environmentalist*. Cambridge, Mass.: MIT Press.

Watershed Writing Collective. 2000. *Recovering Pine River*. Alma, Mich.: WTW Publications.

Williams, Terry Tempest. 1991. *Refuge: An unnatural history of family and place*. New York: Vintage.

❋ TERRY GIFFORD

Teaching Environmental Values through Creative Writing with School Children

ECOCRITICAL PRACTICE

"Why are the activities aboard the *Titanic* so fascinating to us that we give no heed to the water through which we pass, or to that iceberg on the horizon?" The question Glen Love asked his fellow American literary critics in 1990 has begun to be answered by British critics such as Jonathan Bate in *The Song of The Earth* and by the formation of a United Kingdom branch of the Association for the Study of Literature and Environment (ASLE), of which I am currently the secretary. In the UK, Laurence Coupe's *The Green Studies Reader* (2000) has followed the publication in the United States of Glotfelty and Fromm's *The Ecocriticism Reader* (1996) in which Glen Love's question is to be found (229). We know that we are living through an environmental crisis, and some teachers of English in universities are beginning to catch up with some teachers in schools by giving attention to the role of the environment in their teaching and research and by developing an ecocritical practice that informs both activities. It was logical that my own ecocritical research should develop from a study of the social construction of nature in contemporary British poetry (Gifford 1995) to the theoretical elaboration of the theory of the "post-pastoral" (Gifford 2000). As a teacher of creative writing as well as literary theory, I have an interest in the relationship between ecocritical theory and pedagogy, especially in the residential writing courses I run in the Lake District. Elsewhere I have detailed the residential week in Grasmere for Bretton Hall's final year BA English students' optional module "Landscape and Poetry" that I have developed over sixteen years (Gifford 1999). Here I want to consider my weekends as writer-in-residence for Wigan schools at Hinning House, Dunnerdale, Cumbria, where I have developed a programme and techniques that engage with the mountain environment through a variety of forms of writing, leading to a debate about environmental issues located in that particular valley.

THE HINNING HOUSE PROJECT

This is a project I have been evolving on three weekends a year for the last ten years at Wigan Local Education Authority's Hinning House Outdoor Centre, Cumbria. The Duddon Valley, where the house is located, is the most secluded valley in the South West Lake District. Wordsworth wrote a sonnet sequence about following the River Duddon to the sea at the west, and Ruskin's Brantwood home is in the next valley. After travelling north for two hours from industrial Lancashire, pupils must transfer from their coach to smaller minibuses for the journey to what is almost the last house in the upper dry glacial lake bed. Hinning House Outdoor Centre is one of two owned by the Wigan Local Education Authority and is used as an outdoor activities centre, so a writing weekend is unusual. Hinning House accommodates and caters for twenty-four pupils and their staff. What I describe here is the latest evolution of a programme I have adapted for primary, secondary, or sixth-form pupils. The objectives of this project are to raise awareness of environmental issues through activities that include oral work and persuasive writing as well as imaginative narrative and poetry writing. (See Cooper 1998, *Outdoors With Young People*, for the placing of my writing exercises in the outdoor education programme provided by these centres.)

On Friday evening, after they have been given their personal equipment and the rules of the house, I introduce myself as a writer and my interest in the valley. The dialogue includes reference to the windy road they've travelled, to the wall map locating us in the Lake District (with its lakes like the spokes of a wheel), to the notion of the National Park, and to the special quiet remoteness and wildlife of this valley. I read my poem "Dunnerdale 1979" (Gifford 1987, 32). But I also mention the tradition of weekend visits to the Lake District from Lancashire industrial towns like Wigan. Then we go out for a night walk. If it is a dark winter evening the pupils do not carry torches, although they are in the pockets of staff. It is rare for a vehicle to pass us whilst we are walking the lanes of this valley at night. We make a series of stops for note-making in pairs. (If it is dark, instead of writing notes, pupils are asked to respond to a series of questions after talking in pairs. The questions take them through much the same process as the written note-making.) In my instructions for the prose note-making, I am developing a formula that produces heightened language from observation, with a focus on the senses. My guidance goes like this:

> List three words that sum up the atmosphere in this place at this moment (e.g., peaceful, scary, threatening). Circle one of these words (e.g., peaceful). One inch in from the left-hand margin list three actual things to represent, or contribute to, the word you've circled (e.g. sky, hills, sheep). In front of each of these three words write a descriptive word. Look carefully and make it precise to this place now (e.g., calm sky). Each of these three things is doing something. Write what it is doing using an active verb (e.g., calm sky waits). Add a word ending in 'ly' that describes how it is doing it (e.g., calm sky waits contentedly). Add to each line the word "like" or "as though" and finish the phrase (e.g., calm sky waits contentedly like a blanket on the bed). You now have three lines based on the formula adjective, noun, verb, adverb, simile. Let's hear some. Now using this formula write a line about the shape of something else that contributes to the atmosphere here.

At a second stop along the lane I will ask for a line, using the formula, about the texture of something, then a line about a sound, then about an aroma. At the third stop pupils will be asked to vary the formula to make a metaphor rather than a simile. This will be about the way something moves (e.g., The slow river is a silver thread winding through the fields). The next metaphor will be about the stillness of something. Finally they will be asked for a line about something they have not noticed so far.

At an ice-smoothed and striated rock, I point out that it has been formed by fire (it is volcanic rock) and later shaped by ice. It represents the glaciated volcano from which the present landscape of the Lake District is formed. Then I mention the way more recent water and weather has shaped the features of this valley that we have been describing: fells and fields, river and ravines. Human uses of the landscape in front of us are observed and listed. I like to draw attention to how at ease we have become in this apparently wild, now dark, or darkening, place. It is important at this early stage of the (as yet, undeclared) project to be aware that our species has been at home in this landscape for a long time: "Country people have been walking these lanes and footpaths without street lights or torches for centuries." (Later, Kerry Daniel, aged fourteen, wrote this remarkable Thoreauvian sentence: "We had been the animals of the night, fear an insignificant factor in our lives.")

So we travel and pause for listening, looking, and note-making after the lane and the rock, on into the dark wood, across the open pasture, back up the lane by the river, then across the fields (with a stop to call up the owls) toward the house lights. Indoors, pupils work on the first draft of a poem titled "Nightwalk in Dunnerdale," using a model from previous Wigan pupils in the twelve-page anthology I've prepared for everyone. I show them how to find a form through redrafting, breaking the phrases and lines differently and spacing them on the page differently to see how form changes possible meanings before settling on a final draft:

1. The calm sky waits contentedly
    Like a blanket on the bed.
2. The calm sky waits
      contentedly
         like a blanket on the bed.
3. The calm sky waits
    Contented as a blanket
    Over the bed of the valley.

Pupils are often absorbed in this until surprisingly late at night. When the pupils have gone to bed staff begin typing the best of these into the computer for the Sunday publication that will contain one work from everyone.

On Saturday I set up the weekend's project with a conversation that starts with the summer watering restrictions in Wigan and its reasons, which takes us toward mention of concepts they've learned at school like the ozone layer and global warming. "Many of the lakes of the Lake District," I point out, "are actually reservoirs supplying Manchester and Wigan with drinking water. Soon there will inevitably be a proposal to flood the upper Duddon Valley. If we look outside the window we can see how suitable it would be, with a dam across Wallabarrow Gorge where we walked last night." We brainstorm the advantages for and against, for locals and visitors, that will come from the widening of the road and the consequent possible tourist developments. To children water sports are very appealing and better access, for everyone, in coaches, to this wonderful place seems like a good idea.

I divide Friday's pairs into four groups and allocate to two groups the task of developing arguments *for* the proposal to flood the valley, and to the other two the task of finding arguments *against*. In these groups, with this given focus, they now list the arguments we've just brainstormed and try to add more. Their task on Sunday morning will be to make a group presentation to convince their audience of their case, using any writing produced over the weekend, plus quotations from reference books in the house library and from the anthology I've put together for them. After the presentation they will have a free vote on an individual voting slip. So everyone knows that, whether or not they happen to be sympathetic to the side of the debate they have been assigned to represent, they will have a personal vote on the issue at the end of the weekend. This produces running informal discussions between pupils on what they personally think about the arguments they are collecting for the group presentations. The difference between recognising arguments that can be made and the personal evaluation of these arguments in terms of the personal vote to be cast produces a sophisticated handling of environmental ethics that does not ignore personal sympathies and emotions but avoids foregrounding them as the first response expected. The vote is therefore made as a result of the whole weekend's process of debate and reflection.

Now I read from *The Iron Woman* (Hughes 1999, 10–14). I suggest that in this project they are really listening to, and speaking for, either Water Spirit, who knows the benefits of flooding, or Mountain Spirit, who is threatened by flooding. I invite them to write the story of "The Coming of the Mountain Spirit or Water Spirit," like the Hughes story, which must end with the plea "Help me!" Here is one example, like all those used here, from a weekend with fourteen-year-old pupils from Byrchall High School, Wigan:

The Coming of the Mountain Spirit

Laura apprehensively walked through the dark eerie forest, the bracken and leaves crunching beneath her feet and the deep evergreens towering above her. The tranquil atmosphere and gentle flow of the river soothed her. She felt she was alone.

Suddenly she heard a faint noise. Did she imagine it? Perhaps its the whisper of the wind through the trees, she thought. She shrugged it off and continued through the forest.

A familiar smell enveloped the forest, the smell of nature, the fresh damp smell of the country. It comforted her, made her feel safe and secure.

She walked aimlessly through the forest in a dream world of her own until suddenly a bright piercing light attracted her attention in the distance. Very slowly the blurred image of an old man began to emerge in an array of colours. She slowly began to distinguish his features. The piercing blue light was his eyes, as bright as the sky on a hot summer's day. The wrinkles on his face were creased like the rocks sporadically arranged across the valley.

He began to speak, his words slow but steady.

"Help us," he whimpered. "Our time is almost up."

"I don't understand," Laura cried in a panic-stricken voice.

"I am the spirit of the mountain."

Laura began to realise the pain of this man and her fear was lost. A man who had stood alone for millions of years watching over the valley, protecting it from danger, the mountain that shaped the valley—and now this magnificent being was asking for her help.

Sarah MacRae

Now we leave for a woodland walk. After crossing a stream to enter these springtime bluebell woods, I draw attention to the birds, fungi, flowers, dry oxbow lake, the path itself (and lack of litter), ant hills, and the ants' trails. This takes us to a bankside at the entrance to Wallabarrow Gorge, where we sit. I invite note-making on the journey of two people, A and B (any relationship) that was the same as ours this very morning. A was showing B the things we had just seen. I give out the anthology *Romantic Ecology* from my rucksack and read Ruskin's three principles of political economy (Bate 1991, 59–60) before asking pupils to make notes on the elements of air, water, and earth in this place. We cross the river by the stepping stones, at which I read from the anthology Wordsworth's Duddon Valley sonnet IX written in 1818 (30).

So we proceed through Wallabarrow Farm where the unexpected lies around every corner: a llama called Wesley, a Vietnamese pot-bellied pig, a golden pheasant, the old farmer himself, exotic doves, and a barn-owl hole in the architecture for the resident rat catcher. On the rising path beyond the farm we pause in woods halfway up to Wallabarrow Crag for an update in the note-making for this journey. Here I ask writers to inject into their fictional relationships an anxiety about something that A has been feeling lately about B.

We scramble up below the crag to a belvedere where we stop to write an amulet. This is *the* ecological poetic form. I quote John Muir: "When we try to pick out anything by itself, we find it hitched to everything else in the universe."(Gifford 1992, 248) "Look," I say, "everything is joined to everything else, sometimes in ways that are invisible. In front of us there are invisible chains that make the most unlikely connections. What is the chain that connects these rocks with those clouds? Make a list of the chain that links any three things (e.g., clouds, rocks, ferns). Now make a list that links any eight things, but make the chain return to the first thing (e.g., clouds, rain, wind, rocks, earth, roots, ferns, clouds). Put in the verbs of what one thing is doing to the next thing (e.g., clouds spew rain, rain rides wind, etc.). Add adjectives to the things. Write an amulet based upon my poem "Bat Charm" in the anthology (Gifford 1991, 37). Look at the amulets written by previous Wigan pupils in the anthology. Some begin with a common linking word, but the basic idea is that the last word of each line will provide the first word of the next line."

Amulet

Below the grass dripping moisture
Below the dripping moisture crawling creatures
Below the crawling creatures hungry hearts
Below the hungry hearts living love
Below the living love the grass
Below the grass dripping moisture

Anya Smith

At the summit, after another steep scramble, we perch in the wind, above everything. We write notes on how this view and the achievement bring a clearing of perception about the anxiety in the relationship. Character A makes a resolve to do something upon return. Summit experiences can do this. In many European cultures they are the location for churches. These notes become a poem in which images from this view are used to stand for processes at work inside the character. The trick is to suggest emotion through the way the character sees the elements of the view, rather than stating the precise anxiety and its actual resolution. "Try to end with a gesture or an action that suggests a resolve to do something."

Summit

The barbed wire
Trapping him.
The silence
Buzzing in his ears.
The dizzy mountains
Spinning around his head.
The silent rock
Standing
Wide open to the world.

The disturbance of a machine
Had no effect on his hazy mind.
He wanted to be alone
To untangle.
His mind pulled with the powering clouds above,
He looked at his friend
Then at the mountains closing in on him.
As he walked away
They seemed to move back with him.

Beth Morell

After lunch the walk takes us past ancient piles of field-clearing stones, Grassguards Farm's chickens and dogs, a ford, a pied flycatcher stream, steep beechwoods, more stepping stones, and bluebell slopes up to the road. So we return to Hinning House for some (supervised) free time in the fields and stream.

After tea, groups prepare questions to ask "four local visitors who will be arriving this evening." They are the Vicar (against flooding), a local teenager (for), the National Park warden (against), and a farmer turned developer (for). These visitors are actually role-played by teachers and myself who circulate around the groups. This produces some of the most engaged work of the weekend with passionate debate. This is unrecorded oral work, although the recording of key statements by an assigned note-maker allows for later quotations from these interviews to be used in the presentations. In these interviews and the animated discussion that always follows each one, land-use ethics are being debated with great intensity as the pupils eagerly take on their roles in the debate against or with the role-played "visitor." Here the ethical issues are not distanced or abstract but about a valley they know and a threat or opportunity they understand and have already considered. Sometimes a "visitor" will actually be persuaded by a group's arguments and will modify or reverse his or her stance on the issue. Always the group presentations include some quotations from what the "visitors" have said, or have been manoeuvred into saying, in order to make a point in the debate with the authority associated with a statement from an adult. Some of the land-use approaches adopted by the "visitors" may be over-simplified caricatures, but they will be new to these pupils and produce shocked outrage that such ethical positions could be held. Noise levels do get quite high.

To calm everyone down I give a slide-illustrated introduction to John Muir, showing his home in Scotland, the site of his cabin in Yosemite, the

Sierra landscape he interpreted, and his house in Martinez. I emphasise his proto-ecological vision, his being at home in the natural world, and his role in inventing the idea of national parks. I end with slides of places bought by the John Muir Trust in Scotland recently and talk about the urban need for wild places to visit, bringing us back to the Wigan-Dunnerdale link.

After dark, if the weather is clear, we go outside and lie on the grass in silence, stargazing. For urban pupils this may be the first time that they have seen the universe they inhabit, or have felt the earth beneath them, making the quality of bodily connection that David Abram suggests we have mostly lost, to our cost. Abram calls this kind of activity "the recuperation of the incarnate, sensorial dimension of experience [that] brings with it a recuperation of the living landscape in which we are corporeally embedded" (1996, 65). This can produce quite revelatory poetry on return to the house:

Stargazer

My eyes are dazzled.
The brightness jeers at the dark.
In a glance
The dead stars increase ten-fold.
So comforting,
Yet not,
They are a smothering blanket of safety.
Reaching out,
Stars are an imaginary cluster in my clumsy hands.
My eyes turn fuzzy.
How many needless hands reach?
How many oblivious eyes see?
Unknowingly,
The whole universe is looking
At my small shooting star,
Alone in thought
Yet connected with the world.

Claire Witherington

❀

On Sunday morning we go for a last walk and I encourage talking in pairs about the arguments to be presented. Then back at the house pupils prepare their presentations. I write on the board, "Possible elements in your presentation: introduction, nightwalk poem, amulet, 'The coming of the . . .,' summit poem, journey prose, interviews, quotations from Ruskin, Wordsworth, Muir, Gifford, or others, a poster, a slogan, a summary of key arguments, conclusion: why you should vote for or against." Groups choose how they want to structure their presentations, whose work to include to represent the elements they have selected for their structure, and who will read which parts. We try to make time for a rehearsal before the four groups actually make their presentations for their assigned side of the debate. These are often by now impassioned and impressively structured arguments. The attention is focused by the fact that a personal vote is to be cast following these presentations. The creative work is introduced as evidence for what is either to be lost or offered to greater numbers. Poems and narratives originally written without an ethical position are now marshalled into the arguments about land-use at the climax of the weekend's project. Such "evidence" of varied kinds is being manipulated for a persuasive purpose. The videos some schools make of these presentations provide interesting material for further teaching about the use of evidence in environmental debates and the evaluation of issue-based arguments.

Now voting slips are offered by the returning officer, after a briefing earlier about how to make a vote. In the most recent vote two pupils were so convinced by their own arguments that they voted "for" and the remainder "against." On another occasion the votes were cast equally on each side.

During the night and Sunday morning the teachers have been preparing the publication containing one piece from everyone, including staff, for duplication and distribution. During lunch this booklet is distributed and we celebrate the publication by asking pupils to "choose one you like by somebody else and read it for us." The quality of the work induces instant admiration of poets who had arrived in this place unaware that they were poets.

In quick order, we clear up the house, load the minibuses, and wave goodbye to a magic weekend that is not dependent upon a magician. The techniques and the programme I have described could be taught by anyone. This is important, in my view. To be a teacher, which is what writers in this situation are, is to offer an empowerment through language that, when it is working, feels like being a magician. But the success of this project should not be dependent upon the special powers of a charismatic writer/teacher.

WHAT ENVIRONMENTAL VALUES HAVE BEEN TAUGHT HERE?

Ten tentative reflections:

1. Objects have become subjects, mediated through language, listened to, seen closely. Patrick D. Murphy has written that "Nonhuman others can be constituted as speaking subjects, rather than constituted merely as objects of our speaking" (1995, 14). Through these writing activities special attention has been paid to speaking subjects, through finding the voices of "Mountain Spirit" and "Water Spirit," for example. What began as the objects of descriptive writing have been given voice through this mythical character. "Letting the land speak through us," as Murphy puts it, sounds a sophisticated concept, but children can make the imaginative ecocentric leap with great facility, given a model example of a mode of doing so in the story by Ted Hughes.

2. "At the end of the weekend a lot of people had produced work that they were proud of" (Laura Davenport, in a pupil evaluation). "Some brilliant poets had been discovered" (Joanna Heaton, pupil evaluation). Where does the quality of the writing derive from? I would suggest: from a structured engagement with a place that is felt to be special in the heightened, concentrated language that comes from a residency away from home. These writing exercises are transferable to any landscape, as is the notion of the issue-based environmental writing project as a whole. It helps, of course, to have a sense of the distinctiveness of a landscape and its land-use tensions, but these things are not hard to find. The heightened language comes from the pupils finding the specialness of place with the right guidance for the attention, the note-making, and the final shaping of the work.

3. Where do the weaknesses in the writing derive from? From the pastoral clichés we all bring with us about "beautiful landscapes" and from the temptation to overwrite, to use two adjectives where one startling one would be better. Where the quality of attention is poor, the language that is supposed to be expected by the teacher is substituted for the sharpness of surprise that comes from looking and listening beyond the obvious or the expected.

4. Processes and connections in nature have been emphasised. These are slightly different perceptions and are taught by the amulet and the summit exercise in particular. Form here provides a way of seeing. This, in turn, informs the quality of the ethical debate in the project. (Processes and connections in the making of what is now called "nature writing" have been learned too, through note-making, drafting, and integrating

forms of language from oral work to writing questions, reports, polemic, narrative, and poetry. The integration of cultural resources in the service of the environment and our relationship with it is one of the implicit aims of this project. This model of a direction for English teaching should not be lost on the teachers present.)

5. Dialectical debate has been taught through arguing the claims of the environmental versus social, local versus national, human versus non-human, work versus leisure interests. These are the common tensions raised by the role-played interviews and subsequent discussion. They have not been raised in the abstract but in passionate debate about what is more than a case study. It is about the very land on which we are living for the weekend, these lanes we walk, this river we enter, these meadows we cross, this house in which we work and sleep. In a sense the writing of poems is a sensitising process that is necessary preparation for the land-use debate toward which the project is directed. Pupils come away feeling that they have resolved something on behalf of this valley. They often ask before leaving, "Is this valley really threatened with flooding?" The answer is, "If not this one, then another, or at least the raising of water levels in an existing lake." When they next encounter an environmental issue inside or outside the curriculum, it is to be hoped that they might recognise some of the tensions, some of the arguments, and some of the rhetorical strategies with which they have engaged in this project.

6. This project has been an introduction to environmental pressure-group politics and the balloting process. The presence of the final personal vote turns the function of the presentations into pressure-group politics rather than academic argument. The details of designed voting slips, their allocation, the voting booth, ballot box, and declaring officer's announcement provide the experience of the dignity of democracy in action. Pupils might remember what a "spoiled paper" is when they reach eighteen and might make use of their vote correctly, since they will be familiar with the process. They might even remember having enjoyed political debate. They might think that environmental issues are worth voting about—that debates concern real places.

7. Interdisciplinary sources of information have informed the variety of writing and language forms. Information about history, geomorphology, hydrology, ornithology, botany, economics, land management, literary history, and literary forms have been introduced without the alienating boundaries of naming these disciplines. What is missing from this project is an engagement with hard scientific evidence. With different sources of knowledge and skills in the teaching staff more could, perhaps, be offered

to the project, although there are limits to what can be absorbed in the outdoor context of much of the work during the weekend.

8. The summit exercise in particular is intended to lead toward an understanding of the inner through its parallel in the outer. Literature, especially perhaps oral poetry, has traditionally used images from nature as icons or symbols of natural processes by which to understand emotional forces or the paradoxes of the inner processes of relationships. The English folksong "The Seeds of Love" would be as good an example as Blake's worm in "The Rose." That what is now called "the environment" provides us with reminders of our continuity with it as much as our current alienation from it is a literary tool as old as oral literature itself (see Gifford 2000, 157). This is a preoccupation of my own poetry and an "environmental value" I am keen to pass on (see Waage 1985). The physical continuity experienced by pupils when this is successful is not to be understood as a vague "at-one-ness" but a recognition of difference at the moment of seeing that outer forces can help us understand our inner forces at a personal level.

9. Rather than encourage a vague notion of the "equality" of our species with the rest of the organic world, this project has observed differences between all living things, recognising their individual features and qualities. This is essential to learning to live with, rather than in, our environment. Clearly as a species we do not have equality with others in a simplistic sense, because we have a sense of responsibility. A respect for difference, a celebration of otherness, and a listening alertness to what is often now called "the more-than-human world" is the foundation of this project.

10. A danger of working in this "beautiful" mountain environment and emphasising its special qualities might be the implication that environmentalism is concerned only with places like this and not with the pupils' local environments. Indeed, the contrast is what first strikes them: "In this secret haven I have noticed that grass replaced concrete, people were replaced by sheep, and chaos was replaced by calm" (Jennie Lutas, pupil evaluation). (See Turkle 1999.) It is crucial to recognise that this kind of project is not dependent upon the mountain environment. From another location, using a Youth Hostel as a base for a weekend environmental-writing project, I have focused the writing and oral assignments around the issue of whether to by-pass a linear town of narrow streets by sacrificing a neighbouring quiet valley. The final vote by these thirteen-year-olds was sixteen to six against the by-pass. But the project could usefully take place around the pupils' school in Wigan.

Recently I have been able to visit the school of a group that came to Hinning House and extended their thinking and writing about their local environment. With Guilded Hollins Primary School, Wigan, I ran a school-based weekend of environmental creative writing with pupils and their parents using the school grounds and a local park. This was an exercise in reconnecting with the processes of nature available within an urban neighbourhood and considering the threats to such environments. (There has been a strong temptation in the UK over the last decade for urban schools to generate capital by selling off parts of their playing fields in areas of great housing demand.) Here the children were able to guide their parents in the writing exercises in shared creative writing. A subject for further research would be to find ways in which this Hinning House project could give pupils a sense of having gained transferable skills. In the future, as the energy crisis begins to bite and we all are forced to travel less, we will have to "hunker down" where we live, as the American "deep ecologist" George Sessions recently put it to me. But it is important now that teachers find the "specialness" that is just around the corner from home, rather than in the mountains. The programme and techniques of creative writing described here should have something to offer all teachers concerned to raise awareness of the environmental issues facing our species.

It should not be difficult to translate this issue-based project for creative writing to a college level. Teachers of writing have a model here for a field-trip that avoids too much logistical concern with camping gear or cooking. Teachers with a specialty such as geography, environmental studies, local history, or science have a model here for inviting a writer/teacher to work in collaboration to raise awareness of environmental values. Here's the excuse to take students to that "special place," turn on the enthusiasm for it, and do something for its future. Alternatively, here's the excuse to discover the specialness of the locality or campus where you teach and do something for its future by using the curriculum and the teaching skills available to develop both environmental values and communication skills. Isn't that what our planet needs right now—informed, questioning, empowered, environmentally aware citizens?

References

Abram, D. 1996. *The spell of the sensuous.* New York: Vintage.

Bate, J. 1991. *Romantic ecology.* New York: Routledge.

———. 2000. *The song of the earth.* London: Picador.

Cooper, G. 1998. *Outdoors with young people.* Lyme Regis: Russell House.

Coupe, L., ed. 2000. *The green studies reader.* New York: Routledge.

Dawson, J. 1988. *Wordsworth's Duddon revisited.* Milnthorpe: Cicerone.

Gifford, T. 1987. *The stone spiral.* Clapham: Giant Steps.

———. 1991. *Outcrops.* Todmorden: Littlewood Arc.

———. 1995. *Green voices: Understanding contemporary nature poetry.* New York: Manchester University Press.

———. 1999. Teaching post-pastoral poetry of landscape in the mountains. In *Creative writing conference 1999 proceedings,* edited by J. Turner, D. Broderick, and P. Hartley, 145–52. Sheffield: Sheffield Hallam University.

———. 2000. *Pastoral.* New York: Routledge.

Gifford, T., ed. 1992. *John Muir: The eight wilderness-discovery books.* Seattle: The Mountaineers.

———. 1996. *John Muir: The life and letters and other writings.* Seattle: The Mountaineers.

Glotfelty, C., and H. Fromm, eds. 1996. *The ecocriticism reader.* Athens: University of Georgia Press.

Hughes, T. 1993. *The iron woman.* London: Faber.

McFadden, M. 1985. The I in nature: Nature writing as self-discovery. In *Teaching environmental literature,* edited by F. O. Waage. 102–7. New York: MLA.

Murphy, P. D. 1995. *Literature, nature, and other.* New York: SUNY.

Turkle, A. 1999. Pedagogy of place: Teaching a reusable sense of place. *Writing in education* 17: 23–27.

Waage, F. O., ed. 1985. *Teaching environmental literature.* New York: MLA.

❊   LIZ NEWBERY
    BOB HENDERSON

Going Out as a Way In

Social, Cultural, and Ecological Learning and the University Field Trip

W e teach a course in adventure education in which we spend a good deal of time talking about different labels thrown about in the field: risk, comfort zones, flow, and edgework, to name a few. What is so often lost in such a course premised on learning through challenge is that the greatest challenge we humans may face is simply, and perhaps difficultly, to live well—with each other and with the earth. It is such social and ecological learning that we seek in our outdoor education classes at McMaster University, and the field trip is one of our principal tools.

This article is a series of stories about an education that attempts to move toward living well; an education influenced by theories of outdoor education, experiential education, and critical pedagogy, that uses the field experience and a "change of place" to romance students.[1] We try to lure them into a greater depth of learning. Sometimes a field trip arises because it is an attempt to teach existing content in a more meaningful way. Sometimes the field trip forms the backbone around which a course is built. Either way, and perhaps in both ways, going out of the classroom can be a compelling way in to learning.

A critical transformative educational agenda attempts to cultivate critical thinking, such that learners are encouraged to question their world, in the hopes that they do more than fit into it, that they rather change it for the better (Miller 1988). We might argue at great length about what constitutes a "change for the better," but we do not think it too controversial to say that there are social and ecological crises abounding, and the world urgently needs more critical actors, not more people who happily settle for the way things are. We suggest that there are three related dimensions of transformative learning: *ecological*, *cultural*, and *social*. The first implies a critical analysis of environmental issues, as well as a personal ecological consciousness. The second, which might also be called cultural literacy, implies the ability to look within one's own culture, to begin to see and then to critically assess what cultural myths and stories we live within and perpetuate. The idea here is that we can write new cultural stories in which to live, better ones. The third dimension implies the development of a critical consciousness around issues of social oppression, resource disparity, and our own places within this. These dimensions are obviously intricately linked, as, for instance, both environmental and social crises can be understood as grounded in crises of culture. Yet we have delineated them here as they can all too often be understood as existing separately. Not all environmentalists have strong social analyses and vice versa, for example.

The stories offered here will highlight three separate field trips from the undergraduate outdoor education courses we teach in McMaster University's Department of Kinesiology. Each relates a way in to a different area of critical learning described above. Our goal is to disorient our students' and our own conventional notions of schooling, culture, and self in the hope that we might fuel the ongoing process of reorienting in patterns that are more meaningful, just, and sustainable. Our means to this end is the immersion in experience.

ECOPSYCHOLOGY: THE ECOLOGICAL UNCONSCIOUS AND CREATING ECOLOGICAL CONSCIOUSNESS (LIZ AND BOB)

. . . in a forest of stone, underneath the corporate canopy, where the sun rarely filters down, the ground is not so soft. . . . I am foraging for a phone booth on the forest floor that is not so soft, I look up and it looks like the buildings are burning but it's just the sun setting, the solar system calling an end to another business day. . . . (Difranco 1991)

Students move in for a nose-length and novel view of the imposing cement structure that houses their classrooms and gymnasia. The cassette player that Liz holds lyrically chants this lament for a culture that has lost its forest floor, a culture where the ground, and life itself, is not so soft...

"You weren't expecting this class to be normal, were you?" Liz grins at the students from atop the cement stairs. This marks the beginning of a two-hour foray into the arts and ecopsychology, featuring imaginary guests and enthusiastic mucking about in the woods. The theoretical content behind this field trip? We are born with an innate relationship with and love of nature, and humans are deeply *a part of*, not *apart from* the natural world. The strength of our connection to nature means quite simply that you cannot have healthy people on a sick planet (Henderson 1999).

To lead us away from that place where the ground is not so soft, a dramatized Michael Cohen of Project Nature Connect comes out from behind a tree, inquiring, "Are you the group from McMaster? I was supposed to meet a third-year kinesiology class here." This is just weird enough to enchant our students, we laugh to each other.

Following "Michael" just past the edge of campus, and down into the ravine trails, we are invited on a silent walk to wake up our senses.

"You know that there are fifty-two senses," Michael tells us matter-of-factly. "And to think, most people believe there are only five!"

In mid-January, in the middle of an otherwise routine school day, we ask our students to bury themselves in leaves, smell mud (or snow, depending on the weather), feel bark, climb trees, crawl belly-first through the underbrush to get the best underside view; in short, we ask them to fully and sensually explore.[2] We become children, and a hawk watches us dubiously from the top of a dead tree while we play.

After some healthy, unstructured wandering, everyone is lured back to a central place by a small campfire and a guitar. There is something of ecopsychology that is expressed more easily in the poetics of music, prose, and visual representations than in the stripped-bare language of the academy. So that is necessarily where we begin: with former students' journal excerpts, with warming our hands at the fire under a winter sky, with a guitar and a turn at "Big Yellow Taxi" by Joni Mitchell or "Woodsmoke and Oranges" by Ian Tamblyn. Enter "Chellis Glendinning," who just happens to be passing through this Hamilton wetland on a short walk from her New Mexico home. "Chellis" is perhaps best known for her aptly named treatise *My Name is Chellis and I'm in Recovery from Western Civilization*.

"Oh hey!" she greets us. "How's your primal matrix doing today? Just kidding! Except that I'm not, really. That's the question we should all, always be concerned about!"

People stare at her, a bit confused. "Our primal matrix," she explains, "is a healthy, wholly functioning psyche in relationship with a healthy, wholly functioning Earth" (Glendinning 1994, 5). She's evidently excited about this topic as she hardly pauses. "Okay, so we possess an innate wholeness. But it is fractured by the ills, by the fundamental pathology of western civilization. So some people become obsessed and addicted to coping mechanisms: consumerism, drugs, technology. Our *society* is sick, and our primal matrix has become lost to us. We must seek wholeness," she concludes, "and seek it in the natural world" (Glendinning 1994).

"Well, I must be off!" She gets up from the campfire circle. "So much work to do! Personal healing, families to nourish, children to teach in the ways of nature. I just ask one thing before I go—strive to turn off your TVs and spend more time in this place, just minutes from where you live and study." And just as suddenly, she is gone, replaced by a prof, a bit boring in comparison.

After another guitar interlude, "Theodore Roszak," who originally coined the term ecopsychology in 1992 (and possessing a remarkable likeness to a local professor), conveniently appears and helps to fill out some of the theoretical background of Chellis's standpoint.

"Most therapists," he explains, "focus on the relationships with and alienation from self, family, parents. Ecopsychology is rooted in the understanding that the fundamental relationship to heal is that between the self and the natural environment. Furthermore, there is a crucial connection between planetary well-being and personal well-being that desperately needs to be acknowledged."

Pausing to consider the fire, he scans the students' faces and looks to the treetops above. "You know," he continues thoughtfully, "for an ecopsychologist, it's the repression of the ecological unconscious that's of concern. That causes the kind of mass madness of industrial society. Accessing our ecological unconscious . . ." and he leans in close for effect, ". . . may well be the most effective path to sanity" (after Roszak 1992, 320–21). Lofty and uncertain goals, perhaps, but we are well on our way, here, where the scent of half-rotten leaves is heavy on the air.

Students begin talking about their own experiences of connectedness and disconnectedness to places natural and of their reactions to the visits of Glendinning and Roszak. We let the fire die out and decide to end by way of beginnings. There are many trails that lead out from where we sit. Why necessarily follow the path back to the concrete building? There are other paths to journey home.

The origin of the field trip described above lay in the need to create a hands-and-minds-on experience dealing with ecopsychology. Each week in this third-year outdoor education survey course we have a two-hour practical workshop, followed later in the week by a one-hour lecture that provides background theory. For a bioregional education class we stage a campus-wide scavenger hunt that sees the students more consciously answering the question: where is here? For an environmental-education class rooted in a nature-interpretation tradition, we carpool to a local conservation area to visit a dynamic teacher "in her natural habitat." It seemed ludicrous and more than vaguely contradictory to teach about ecopsychology in a lecture hall with fixed seats and no windows. Instinctively, we had to go outside. This two-hour field trip arose to meet a curricular need—we had content we had to cover in the context of a university course. This was the most effective way, we deemed, to teach it. What made it work was a flair for the unusual, our propensity toward self-mockery, some pedagogical risk taking, and students who were, we believe, desperately ready for something different. Most importantly, we knew enough not to fill the space with our words but to let the land do its teaching. The *place* had to be central.

There are students for whom I suspect this class is difficult, those who, when invited out for a short solo nature sit, clump together on the path and talk. They are a small 10 percent of our class. And they are probably still enjoying themselves and getting something out of the eclectic workshop. At the very least, they are spending two hours in the woods, which they would otherwise not have done.[3] From those who more eagerly delve into the possibilities we present we hear remarkable things.

Later in the term, students are asked to write an environmental autobiography. One student felt it appropriate to begin hers with that time we spent together in the ravine behind campus:

> Found: One long-lost friend on Saturday, February 3rd, 2001 in Cootes Paradise. Under the canopy of the trees, Sharon and Nature were triumphantly reunited. The relationship needs minor repairs, but the strong bond is still intact.
>
> If my life read like a newspaper the above clipping would have summarized the front-page story. Inspired by my Outdoor Experiential Education class outing to Cootes Paradise, I returned the next day and made a miraculous discovery. In the woods that day I found something that lay hidden within me. I rediscovered my love for nature. Before this experience, my love for nature was hidden beneath a blanket of general malaise. . . . Unable to pinpoint the cause of my dissatisfaction, my frustration grew. I felt spiritually disconnected. I felt lost, unsure of my place and purpose in the world. In the woods I experienced two strong, yet opposing forces. I was drawn into a spiritual bond with nature and simultaneously was set free from my own self-doubt. Alone in nature, I felt like I had come home. In this home I found my place and my purpose.

Several days after another year's workshop, we received this unsolicited e-mail from a student we hardly knew:

> I have no real reason for writing, other than the fact that I really want to convey to you how much the eco-psychology class last week meant to me. . . . The last two months, I have been struggling with anxiety and insomnia. . . . That 10 minutes of time that I spent on the top of a hill, sitting on a fallen willow tree, I regained that sense of connectedness with nature, the connection that I had forgotten because my brain was swimming in a pile of worries. That night as I lay in bed, no longer did thoughts pervade my every waking moment, I fell asleep. I had the most peaceful sleep that I have had since December. I was at peace with nature. I was at peace with myself. Thank you for opening my mind.

These students seem to be not really *learning about* ecopsychology so much as *experiencing* it. Among all of the classes we throw together for this course, it is the ecopsychology workshop, so simply performed in our backyard, literally three minutes from our office, that consistently astonishes us with its pedagogical significance. What we set out to do was convey some content in an engaging way. We suspect that we may have done much more than that. Many of us who guide extended "wilderness" expeditions have long noticed the sense of wellness, balance, and peace that is brought to ourselves and our students when out on trail; the very stuff of ecopsychology. We had not expected the same from our brief midafternoon journey. Perhaps we underestimated the ecological unconscious!

We've become convinced of the power of a pedagogical approach that attempts to *live* the curriculum instead of merely talking about it. Even if we were brilliant and charismatic teachers, we would never have been able to achieve from inside the classroom the depth of learning that we actually did. In retrospect, what we think we did was go beyond the typical university-bound intellectualization of content to engage the emotional and spiritual realms. It matters little whether what happened involved excavating the ecological unconscious or raising some ecological consciousness. What matters is that for many students there seemed to be something transformative about this field trip in ecological terms. There aren't likely any environmental heroics arising out of our work that day or any complex enviro-political analyses about capitalism, globalization, or environmental justice being generated. But we think many of us may have re-remembered how important the earth is to our own health, re-remembered that we *do* belong here. And, after all, the most effective environmental politics may begin with how we think about and live our everyday.

SNOWSHOEING AS A VENUE
FOR CULTURAL CONSCIOUSNESS (LIZ AND BOB)

"Well, Hubbard was having trouble finding an aboriginal guide to lead him in his obsessive search for Lake Michikamau and the George River beyond." Alex's enthusiasm for this classic story is contagious. She draws us in with her detail, reconstructing for us a particular version of the Labrador of 1903. We all move a little closer to the fire as the story winds on, her voice punctuated by the occasional crunching of snow underneath us. We laugh at the naivety of Hubbard contrasted with the matter-of-fact wisdom of the local peoples. At the same time, we can't help but be awed by the task that Hubbard set out for himself. As if she'd planned it, we all slide into a numbness while the fire dies out and her story nears its inevitable end of Hubbard freezing to death. As guides, we are aware of the faint blueish tinge many faces have taken on. At least we have a wannigan full of food and a stack of already cut firewood. We'll fare better than Hubbard. For the moment, we are well set up to live here in this hemlock grove. We build up the fire, revive ourselves with hot chocolate, and share our thoughts about adventure, hubris, cultural views, leadership, and Hubbard. Another typical winter-camp evening unwinds its way toward eventual sleep in the wall tents and quinzhees—Athapaskan snow houses built from loose snow.

Since we are a "northern" nation, winter is a part of our national mythology, if not our psyche,[4] and the expedition is prominently part of the outdoor education tradition in this province. Years ago, Bob accordingly decided to create a winter travel course based around a snowshoe journey. The faculty curriculum committee wouldn't go for it; they held the apparent view that such an expedition didn't constitute "real" learning. Perhaps it sounded like too much fun, not serious enough. We have so thoroughly been schooled in the notions that learning cannot be fun, that it must be somber, and that hard work involves abstract content, memorization, pen, paper, and computer. This "high status knowledge" as described by Bowers (1997) arises out of a human-centred perspective that relies on experts and worships "progress"; this knowledge tends to be treasured as "real learning" by our institutions of schooling. Ecologically centred learning is relegated as "low status knowledge," and, in our case, was seen as not being academic enough. Bob changed the course title from "Winter Travel: Traditional and Contemporary Techniques" to "Winter Travel: Story, Place, and Technique" and resubmitted the proposal. With new language that framed the travel experience within academic interdisciplinary themes the travel experience was legitimized. The committee bought it and the McMaster winter-camp course was born. The strategic use of a few hot academic words can apparently go a long way in supporting what we instinctively already know is valuable learning.

Perhaps it was well thought out, or perhaps it was inadvertent, but when Bob attached those three words to the trip, what he essentially did was wrap rich, productive and culturally disorienting curriculum content around the mainstay of the expedition. How this played out pedagogically led to the major insight that we will elaborate here: *a course in outdoor education can serve as a valuable window for viewing cultural practices and assumptions in new light. It can in fact be an excellent anthropology course in which the culture of study is our own.*

The foundation of this course is a carefully crafted and selected reading kit, a reading kit drawing on multiple disciplines around the themes of Story, Place, and Technique. It helps that our class size is quite small (ten to twenty students) so the discussion of these articles can become very rich. We spend a couple of three-hour workshops exploring each theme and throughout the course we continue to draw learnings back into the themes. The week-long trip occurs two thirds of the way through the course and experiences on the trip are later viewed through the academic lenses already introduced. The final assignment is a take-home exam: an expressive course-end representation of the students' learning in the form of a creative concept map.[5] These have provided impressive indications of the kinds of links our students are making with the theoretical material, the field experience, and their own selves.

Story

"We lead storied lives," the narrative researchers Connelly and Clandinin (1990, 2) tell us. Indeed we do. And as educators we explore the many meanings of this. Our task: to make the innocently simple and childlike notion of "story" both strange and complex.

We begin quite obviously by telling a story. This illustrates techniques students will later draw on in their excursion into the role of storyteller. It also allows us to initially explore the notion of cultural stories: what widely held perspectives did characters in the story draw on? While on the expedition, we ask each student to tell a twenty-minute story to the rest of the class. We find that this experience is more rich and difficult than any conventional school presentation. It is a challenge not unlike, yet perhaps more unique than, a ropes course. They are performing, must know their material well, and are encouraged to choose stories within which there is a richness of cultural exploration possible. Each story is followed by a discussion, and we relate the story to our own lives. Storytelling, in this way, becomes pedagogy. In telling and sharing stories we are telling/sharing our understandings of the world (Henderson 1995). It is this sharing of understandings that renders storytelling a tool for self-understanding, for education, and potentially for change, because "what makes storytelling political—and therefore transformative—*is the fact that other stories may also be told*" (Lewis 1993, 17, my emphasis).[6]

To explore notions of story as theory, we play, with permission, interview segments from research participants in a study of gender and outdoor education. A woman on tape animatedly describes her first canoe trip and the intense freedom found in her dirty t-shirt. Our students laugh as they picture this t-shirt transformed into tea towel and all-purpose rag. They smile thoughtfully as the woman talks of her sense of freedom and power. We pause and ask: "So what do you think this story is about?" For the moment, we become narrative researchers, trying to understand the many layers of the research story and trying to discern what these stories can tell us about the world. Later we introduce the concepts of discourse and ideology to explain how some philosophies describe how we make meaning out of the world through stories, or how we might understand the world through the stories we tell of it. Gently we hint: "our world is made up of stories. We live in a story."

Ah, and then there's the "who am I story" (Henderson 1995), as Madan Sarup suggests: "The concept of home seems to be tied in some way to the notion of identity—the story we tell of ourselves and which is also the story that others tell of us" (1996, 3). On trip we will generate new stories for ourselves within our collective experience. We will find our own freedom and power in our own dirty t-shirt symbol. Novelist Douglas Coupland put this another way; "Either our lives become stories or there is just no way to get through them" (1991, 8). Getting out of a sleeping bag to stoke a fire in our sheet-metal stove within our once-cozy-now-frigid wall tent is a story for some. A polar bear swim, falling into an otter's tunnel system, having that epiphany of total contentment despite being outside all day at minus-twenty degrees Celsius: all these are the stuff of story and exploration of self.

Technique

Returning to the university, our students laughingly related the story of their struggles in deciding whether or not to wash their trip clothes. The problem, it seemed, was that while washing, at one level, seemed necessary, it would also remove the lingering smell of woodsmoke from the clothes. This smell remained as a reminder of a place and a trip that had been engaging, simple, and meaningful. The significance of woodsmoke, we believe, lies in its connection to an entire way of living, more so than its mere connection to "a bunch of good trip memories."

Explained more clearly with an example, students look forward to hauling and chopping wood. They pose for photographs beside the chopping block. Wood heat is simply a fundamentally different technology that requires a fundamentally different way of living than a gas-powered furnace. There is a sense of whole process in the selecting, gathering, sawing, chopping, lighting, and feeding; rather than being a burden, this work seems to bring the enjoyment of holistic living. We are connected and engaged in a way that we may never be to that switch we flick to turn on lights or to turn up the heat. In class, we talk about the "intimations of deprival" (Grant 1969, 140), that hint of loss we might sense with the embrace of the new and improved. What richness are we depriving ourselves of as a culture, living the way that we do, with all of our lives' alluring conveniences? On trail, we try to live with holistic, connected technologies—wood heat, simple sleds, Egyptian cotton wall tents, home-cooked meals. We travel according to the weather and things take the time that they need. There is no rush. The contrast between this experience and modern urban living helps to make explicit the technological stories of our culture. Through our readings we examine the counterstories, if you will, told by theorists such as George Grant, Jacques Ellul, and David Strong. What is unique about this winter course is not that we winter camp, nor that we use the hand-crafted Ojibway wooden sleds called o-daw-bans alongside the ten-dollar Canadian Tire plastic sleds. What is unique is that these technologies and the wider impacts that they have on our lives become our curriculum content.

Place

While on trip, *place* is ever-present as a theme. In very basic ways, we learn how to live in this place, right down to chopping the ice hole and knowing which wood will burn. This contrasts well to a "living apart from place," the way so many of us perhaps reluctantly do in our homes that insulate us so well from the world outside. On trip we discover that the hemlock trees that minimize the snowpack for easier foot travel throw a spark when they burn and so are not choice firewood. We hear and tell some of the many stories told of this place: the mysterious death of famous painter Tom Thomson just up the lake, the local history and culture of the generations of summer campers who have paddled these waters we now walk upon, the national mythology surrounding Algonquin Park. Amazingly, even the technologies of snowshoes were intricately connected to the places where they were developed. More rounded shoes were used in heavily wooded landscapes. Longer and narrower shoes were predominant where wide-open lake travel was prominent. Aboriginal people seemed to have a knack for developing and using technology appropriate to their place. Back at school, we decide that a "change of place" is paramount for the success of our theoretical exploration. A quiet evening walk leads us to a neighbourhood coffee shop where a corner "space" becomes, for us, a "place" as we imbue it with the meaning and memory of an evening's discussion. Sipping hot drinks, we relax into the couches and together wrestle with ideas and theories: the myth of wilderness, sense of place, environmental nostalgia, diaspora and notions of home.

This curriculum, enhanced by the experience of winter living on trail, takes the university well beyond the expected conventions of content and course requirements. We enter a realm of culture study and life investigation. Throughout this course and using the lenses of story, place, and technique, we strive to make visible the cultural myths that we live within, the stories that, as a culture, we tend to label as "truth" and "common sense." In a hopeful, uncertain, and exciting way, seeing these stories as fictions opens up the possibility of constructing better and more meaningful stories for our lives. In this productive space of unwriting/rewriting, we believe, lies potential and hope.

UNPACKING ADVENTURE: A SOCIAL EXPLORATION IN URBAN SPACE (LIZ)

Sandwiched between the shelf of pitas and the display of pies, five young women are huddled in an intense discussion over the bag of dinner rolls in their hands. Shopping carts whirl tight corners around them. "We could take some bread to the men's shelter when we go," one woman ventures.

Another looks puzzled: "Well, I'm worried about . . . a kind of tokenism or something. Like how can we take so little to a place that feeds so many and has so much need."

"Yeah, maybe. What is a random act of kindness, anyway? Here we are planning it. How is that random? I wonder if it's just about how you choose to live with people around you."

Their conversation goes on, spilling over into the frozen-food section. Across town, several of their peers are sharing a cup of coffee with a Hungarian fibre artist who recently emigrated to Canada. Others are elbow deep in soapsuds washing dishes in a soup kitchen. On a damp street corner several blocks over, three young people are discovering some of the black history of their city through a series of murals painted by local youth. The young women eventually fill their backpacks with canned goods destined for a food bank, and, keeping within their budget, leave the grocery store with assorted items for their own lunch. Picnicking on a roadside curb, they offer some of their lunch to the older woman sitting alone on the bench beside them. Her face warms up, and together they dig into the five-dollar feast. Their questions about kindness, disparity of wealth, and community, however, linger on.

In the spring of 2001, I taught a fourth-year kinesiology course called "Adventure Based Learning." All students take part in a weekend field experience that involves intensive initiatives and ropes-course work and follow up the weekend's learning by studying selected topics from risk management to adventure therapy. Toward the end of term we increasingly add complexity to our understandings of both adventure and education. I conceived the urban field experience described here as part of this task. It ended up being much more.

Using the elements of surprise and mystery, I didn't tell students much about the field trip beforehand. This is what I sent them:

The Urban Canoe Trip

Here's a checklist to help you pack for your expedition.
- —McMaster student card (this functions as a bus pass)
- —first-aid kit
- —one dollar
- —a quarter
- —an open mind
- —a sense of adventure
- —a willingness to challenge your ideas about adventure education
- —outdoor clothing
- —absolutely no cars

—a journal and pen

You will undertake your own small group expedition, navigating new physical and hopefully conceptual and social terrain. Details to follow Friday.

Students gathered midmorning in the field behind our physical education complex. They put themselves into groups of four or five and were given a set of instructions that included a map. The expedition boundaries were clearly laid out: it was to take place between four major east downtown streets, they were to stick together, they were to travel only via foot or public transport, they were to complete as many of the given tasks as reasonable, desirable, and safe, and we were all to meet up five hours later in a donated downtown church room for debriefing. Following are some of their tasks:

Talk with someone who leads a very different life from you and find out about that person's life.

As a group, buy lunch. Pay no more than $1 per person.

Visit the murals in the urban core. What do they say to you? What is their significance? Why are they here? Who painted them?

Visit a cultural association and find out what they are about and what kind of services/resources are available at the centre. Visit one important cultural site in the downtown core that is recommended by the people at the centre. Similarly visit a social service agency.

Commit at least one random act of kindness.

Interview a local artist/musician. Find out about that person's contributions to the community.

Walk blindfolded through a neighbourhood, being guided by a member of your group.

Find a busy street corner that interests you. Have a seat and take it all in. Sketch a picture of it.

Find somewhere to volunteer for a while.

Talk with an elderly person and find out some of the history of this neighbourhood.[7]

I was pleasantly astounded at the enthusiasm and richness of stories and learning that this day generated. Most people were surprised at the potential for learning, excitement, and risk-taking in an urban space and in their own backyard. A new educational resource was explored by the students, many of whom have since moved on to teaching careers. More interesting were many of the observations students had of their hometown. The students can best speak for themselves here.

Everybody I see walking the sidewalks are head down, not wasting any time because they have things to do, people to see. . . . A simple smile can change a person's mood. . . . But most are in too much of a hurry to notice these gestures.

It wasn't so much that the experiences were new or out of the ordinary that made the afternoon so interesting, however. It was that I developed a relationship with the city—with individuals, history, and politics. It was that I experienced a connection with Hamilton in a way I never have before.

I don't think that society spends enough time acknowledging and really putting an effort forward to getting to know each other . . . and I really realized this after I spent time meeting and talking with some of the friendliest strangers in the world.

There are strict norms of urban interaction that many of these students challenged that day. By virtue of the tasks I had laid out for them, and the fact that their minds were attuned to "adventure," they explored their downtown core with a very different set of eyes and a different attitude to people on the street. One group met a particularly warm couple who owned a bakery where they stopped for a visit. Astounded by their hosts' generosity, and so thoroughly enjoying their stay, they made a thank-you card for the couple and sang a song to them before they left. This type of social interaction doesn't regularly happen, and I don't think the importance of "a simple smile" and an uninhibited song of appreciation can be underestimated. Just this kind of reaching out promotes community. It is a figurative reaching out of hands, to strangers on the street, to citizens who share the same city. Furthermore, I don't think it's farfetched to say that building community can be a radical and socially transformative act in itself; it promotes a healthier place of living as well as promoting the conditions whereby people can better work together for change.

Most of my students were astonished that they had spent four years in this city without ever once venturing into the neighbourhood where I sent them. Only a fifteen-minute bus ride from campus, it was approximately three hundred meters east and north of where most of them would regularly go to see movies and visit clubs. It is a less affluent and more culturally vibrant area of town than the neighbourhood that houses the university and most student homes. East Hamilton is often seen as the "Other" by West Hamilton but most certainly not by the people who proudly call it home. In some ways, the urban adventure could be understood to have begun the process of building bridges across notions of difference in Hamiltonian geography, class, culture, and race.[8]

> Of course I've always known of the enormous cultural diversity that exists in Canada/Ontario/Toronto/Hamilton, it's just that I've always experienced it from the window of a car, or in brief passing by. I have never really embraced it. This is how I would describe the urban adventure. The first time I have really embraced the different cultures and ways of life that exist around me.
>
> . . . Many people, myself included, realized just how much we take for granted. . . . Talking to people you normally wouldn't come into contact with and seeing how they survive on so much less than we have is really grounding. Living in the university environment, I think most people tend to forget that there is life outside the microcosm that is McMaster. . . . I have really made an effort since then to put my life into perspective and appreciate the good things in it.

There is something promising, yet simultaneously troubling to me here. I think it's important that we realize that our world is much wider, bigger, and more diverse than the scene outside our windows. We so often have a blindness to difference—different people, places, and ways of living—and these students aptly describe how the urban adventure has widened their understanding of the world. This is good. At the same time, however, a mere celebration of difference doesn't adequately critique how difference is differently privileged, nor does it lead to action. There is a sense of the tourist in the task that I set out for my students that I am uneasy with.[9] Bell hooks's work on appropriation and appreciation is useful here in critiquing some of the traps of exploring and celebrating the diversity in this neighbouring part of town. Hooks renders the desires for the body, art, and experiences of the Other problematic because they occur within the context of "white supremacist capitalist patriarchy" (hooks 1992). She describes the consumption of racial difference as "a new dish to enhance the white palate" (hooks 1992, 39). I wonder about the urban exploration as an educational experience to enhance the already educationally privileged, appropriating some kind of "authentic" experience of poverty and Otherness.[10] Key questions that I ask myself here involve the power context of the exploration and the depth of positive affective and behavioural learning that might come out of the experience (however "positive" might be assessed). There are enormous political issues unresolved within this field trip, yet it seems to have provided a concrete means to further understand one's own life and privileges:

After buying some bread and peanut butter we went to Tim Horton's for lunch, where we bought a box of timbits to justify our stay, and began to spread our peanut butter. We certainly got a few strange looks, and it made me question the reality of our day . . . if we had not been well-dressed, and looked pulled together . . . would we really have been able to eat our peanut butter sandwiches in Tim Horton's? Further in the day I questioned this further, as I desperately had to go to the bathroom and we stopped at a gas station where they quickly gave me the key to use the facilities. I doubt they would have handed over the key so easily had I actually looked more desperate.

I find the recognition of privilege here intensely hopeful. This kind of consciousness is a first step toward taking action, toward change. These students are bringing a seamless hegemonic discourse into view and examining it as not common sense; our previous assumptions about wealth, hunger, poverty, and ourselves are being slowly taken apart and inspected. It is what we do with privilege and power relations once we recognize them that is important.

Some students after visiting a food bank decided to organize a class-wide food and clothing drive. Another student, after visiting the MS Society, returned to volunteer there, helping with yoga classes on a long-term basis. These are two concrete examples of actions that came out of the field trip. Our actions and reactions to inequities can be placed on a charity-justice continuum (Fenton 1975). Charity is important, but it is not the same thing as working for justice, which implies both an analysis of power relations and working for structural change. Furthermore, charity sometimes functions to hold inequities in place. Understanding where our actions fit on this continuum may help us to avoid deluding ourselves that our acts of charity are acts of justice.[11] Donating to a food bank is important, and undeniably a good thing to do, yet it doesn't ultimately challenge the structural inequities that create the need for (chronically under-funded) food banks in the first place. Nor does it cause recognition of how the wealth of some is predicated on the poverty of others.

The debrief of this exploration, then, necessarily must provoke reflection on issues of justice, charity, power relations, and change. The field experience is no substitute for theory, and we must both build theory out of, and bring theory into, a debrief in order to extend our insights. My debrief centred around storytelling and organized small-group discussions on selected topics. The "now what" (Priest, Gass, and Gillis 2000) stage of the debrief is of utter importance here. What now? What does one *do* with insights from a day like this when one is firmly nestled back in "the microcosm that is McMaster"? My hope is that a sense of praxis might emerge for some of us; through reflection, a recognition of privilege and a taking responsibility for it.

I believe that this field experience was a very complicated pedagogical event—it could not be said to be a straightforward or wholeheartedly beneficial day. For, as a critical educator, I believe we are always courting and drawing on dominant discourses even as we try to interrupt them. Were we tourists, voyeurs out for a one-day adventure into the terrain of the less advantaged? Were we learners who developed an important sense of social consciousness and awareness of community through an immersing experience?

We were, perhaps, both. But I do know that this field trip originally designed to debunk mainstream notions of adventure as adrenaline-based, wilderness endeavours became a pivotal site of learning for students. Five hours of structured exploration provided richer learning for my students than I was ever capable of orchestrating in the classroom. As a teacher, my mind is troubled by social inequities and so I try to trouble my pedagogy accordingly. This simple field experience provided a very tricky and contradictory route into a troubled/troubling critical pedagogy.

CONCLUSION AND POSTSCRIPT

If "to propose a pedagogy is to propose a political vision" (Simon 1992, 57) then the political vision wrapped up in our pedagogy involves learning how better to dwell with ourselves, each other, and the earth. There is nothing neutral about this; we seek change. Understanding our pedagogy as cultural work, the cultural productions we orchestrate are rather more like delayerings; we somehow seek to unlearn as much as to learn.

The three examples that we've shared here are but short stories of passionate attempts at a pedagogy that transforms—in ecological, cultural, and social realms. The immersion in these field experiences seems to have been more successful than the best laid pedagogical plans. And yet they are just complicated beginnings.

There are important questions, as yet unanswered, to ask of any pedagogy based on experience: How is experience constituted? Does experiential education assume a transparency of experience and a linear simplicity in the process of making meaning out of experience? That is, is the experience we theorize decontextualized from the dominant liberal humanist philosophy that mediates our everyday? In reflecting on the stories in which we ostensibly tell about the challenges, contradictions, and possibilities in thinking about a critical, experiential education, we wonder, in retrospect, if we ought to continue doggedly in our hope for a meaningful pedagogy and a better world while wearing these notions of "transformation" more lightly and cautiously. Transformation is a compelling but perhaps too loaded a word, we agree to each other, as we prepare our gear for the next class.

Acknowledgements

Thanks to M. J. Barrett, Gary Bunch, and Paul Tarc for useful feedback on early drafts. Thanks also to the many former McMaster students who agreed to have their voices included in this piece.

Notes

1. Romance is a term used by British philosopher Alfred North Whitehead (1929) as part of his rhythms of education. Romance involves the stirring of imagination, a novelty of inquiry and enterprise. Students are "romanced" and then crave the academic content principles, definitions, and models that follow as Whitehead's next rhythm: precision. Upon return from a trip, Whitehead's next rhythm of generalization may be experienced. Here students return to a romance for the academic content with a freshness of ever-deeper inquiry.

2. We recognize here that ours is an ecosystem that is relatively safe and friendly to explore in such a way. There are no poisonous snakes or insects to worry about and few needles, thorns, and spikes to impale ourselves on. This approach may not be appropriate for all places.

3. As educators we are well aware that we may never know how students are taking up the intended and unintended content of a class. Such things are not reliably predictable or knowable.

4. Wilderness, winter, and north figure in our national mythology in romantic, alluring, and also very problematic ways. The power relations implicated in these nationalistic space myths are well described by Shields (1991) and Francis (1997).

5. Other assignments include presenting a field interpretation/natural history lesson, telling a story, and creating a journal that includes reflections on field experiences and readings.

6. We are mindful of the need to employ "storytelling as pedagogy"

and "storytelling as inquiry" very critically. The telling of stories from a position of marginality can be very risky and sometimes serves those who hear at the expense of those who tell. How stories are heard is not always how they are told; our own social locations have everything to do with how we hear and know (Razack 1993).

7. I've heard it said that good teachers know what is worth stealing. I was lucky enough to inherit the "Adventure Based Learning" course and the backbone of the urban adventure from Brian Lisson of Adventure-works! In turn, I believe he created the activity with inspiration from the Outward Bound expeditionary learning reader by Cousins and Rodgers (1995).

8. Yet there are times when I am less sure. I also wonder if the very structure of this activity re-entrenches the distance/difference between Self and Other.

9. Even the act of referring to this activity as an adventure is steeped in power relations. There is an assumption of privilege in what I set out for students to do. Buying lunch for $1 or visiting a social service agency is hardly an adventure for someone whose everyday reality encompasses these tasks.

10. Thanks to Paul Tarc for helping me develop this critique.

11. Karen Warren (1998) in a related vein describes how to promote social change versus social service in service learning projects.

References

Bowers, C. A. 1997. *The culture of denial: Why the environmental move-ment needs a strategy for reforming unversities and public schools.* Al-bany: State University of New York.

Connelly, S. M., and D. J. Clandinin. 1990. Stories of experience and nar-rative inquiry. *Educational Research* (June-July): 2–14.

Coupland, D. 1991. *Generation X: Tales for an accelerated culture.* New York: St. Martin's Press.

Cousins, E., and M. Rodgers. 1995. *Fieldwork: An expeditionary Out-ward Bound reader,* vol. 1. Dubuque, Iowa: Kendall Hunt.

DiFranco, A. 1991. Not so soft. *Not so soft.* New York: Righteous Babe Records.

Fenton, T. 1975. *Education for justice: A resource manual.* Maryknoll, New York: Orbis Books.

Francis, D. 1997. *National dreams: Myth, memory and Canadian history.* Vancouver: Arsenal Pulp Press.

Glendinning, C. 1994. *My name is Chellis and I'm in recovery from western civilization*. Boston: Shambhala Publications Inc.

Grant, G. 1969. *Technology and empire: Perspectives on North America*. Toronto: House of Anansi.

Henderson, B. 1995. *Outdoor travel: Explorations for change*. Unpublished Ph.d. thesis. University of Alberta, Edmonton, Alberta.

———. 1999. The place of deep ecology and ecopsychology in adventure education. In *Adventure programming*, edited by J. Miles and S. Priest. State College, Pa.: Venture Publishing.

hooks, b. 1992. Eating the other. In *Black looks: Race and representation*. Boston: South End Press.

Lewis, M. 1993. *Without a word: Teaching beyond women's silence*. New York: Routledge.

Miller, J. 1988. *The holistic curriculum*. Toronto: OISE Press.

Priest, S., M. Gass, and L. Gillis. 2000. *The essential elements of facilitation*. Dubuque, Iowa: Kendall Hunt.

Razack, S. 1993. Story-telling for social change. *Gender and education* 5 (1): 55–70.

Roszak, T. 1992. *The voice of the earth: An exploration of ecopsychology*. New York: Touchstone, Simon and Schuster, Inc.

Sarup, M. 1996. *Identity, culture and the postmodern world*. Athens: The University of Georgia Press.

Shields, R. 1991. The true north strong and free. In *Places on the margin: Alternative geographies of modernity*. Routledge.

Simon, R. 1992. *Teaching against the grain: Texts for a pedagogy of possibility*. Toronto: OISE Press.

Strong, D. 1995. *Crazy mountains: Learning from wilderness to weigh technology*. Albany: State University of New York Press.

Warren, K. 1998. Educating students for social justice in service learning. *The Journal of Experiential Education* 21 (3): 134–39.

Whitehead, A. N. 1929. *The aims of education and other essays*. New York: Macmillan.

On the Path, Off the Trail

Teaching Nature Writing as a Practice of the Wild

I

I'm sitting on a rocky ledge at the top of Black Mountain, a rounded granite summit that looks out over the West River valley in southern Vermont. Scrub oaks and low-bush blueberry spread out close to the ground in the depressions and crevices between the ledges, and a few scattered red pines grow straight and tall. Nearby, a couple of pitch pines stretch their scrawny branches in grizzled, awkward gestures. I've hiked here with an all-day nature-writing workshop, and I've just given them their final "assignment": to spread out and explore on their own until they find something that particularly intrigues them and then to write about it—first describing what they see and then letting their writing leap to whatever comes to mind.

I'm drawn off the open summit toward a path that leads through the woods. I take off my shoes and feel my way along the rough textures of granite, pine needles, and lichen, as I work my way over to the forest's edge. Soon I'm walking over soft layers of oak leaves and pine needles, along a rough path, perhaps an abandoned trail. The way keeps opening out, leading me around each bend. I see a broad patch of sunlight up ahead and I keep on going toward it.

In the clearing, a granite shoulder rises up out of the soil, like the smooth rounded back of a whale. Mt. Greylock supposedly gave Melville some of his inspiration for Moby Dick. I remember a dream I had last fall, in which I was paddling along in a canoe, and suddenly beside me in the water the back of a great gray whale floated near me, on its back a Japanese meditation garden complete with a bench for meditation and a tiny bonsai tree.

Here, on this whale-back, a small birch sapling sprouts from a cluster of stones, clumped cairn-like in the center of the granite slab. How these gray birches sprout in such unlikely places! I remember one such gray birch that grew from a rock on Eagle Crag, near my solo site when I was leading my first outdoor camping course, many years ago in the White Mountains. I lit a candle then and sat for hours in the dark, stars wheeling overhead, candlelight reflecting on the small green leaves and pencil-thin branches. I felt such kinship with that small tree, perhaps because it had made its home in that high, spare landscape, a place where I was beginning to find my home as a teacher. And now, I have discovered another mountain birch in a place where I have come to lead a writing group.

Then it hits me how much the experience of writing all this down feels analogous to my experience of walking along the path. As I walked, I followed the path around each corner until it led to a place where I found something I had not seen or imagined when I started. And as I wrote, connections led me through the terrain of my inner world: Moby Dick, a whale, my dream of a meditation garden on the back of a whale, a miniature bonsai tree, and finally a small birch on top of another rocky summit, which brought me back to an earlier stage of my outdoor teaching life.

Several days later I'm up at dawn to go searching for vernal pools on Putney Mountain with my friend Mary. We're tramping off through the woods on a sunny morning in early May. Mary has a pretty vague idea of where these vernal pools are supposed to be, so we've been bushwhacking off the trail for over an hour now, with no success. We stop to rest and reconnoiter, and looking up I see a small bird flying with something white trailing from its beak. It disappears and then reappears perched on a branch. Mary notices a swatch of forest duff collected in the crotch between two branches of a tree. On closer inspection, we see it is a nest in which a major ingredient seems to be birch-bark strips. Another bird appears and perches on the nest. Closer up we identify it by its conspicuous eye ring: a solitary vireo. Now we watch as a pair of solitary vireos work together to build a nest. The male flies off and returns with more strips of bark, while the female sits on the nest and adds them to it. When the male starts making agitated alarm calls, we walk on.

Five minutes later, we still haven't found any vernal pools. Mary sees a chickadee fly into a hole in a tall snag. Shortly it reappears with a wood chip in its beak. Then another chickadee appears and plops into the hole like a ball into a pinball machine, soon reappearing with another wood chip. Together this pair of chickadees is excavating a nest from a hollow snag. How many times, I think, have I walked the trail to the summit of

Putney Mountain, or any mountain for that matter, yet never seen a pair of chickadees or vireos engaged in the act of nest building? Yet when we stepped off the trail to saunter into the woods, there they were. And is not this also true of writing? When I step off the path and enter unknown territory, that's when the most exciting discoveries occur.

So writing is like walking a path. And writing is like stepping off the trail. The more I think about this paradox, the deeper I see into the writing process, and the teaching of writing. Writing is a discipline, a path of sorts that can lead us to new discoveries. Yet at the same time, the discipline itself involves a kind of wandering off the trail, which often leads to the strongest writing.

A number of writers have likened the writing process to following a path. Annie Dillard opens her book *The Writing Life* with this image: "When you write, you lay out a line of words. The line of words is a miner's pick, a woodcarver's gouge, a surgeon's probe. You wield it, and it digs you a path you follow. Soon, you find yourself deep in new territory. . . . You make the path boldly and follow it fearfully. You go where the path leads" (1989, 3). Dillard's use of the image is intriguing in part because the path she speaks of is a path that we create for ourselves as we go. By writing our way into new material, we see the path behind us as we look back, but before us is still a pathless way.

Gary Snyder examines the virtues of going "off the trail" in his essay "On the Path, Off the Trail," in *The Practice of the Wild*. He interprets the first line of the *Tao te Ching*: "'A path that can be followed is not a *spiritual* path.' The actuality of things cannot be confronted within so linear an image as a road." He develops the metaphor: "There are paths that can be followed, and there is a path that cannot—it is not a path, it is the wilderness. There is a 'going' but no goer, no destination, only the whole field." He applies this notion to the art of sauntering "totally off the trail—away from any trace of human or animal regularly aimed at some practical or spiritual purpose. One goes out onto the 'trail that cannot be followed' which leads everywhere and nowhere, a limitless fabric of possibilities, elegant variations a millionfold on the same themes, yet each point unique" (Snyder 1990, 150, 152, 153).

Snyder concludes his essay with the statement that "you must first be on the path, before you can turn and walk into the wild" (1990, 154). This statement frames eloquently the paradox of the pathless path. Though Snyder writes about a spiritual practice that is not specific to writing, he suggests implications for writing as a practice. How might this paradox illuminate the writing process, and our teaching of writing? I know that my most powerful writing usually happens when I am able to release myself into a process beyond my control and saunter around in territory I have not yet explored. Yet I also know that certain practices help me move into that place "off the trail." How then do we as writers place ourselves on this "pathless path"? And how can we help our students to move through a process—a path—that enables them to step off the known trail and move into that "limitless fabric of possibilities"? These questions take on even more significance when we take the teaching of writing outdoors.

II

I have come to distinguish four disciplines or practices of writing—we might call them attitudes or states of being—that have helped me and my students to venture off the path into the wild: attentiveness; spaciousness and freedom to explore; receptivity to interconnections and stories; and openness to sharing within a community of writers. While each of these is a practice, a path that helps us in the writing process, each path is also, paradoxically, a way of walking off the trail, leaving behind that which we know, to move into the unknown.

The first practice, attentiveness, is perhaps the most basic discipline of good writing about nature. In order to have something worth writing about, we need to pay attention to what's happening around us. Here the practice of going off the trail is most literal, as we wander off our accustomed routes and begin paying attention to things in the landscape we have not noticed before.

When I became interested in writing about nature, this was my first major challenge. I loved to explore the feeling of being in nature, the ideas that inspired in me, but I had a very difficult time just looking closely and describing what I saw. I find this is often a major challenge for beginning writers. Unless they have been trained in the natural sciences or visual arts, they may not have been schooled in this most basic discipline of all: seeing.

I often begin a class or outdoor workshop with a poem that invites listeners to pay attention. Many of Mary Oliver's poems are ideal for this purpose. One of my favorites is "The Summer Day." After describing in detail a grasshopper that sits in her hand and then flies away, she reflects:

> I don't know exactly what a prayer is.
> I do know how to pay attention, how to fall down
> into the grass, how to kneel down in the grass,

how to be idle and blessed, how to stroll through the fields,
which is what I have been doing all day.
Tell me, what else should I have done? (Oliver 1992, 94)

David Wagoner's "Lost" also speaks with vivid images of the importance of attentiveness. Inspired by the initiatory quests of traditional
Northwest coast peoples, he imagines addressing a young person who has
become lost in the forest. "Stand still. The trees ahead and bushes beside
you / Are not lost. Wherever you are is called Here." He invokes listening—"The forest breathes. Listen. It answers, / I have made this place
around you"—as well as seeing—"No two trees are the same to Raven. /
No two branches are the same to Wren. / If what a tree or a bush does is
lost on you, / You are surely lost" (Wagoner 1999, 10). These poems
provide a good way in to the writing process when the group doesn't have
immediate access to the outdoors. On the first session of a writing class I
often read "The Summer Day," and ask the students to write about a similar "moment of awareness," when they felt especially present and attentive, describing what they saw, heard, felt, etc.

A non-writing activity such as a contour drawing can be an excellent
way to engage the senses: look only at the object, and draw it without
looking at the paper, keeping your pencil in contact with the paper.
Though the overall shape of this drawing is often very different from the
object itself, the quality of attention and the details that show up in the
drawing make it a worthwhile exercise in seeing.

One of my favorite activities is to have people bring in natural objects.
We pass them around one at a time, and I ask the group to suggest different words or images to describe each object. This sense of permission
to play and try whatever pops into mind, along with the energy of the students' imaginations playing off one another, often brings out fresh and
startling images and helps class members see new possibilities. I often give
examples of arresting metaphors from the work of nature writers to open
up for them the sense of possibility; for example, John McPhee's description of a loon:

> He is out there cruising still, in the spiraling morning mist, looking for fish,
> trolling. He trolls with his eyes. Water streams across his forehead as he
> moves along, and he holds his eyes just below the surface, watching the in-
> terior of the lake. (McPhee 1975, 29)

Outside, a number of writing exercises can be used to stimulate attentiveness:

1) Go find a place, and sit there for fifteen to twenty minutes, and just look, and then describe what you see.

2) Go and find a place, and write from each of your senses, one at a time: what do you hear, see, feel, smell, taste? This can also be combined with a sense awareness meditation that leads naturally into writing from all the senses.

3) In a more extended group, people can find a place to which they are especially drawn, and then go there regularly, and describe what they see, hear, feel, and smell, and notice what changes over time.

4) The "Five minute exercise" from Burghild Nina Holzer's book *A Walk between Heaven and Earth* is a wonderful way to help people capture the essence of a place or moment in a short period of time.

The field journal is another tool for encouraging attentiveness. I suggest keeping one handy for jotting down details and notes on the spot. The dialogue between Ann Zwinger and Gary Nabhan in *Writing Natural History* speaks of the value of the field journal. Nabhan says:

> I depend upon all senses when I'm out there. Unless I do, when I get back to a cozy room with my notebook or a word processor to write something up in essay form, I won't be able to remember the sounds that were there, or what the light was like. When I take a lot of notes in the field, there is a chance that some of the sounds I hear in that landscape will carry over into the sounds of the words I use to describe a place. (Lueders 1989, 78)

Writing inspired by the practice of attentiveness is rich with vivid details and images: visual, auditory, tactile. It also brings to the page fresh, original language that describes things in unusual ways.

The second discipline, spaciousness and freedom to explore, builds on attentiveness to the outer world and gives permission for the writing process to follow the path of whatever one encounters, outer or inner. This can help free up writers to enter into a space of not knowing and to let go of preconceived notions of both the form and content of good writing. Letting go of expectations about "good writing" frees us up to write from a place beyond the conscious linear mind and allows us to tap into the unconscious, from which surprising connections and associations come. It also helps us move beyond cultural assumptions about what things mean into the more fertile territory of one's own universe of meaning. In *The Tree*, John Fowles speaks of this going "off the trail" in the inner world:

> Some such process of retreat from the normal world—however much the theme and surface is to be of the normal world—is inherent in any act of artistic creation. . . . And a part of that retreat must always be into a "wild" or ordinarily repressed and socially hidden self: into a place [of] complexity beyond daily reality, never fully comprehensible or explicable, always more potential than realized. (Fowles and Horvat 1979)

While this freedom is liberating, it can also be disorienting or even frightening and counter to what students have learned about the writing process. So it's worth spending some time discussing this practice to give people a sense of possibility. We often explore and write about the voices that restrict our free exploration in writing: our concern with finished products; our ego investment in having something of good quality; voices of criticism from our past; our inner critics who tell us our work is not good enough. I give examples of famous writers who speak of their writing as an exploration of the unknown, like W. H. Auden's question: how can I know what I think, until I see what I say? My favorite quotation in this regard is William Stafford's description of his writing process, from *Writing the Australian Crawl.* It is especially useful for students and beginning writers because it shows quite specifically the process of a writer's mind at work:

> A writer is not so much someone who has something to say as someone who has found a process that will bring about new things he would not have thought of if he had [not] started to say them. . . . One of the implications of this is the importance of receptivity. . . . I get pen and paper, take a glance out the window, (often it is dark out there) and wait. . . . Maybe I have to settle for an immediate impression: it's cold, or hot, or dark, or bright, or in between. Or—well, the possibilities are endless. If I put down something that thing will help the next thing to come, and I'm off. If I let the process go on, things will occur to me that were not at all in my mind when I started. These things, odd or trivial as they may be, are somehow connected. And if I let them string out, surprising things will happen. (Stafford 1978, 17–18)

Free writing is an invaluable way to help students enter this space of exploration, and Natalie Goldberg's *Writing Down the Bones* and Peter Elbow's chapter on "Free writing" in *Writing with Power* are valuable resources here.

An exercise that combines attentiveness and freedom to explore is the "present moment exercise" from Holzer's book *A Walk between Heaven and Earth* (1994, 42–44). After reading from Holzer's book, I give the following instructions:

> Go off to a place, sit and write for half an hour about whatever you are aware of, being as attentive as you can in each moment of the play of awareness, both inner and outer. Start with what is happening around you, but follow your attention wherever it takes you: notice the dynamic of attention as it moves back and forth between inner and outer, and try to capture as fully as you can in your words the feel of your shifting awareness.

Writing from this exercise often has an unusual freshness and ease about it, capturing on the page the active sense of a person's mind and imagination at work.

Writing inspired by the freedom to explore leads to the emergence of what Peter Elbow calls "voice," the unique sense of the person conveyed through the words on the page:

> Writing with *voice* is writing into which someone has breathed. It has that fluency, rhythm, and liveliness that exist naturally in the speech of most people when they are enjoying a good conversation. . . . Writing with real *voice* has the power to make you pay attention and understand—the words go deep. . . . If you really seek excellence, if you seek to write things that others might actually want to read, you need to stop playing it safe: go for it, take the plunge, jump over the edge. You won't know where you are going. (Elbow 1981, 299–302)

❈

The third practice is perhaps the hardest to define, as it builds on the practices of attentiveness and freedom, and takes them in as many different directions as there are writers. I call it receptivity to interconnections and stories, but it could also be called reflection or a search for meaning. Mary Austin prepares the ground for this notion with her statement that nature writing is neither imaginative fiction nor scientific fact, but a "third thing, the sum of what passed between me and the land, which has not, perhaps never could, come into being with anyone else"[1] Each of us experiences the natural world in a unique way, shaped by everything we bring to the encounter. This notion helps students to recognize the uniqueness of their own experience as a source for writing and to find a way of writing about it that conveys that uniqueness.

This practice has also been inspired by the notion of interior and exterior landscapes, as described by Barry Lopez in his essay "Landscape and Narrative," in *Crossing Open Ground*. Lopez suggests that in addition to

inhabiting an exterior landscape, we also carry within us an interior landscape: "a kind of projection within a person of a part of the exterior landscape . . . deeply influenced by where on this earth one goes, what one
touches, the patterns one observes in nature, the intricate history of one's
life with the land" (Lopez 1987, 65). A good story happens, he concludes, when a storyteller (or by implication a writer) brings together the
inner and outer landscapes. This integration gives great satisfaction to the
listener or reader by restoring the balance between inner and outer that is
often lost in our daily lives.

How do we discover these stories? As a writer becomes able to freely
explore the interaction between the inner and outer terrain through exercises like free-writing and the present-moment exercise, these interconnections begin to appear. By our being receptive to them and allowing
them to develop, the stories gradually emerge.

Often it's useful to explore the notion of story in the work of nature
writers. The dialogues in *Writing Natural History* are rich with suggestions about the power of story. Terry Tempest Williams emphasizes the
importance of connection and relationship: story is "the correspondence
. . . between people and place. . . . It's the umbilical cord between past,
present and future." Bob Finch suggests that "we can only care and connect with that which we have come to love," and "that only by storying
the earth do we come to love it. . . . By storying the place where we live,
it gives us back a sense of who and where we are. Through stories we literally identify with the land." Lopez speaks about how story "creates both
a surface reality and a reality in parallel, which allows you to appreciate
something both directly and indirectly" (Lueders 1989, 46, 41, 16).
These words suggest how we can find our stories by searching out our
connections with place, by investigating the threads of connection with
our past, and by looking to the parallel realities that run through our lives.

I like to tell the class that our lives are full of stories, like the multitudi-
nous phone conversations being carried along a telephone cable. Our task
as writers is to tease out of the tangle of stories the individual threads that
belong together and to search for the underlying patterns and relationships
that give shape to a story. Though the process of discovering these stories
is complex and multifaceted, the heart of it is receptivity to interconnections: being alert to their possibility and open to exploring them when they
appear. One of the best exercises for doing this is the "leap":

> Go off and find something, anything that arrests your attention: an insect,
> a flower, a rotting stump, a hawk soaring on the wind. After you've gotten

down some descriptive detail, then make some kind of leap to your inner world: a childhood memory, a person you think of, a dream, or a feeling—whatever is evoked by the thing you are describing.

Sometimes it's helpful to give examples from writers. Annie Dillard's encounter with the weasel—"I should have gone for the throat" (1983, 15)—and David Quammen's reflections on the chambered nautilus—"For me there have been a number of compartmented phases" (Trimble 1988, 148)—are two good examples of essays with artful leaps that give power to the writing. Dramatic leaps, surprising discoveries in the recesses of memory, powerful reflections on the meaning of experiences—these occur when students are encouraged to explore off the trail in search of connections and stories.

The fourth practice, sharing the writing in a community, may not appear to be a practice of writing as such, but it is for several reasons equally important in walking the pathless path of writing. It is the way we bring back what we have found along the way of our forays off the trail. In Snyder's words, "the wild requires that we learn the terrain, nod to all the plants and animals and birds, ford the streams and cross the ridges, and tell a good story when we get back home" (1990, 24). When students share their writings with others, they create a space in which the wild, both inner and outer, can come to reside more fully in the midst of the human community.

The process of sharing also helps each person's writing to grow. Hearing others' writing opens up new possibilities, and hearing feedback on how our writing affects others gives new insight about it. This growth is also a process of letting go, stepping off the trail into the unknown. When we share our writing and receive feedback, it is no longer our private possession: we experience it as a gift that needs to be passed along. Some students are initially hesitant to share, afraid of exposing their fragile writers' egos to painful criticism. But by setting a supportive space where feedback can be given in a way that supports and encourages growth, they come to feel more comfortable with the process, even to relish it.

Peter Elbow's chapters on "Feedback" in *Writing with Power* are helpful for setting this context: "The crucial question about any piece of writing intended for an audience is not 'How does it measure up against certain criteria' such as good sentences, good logic, or good paragraphs, but *'How does it work on readers?'"* (1981, 242). I encourage students to give feedback based on their own experience of the writing: where it was vivid and engaged their attention; where they lost interest; where they felt energy and voice in the words, and where that was lacking; where they wanted to know more; where they got too much information. This kind of "reader-based feedback," whether positive or critical, gives useful information and helps writers understand how their writing impacts others. This realization is in itself empowering.

III

The four practices just discussed serve as guiding principles for a nature-writing class I've taught for the past ten years in Antioch's Environmental Studies Masters' program. During a fifteen-week semester the class meets weekly and engages in a variety of activities to stimulate the writing process: in-class free writing, a daily journal practice, discussion of nature essays, and writing and sharing of weekly assignments that focus on description, exploration, and story. The highlight of the course is a weekend trip to Cape Cod, where the group is able to take these practices into the field. We stay at a nature center in the midst of the dunes of Truro and spend the weekend walking the dunes, beaches, and swamps of the Cape, and writing.

For the first few years, I found it hard to get students to write while they were there. The excitement of getting outdoors away from school, the beauty and power of the landscape, and their desire to experience the place directly without the mediation of words, all contributed to the difficulty that I, along with many teachers, have experienced when trying to get students to write outdoors. As a teacher new to this process, my own tentativeness was reinforced by their reluctance to sit down and get "serious" about writing. At first, I let people wander on their own and hoped they would write. Sometimes they did, but often the writing didn't happen until they got back and had an assignment. Gradually over time, I discovered that these four writing practices served as a way of inviting the students into a deeper experience of the landscape, inspiring much more enthusiasm about writing outdoors.

The weekend moves with alternating rhythms of structure and spontaneity, group time and alone time. We often start the weekend off with a group hike in the dunes that familiarizes everyone with some of the key features of the landscape and its ecology. This helps the students to begin paying attention to small details they might otherwise overlook and to notice the patterns and relationships that inform the "story" of the land.

We walk along a dune, and I stop to pick up an "Earth-star," a small puffball that grows loose on the sand. Its small central globe is surrounded by star-like points that close around the center during dry spells to prevent desiccation, and open when it's damp like tiny starfish arms attached to a miniature ping-pong ball. We talk about dune ecology and how the dune grass serves as an anchor to keep the dunes in place. Someone points out how each stalk is surrounded by a circle etched in sand as the wind buffets it around. Later as we walk inland I point out how succession shapes the dunes: the farther we go from the beach, the more stable the dunes become. As soil builds up, vegetation changes from bushes like bearberry and bayberry, to larger trees like pitch pine and scrub oak, and eventually to mature forests of beech and pine, and swamps of red maple and white cedar.

Early in the weekend I introduce the theme of attentiveness with the "five-minute journal exercise." I begin by reading a few excerpts from Holzer's description in *A Walk between Heaven and Earth*, highlighting the importance of capturing sense impressions on the page while they are fresh:

> Once you begin to notice that five minutes here, and twenty minutes there, can be used for journal entries, your day begins to take on a different perspective. It is like walking into an open landscape, discovering the small places between the bushes where the first flowers grow after the snow. . . . Take (the journal) with you, catch the scenery of the path wherever you are. (Holzer 1994, 24–25)

This exercise has the virtue of being brief, portable, and flexible. I suggest doing several of these during the weekend, at whatever moments something interesting occurs. Then I encourage people to move with their own pace and rhythm and to choose from a variety of options for landscapes to explore. By Saturday afternoon, the class has usually dispersed into several smaller groups and some solitary wanderers.

On Sunday morning, Donna woke early and walked by herself in the woods near the nature center. Her description of a slug is fascinating, not only for its attentiveness to details but also for the way it tracks the play of her attention as it moves from one point of focus to another until it settles on the slug:

> Here and there—everywhere—spider webs glisten on the grass; dense webs with a funnel-like hole. But I'm not interested in spiders. I'm looking for something, listening for something—I'm not sure what. Suddenly a slight movement against the dun background of pine needles, something same-

colored, but differing in shape and texture, catches my eye. Sensuously embracing a thin, stiff plant stalk, a smooth fat slug slowly slides upward. It doubles back on itself, oozing its body which appears to be all muscle and mucous, headfirst down the stem.

One warm September day, we stood at the crest of a high dune, looking out toward the Atlantic across an undulating expanse of sand. I noticed Beth was getting restless as I introduced the "present moment" exercise. When I finished speaking, she told me with great excitement that she could hardly contain herself because an ant was crawling up over her foot—in the present moment!—and she couldn't wait to begin describing it right away:

> The tiny little black body scurries across the sand, falling here and here into the imprints just made by our feet. These footprints must seem like giant dunes to the little ant that is trying to navigate them. I move out of the ant's way and watch him as he scurries all around my feet. He falls over the edge of one of my dunes. As he tries to grasp the edge to pull himself back out he only succeeds in pulling more sand grains down around him. I worry that he will get buried, as I anxiously continue watching him.

While Beth was describing the ant, Julia's "present moment" was quite different.

> Tiny golden petals waving gray shadows over sun bleached sand—silence carries whispered crackle of long dune grass. . . . Thoughts sent rolling on the dark ball of wet sand unearthed by toes digging into cool, moist depth below the sun baked surface—what would I miss if I just listened to the quaking sound of a distant bird, if I swayed with the breeze rather than try to interpret her words as she whispers easily against my ear?

Tim's present-moment writing is noteworthy for the way his attention shifts back and forth between senses and between inner and outer awareness:

> Wind. Beach grass blown sideways toward the ocean. Sand in the cup of my left hand: pepper, salt, sesame seeds, finely ground cornmeal. Sun casts light and shadow, and then disappears in seconds; everything is flattened again. Grains of hurtling sand pelt my windbreaker, and I thought of rain, thought of how quickly a drop of water would be sucked up, blown away, filtered down. I could spill my whole bottle of water here and watch it disappear. But still, I haven't tried this and am trying to watch my assumptions. My hands are cooling down, and the pen feels heavier, slower. My

fingers are clenched together and trying to push, pull. Grace falls aside. I am just sitting, watching a new burst of light and shadow, feeling the sides of my jacket push against me with the wind, listening to grasses, sand, the jacket's nylon hood beating against my ears.

Sometime during the weekend, I encourage people to begin paying attention to where the interconnections and stories might be. Nicole had been struggling all weekend to connect with this landscape and write about it. She had never been to the Cape before, and felt her connections much more deeply with the desert. She had also had a hard time in class assignments finding "stories" to write about: her essays were vivid, poetic evocations of moments of awareness, but they often lacked the threads of connection that pull together a good story. I suggested she try following her associations with the desert and see where they led. This journal entry became the jumping-off point for a longer essay that finally helped her find "storied" connections she could explore more fully:

> Dunes stretch across the landscape made up of sand like sea salt glistening in the afternoon glow. . . . Shadows cast long patterns crossing like tracks leading down into the bowl. . . . Tracks lead me on and on across the universe. Coyote tracks in the sand washes of Utah. Like here there is life, something is always singing or at least whispering. Rattlesnakes . . . this grass reminds me of rattlesnakes. Perhaps of the time I killed one as a little girl, stoned it to death in Arizona when I was eight because the cowboys said they were bad for the horses and would leap at them from the grass. What did they know? A rattlesnake died because of me and now I hear its stories on the dunes of the Cape.

By the time we come to Cape Cod, the sense of a supportive community for sharing work has already been established. On Sunday morning, a session for reading aloud brings the weekend to a climax and prepares the ground for the process of returning home and working with the material over the next several weeks. I approach this in various ways, depending on the weather, the group's energy, and the readiness of group members to share. Often we'll begin with some focused time for writing, so everyone has something they can read: perhaps the "leap" exercise or if it's a rainy morning we might begin with some quiet indoor journal time.

One Sunday morning I ask everyone to make a list of images from the weekend that have been most compelling for them, what the artist Clare Walker Leslie calls "daily exceptional images." Then each person chooses one image as the starting point for a five-minute free-write. Verna reads about how she's been noticing layers: the layers of sand in the dunes, layers of decomposing vegetation building up in the pools of the cedar swamp. And she thinks of other layers in her life: the layers of her mother's triple-layer cake, the layers of her wedding dress, the layers of vegetation in a cypress swamp she visited once, the layers of her memory. John reads a poem about watching three gulls circling high on the wind, their wings so still at first we think they're hawks. I read from my journal about the fox we saw yesterday. We had all been watching a harrier fly low over the marsh near the nature center when someone cried out "look, a fox!" We watched as it trotted along and then settled in to devour a dead gull. Lea reads about the fox, too, and how it stirred her yearning for wildness.

A good way to bring the weekend to a close is the "group poem." Each person makes a list of "daily exceptional images"—one image for each line, until she has a poem-like sequence of vivid images strung out down the page. Then we do a group reading; someone picks an image at the top of the list and reads it aloud, followed by the next in the circle doing the same. We go around and around until everyone has read the complete list. The group reading recaps vivid moments from the weekend, gives each voice a chance to be heard, and yet makes it easier for the reluctant ones to read without feeling on the spot. This also gives each person a good list of images to take home with him as a way of beginning the next phase of the writing. We sit in a circle in the grass outside the nature center, the sound of the sea a constant background to our voices. Distilling the essence of each image, our words become icons of our experience of this place:

> Rocks and shells strewn in a line, where the high tide last left them
> Crab skeleton slowly picked to death ravaged by seagulls in the sign of a cross
> Mergansers on the water—crested silhouettes against the sun
> The wind's breath hits me like longing
> Tall grasses shift and shudder, become one with the way of the wind.

By the end of the weekend, the sense of intimacy and community has grown, a dynamic I've experienced with many outdoor class trips. But there's another dimension to this intimacy that grows as we explore the landscape together in the context of discovering our connections and sharing our stories. Over the next two weeks, the sense of community grows as the class engages in a process designed to help them continue to explore unknown territory, discover more interconnections and stories, and develop their journal entries into finished pieces.

I ask them to continue writing in their journals until the next class, developing images from their image poems or working with other journal entries to develop them further. Then in class each person reads something out loud and we discuss various possibilities for development. Sometimes we do a series of free-writes: "Pick a line you like from your journal, one that has power for you: underline it and use it as a starting line for another free-write. Pick another line from that one and do the process again. And again." Throughout this process, I emphasize that even though we are back home, away from the landscape itself and our experience of it, we are still in a process of exploration: the meanings continue to evolve and deepen as we write. I also emphasize that when working with journal entries, it's important not to refine the raw "juice" out of them. Often there's a freshness of language that comes from the process of discovery through writing that is important to preserve in the finished piece. The next assignment is to take something from the journal and develop it into a finished essay or poem.

When we meet the following week, the air of excitement from the trip is still present, but with a different edge to it. By now the members of the class have become involved in each others' stories and are eager to see what has grown out of them. Now we finally get to appreciate where the journey has taken us.

John reads his finished poem about the gull, which weaves together other images from the weekend as he explores the paradoxical nature of thought:

> I think
> to try to make sense of things
> to try to get out of
> the tangle of trees
> the sheets of shadow
> the mossy hummocks and murky pools
> that I so often feel lost in.
> Look how elevated we hold this great enterprise.
>
> On the dunes of Cape Cod
> we lie in the sand
> binoculars trained
> on birds overhead
> circling high
> with flattened wings
> never flapping

the flight of a hawk
but the color of a gull
mostly white
silent beauty
floating there
enveloped in blue
reverie.

White globs
falling down
"Oh, my God—it just shit!"
I exclaim to my friend.
The pristine image is falling to Earth
and we
can't stop laughing.

Lea reads from her essay about the fox, which has expanded to include other incidents from her life. She begins:

> I had the voice of a lion until fourth grade. At that point, like many other little girls, I reacted and assimilated to the pressures and societal influences that let us know what is appropriate, and what behaviors are expected of us. The stripping away of the wild nature left me both fearful and insecure.

After a series of reflections on wildness, she brings in the fox:

> I watched a fox for fifteen minutes on a trip to Cape Cod. It glided along the sand path, heading toward the beach, then leaping up onto the hillside. From underneath a scrub oak, it yanked a dead Black-backed gull, eating it in its entirety as we looked on. After finishing, the fox retraced its steps, slinking down the path into the protective dense growth toward home, marking territory with its skunk-like smelling urine.
>
> The fox was wild, her motions smooth and doubtless: eating, marking territory, then returning to the young, to feed and nurture those kits. I want to go wild like the fox.

Maggie, a student in Conservation Biology, skilled in the sciences but uncertain about her ability to write creatively about nature, had struggled all semester with journal and free-writing and felt insecure in a group full of imaginative writers. After the weekend, she wrote this as the conclusion to a nine-page essay that leaps back and forth between her impressions of the weekend and her observations on the ecology of a salt marsh:

The next morning we shared our thoughts and experiences. Lea and Fred both spoke of the fox we had watched the previous day. Fred was fascinated by the fox's consumption of the Great Black-backed Gull. Wavering between the fox as a scavenger and the wing of the gull, he delicately explored the issues of personal growth and death. Lea, full of curiosity and questions, wondered about all that was wild, and longed to act purely on instinct. She found the common thread in all of us as we nodded in agreement. Thoreau once wrote "Give me a wildness whose glance no civilization can endure—as if we lived on the marrow of koodoos devoured raw." That weekend we had a taste of the raw marrow of koodoos and Thoreau's words were no longer black ink on paper: they were nourishment for our souls.

Marshes are productive for several reasons, all resulting from fresh water meeting the sea. Fresh water run-off from the land is often rich in nitrogen, phosphorus and potassium. These nutrients, as well as many others, are insoluble in salt water. As the nutrient-rich fresh waters mix with the sea water, the nutrients precipitate out of solution. Thus the salt marsh acts as a nutrient trap. These nutrients are quickly cycled, used and made available for reuse. Twice a day the tide flows in, trapping nutrients in the estuarine system, and twice a day the tide flows out, dispersing the nutrients of the marsh into the sea.

We flowed into Truro, some of us old salts, others fresh and vibrant with new ideas. Differences met and mingled as we found our common ground along the beach or sat among the dunes. Our diversity allowed a collective energy to precipitate out of our individuality. We built upon the tangled mat of other writers' words as we added our experiences and thoughts to the existing layers of science and literature. Our writing grew both horizontally and vertically as we steeped in the richness of the weekend. We were in a self-made estuary, a productive habitat, which unfortunately is ephemeral. At the end of the weekend we said our goodbyes and flowed out of Truro, dispersing our rich thoughts into the sea.

Maggie's words express the importance of the communal dimension of nature writing as a "Practice of the Wild." Barry Lopez captures the importance of this sharing in a passage from his story *Crow and Weasel,* which I often read at the close of a class or workshop:

"I would ask you to remember this one thing," said Badger. "The stories people tell have a way of taking care of them. If stories come to you, care for them. And learn to give them away where they are needed. Sometimes a person needs a story more than food to stay alive. That is why we put these stories in each other's memory. This is how people care for themselves. One day you will be good storytellers. Never forget these obligations." (Lopez 1990, 60)

I return to Cape Cod on my own in February to walk these dunes, swamps, and beaches, to see what memory stirs for me, and to follow it in my own writing. I walk in the dunes near the nature center and think of Lea's fox and Donna's slug. I walk out onto the high dunes, stand at the crest near where Beth watched the ant crawl over her foot, where Nicole listened to the grass and heard rattlesnakes. I know these stories have been taking care of me, for as I walk among the dunes they come back and refresh me.

I walk farther in and realize that I have become lost, that the trail I thought I was following has led me to a totally different part of the dunes. The sand has shifted, the footsteps have disappeared, and I am once again off the trail.

From a promontory I get my bearings and set my course through a valley that runs through the dunes parallel to the ocean. I've looked out over this valley toward the sea many times but never walked through it. I walk on, eager to see what I will find. I walk among pitch pines, low-bush cranberries with bright maroon leaves and a few bright red berries still clinging from last fall, and gray-green branching stalks of reindeer lichen sprouting up in the sand. Then I walk up over another dune crest and come to the sea. Along the beach, mergansers bob on the waves, and cormorants fly by in a loose formation. After walking the beach, I climb the first ridge of dunes again and stand at the crest. A seal bobs the surface with something in its mouth—apparently it's eating a fish. The sun comes out from behind a cloud and the breakers shine white in the sun. The sea opens like a window from gray into pearly green, like gray-green glass, like polished jade.

I return back through the valley toward the dunes. The light fades around me but a golden sunset glow clings to the dunes above me. Like Nicole, I think of the desert here in this unearthly light. A flash of wings and a white spot, and a harrier swoops low over the cranberries.

Notes

1. Austin's words originally appeared in a 1920 letter to her guide and confidant, Professor Daniel Tremblay MacDougal, as she prepared to explore the Sonoran Desert. The letter is archived in Special Collections,

University of Arizona Library, and quoted in Larry Evers's introduction to Austin's *The Land of Journey's Ending*, reprinted by the University of Arizona Press in 1983.

References

Dillard, Annie. 1983. *Teaching a stone to talk*. New York: Harper.

———. 1989. *The writing life*. New York: Harper.

Elbow, Peter. 1981. *Writing with power*. New York: Oxford University Press.

Fowles, John, and Frank Horvat. 1979. *The tree*. Boston: Little Brown.

Goldberg, Natalie. 1986. *Writing down the bones*. Boston: Shambhala.

Holzer, Burghild Nina. 1994. *A walk between heaven and earth*. New York: Bell Tower.

Lopez, Barry. 1987. *Crossing open ground*. New York: Scribner's.

———. 1990. *Crow and weasel*. San Francisco: North Point.

Lueders, Edward, ed. 1989. *Writing natural history: Dialogues with authors*. Salt Lake City: University of Utah Press.

McPhee, John. 1975. *The survival of the bark canoe*. New York: Warner.

Oliver, Mary. 1992. *New and selected poems*. Boston: Beacon.

Snyder, Gary. 1990. *The practice of the wild*. San Francisco: North Point.

Stafford, William. 1978. *Writing the Australian crawl*. Ann Arbor: University of Michigan Press.

Trimble, Stephen, ed. 1988. *Words from the land*. Salt Lake City: Gibbs Smith.

Wagoner, David. 1999. *Traveling light: Collected and new poems*. Urbana: University of Illinois Press.

Road Trip

Self-Directed Field Work as a Learning Journey

> When someone goes on a trip, he has something to tell about.
>
> —German saying[1]

Back when I taught the mandatory research paper in freshman composition class, I would start by asking students to take out a piece of paper and write some answers to the following question: *What do you want to know?* This exercise, which I'd read about in a book on teaching composition, had two purposes.[2] First, it got students to generate some material out of which a promising research question might eventually be developed. Second, it sent the message that while the research paper might appear to be a tedious, time-consuming academic exercise, it was really an opportunity to use research techniques and expository writing to explore a subject that had piqued their curiosity. Despite the laudable intentions and tactical cleverness of this approach, I don't recall that it generated a great deal of intellectual ferment among my students or paved the way to many memorable essays.

The students and I shared the blame for these disappointing results. Most of the freshmen coming into George Mason University, a state school in Virginia, hadn't arrived with well-developed intellectual lives. As a result, their answers to the question *What do you want to know?* rarely translated easily into promising research questions. Probably another instructor, more skilled and motivated than I, could have helped students uncover the hidden potential in their answers. I don't doubt that the author who'd invented the idea I borrowed, an experienced and committed teacher, got good results with this approach. Part of what prevented me from helping students do better work was my lack of excitement about the whole enterprise. As a graduate student in the university's creative writing program, I had serious doubts about the conventional research essay, wondering if students could really use this format to produce interesting and rewarding written work. I sometimes felt less like a teacher than a writing cop charged with the job of leaning on students to form passable topic sentences and use their sources responsibly.

Now I'm a full-time teacher at George Mason, where I've joined the faculty of New Century College, an integrative-studies program with a strong commitment to alternative pedagogies and experiential education. Students in my writing-intensive classes still do research projects. Instead of asking them what they want to know, I now ask them where they want to go. I'm much more satisfied with the results.

In this essay I will discuss Road Trip, a semester-long research and writing project that centers upon a self-directed journey. Students complete the Road Trip project to earn one of the two experiential learning credits in a six-credit, co-taught literature and history course called Roads and Rivers: American Landscapes in Fiction, Film, and History. This project showcases some of the challenges and many of the rewards that independent field work projects create for students and teachers alike. As a teacher I have been intrigued and heartened to see how "road work" promotes intellectual growth and overall maturity in students by intensifying their engagement with course materials, blurring the often too-rigid boundary between the classroom and the "real" world and helping to redefine the student-teacher relationship. As a *writing* teacher I am particularly interested in the ways the project helps students develop as writers by increasing their investment in what they write, by reinforcing the process-oriented approach to writing, and by highlighting various ways writing can be used as a powerful way of knowing.

I will begin by briefly describing the Road Trip assignment, which opens with a question and a promise. The assignment sheet asks students where they want to go and tells them they will create a piece of writing that could end up on the Roads and Rivers syllabus, which is dedicated to American journey-based narratives and historical studies of important American waterways and roadways. Early in the semester students submit a brief proposal in which they describe the trip they wish to take, articulate at least three learning objectives, and discuss their plans for research they will do before, during, and after the trip. A note on the assignment sheet reminds students that research can take many forms, depending on the nature of the project. In addition to tracking down books, articles, and web sites that deal with their topics, many will want to visit local museums and information centers, view films, interview people, and consider searching for archival materials such as photographs and maps.

After receiving feedback and final approval of proposals from faculty, students undertake the journeys they proposed. The next writing they submit is a follow-up report in which they give a narrative account of the trip, evaluate their learning in light of the objectives they spelled out in the proposal, report on research completed so far, and comment on plans for additional research yet to be done. The last piece of the follow-up report is a proposal for the piece of research-based writing to be submitted at the end of the semester. While this piece must be rooted in solid, well-documented research, and must relate clearly to major themes and topics of the course, students choose the genre that best suits their material and their writing interests. Conventional research essays are welcome, as are personal essays, travelogues, short stories, narrative poems, film scripts, and anything else for which they can make a compelling case. Faculty respond to the follow-up reports with comments, questions, and suggestions. The class conducts a workshop on early drafts a couple of weeks before the end of the semester. On the last day of class students hand in the drafts that will be graded and then swap stories about their travels in brief, informal presentations.

I like to begin by asking students where they want to go because the question foregrounds choice and adumbrates a journey, a departure from familiar places and the old routine, a chance for liberation, for new sights, new people, new experiences. The road trip functions as a concrete experience with active, independent learning and, in many cases, as a metaphor for learning itself. Learning ought to be something we choose to do, not something others impose upon us. In this assignment students choose their destinations, their routes, their means of travel, and the company (if any) they will take along. They define their learning objectives and decide how best to relate these objectives to course texts and themes. They choose the kinds of research that best suit their individual learning enterprises. While on the road, they choose how disciplined they will be about executing their learning plans in the face of the distractions and complications that inevitably arise. They also decide which genre best fits their material when the time comes to transform it into a formal piece of writing.

With all of this freedom comes an equal amount of responsibility. This, to me, is a main point of the assignment. For many people, college can act as the critical stage in the transition from the highly structured classrooms and curricula of elementary and secondary school to the much more fluid learning situations of adulthood. The New Century College motto is "Connecting the classroom to the world." Road Trip promotes this connection not only by sending students out of the classroom and into the "world" but also by helping prepare students to make the most of the independent, "lifelong" learning opportunities that await them after graduation. A crucial part of this preparation is adopting the notion that close observation, thoughtful reflection, and in-depth analysis are activities one can and should do off campus and after hours, outside the usual school settings. No teacher accompanies students on the road to make sure they do the observation, inquiry, and information gathering that will assist them later when they sit down to write. Faculty are available to give feedback on proposals and drafts, ask questions, make suggestions, and offer encouragement. We try our best to avoid (or at least limit) the looming and handholding typical of many well-intentioned teachers, since such behaviors tend to undermine students' sense of autonomy and responsibility.

Road Trip creates a context in which students can see faculty as sounding boards as well as grade givers, as writing coaches as well as writing judges. There are other ways the assignment promotes important shifts in the teacher-student relationship and the learning environment. Roads and Rivers is a carefully orchestrated class developed by a teaching team with a clear agenda regarding course content. Like most teachers, my partner and I have strong opinions about materials that must be covered and concepts we want students to take away from our course. Throughout the semester we model approaches to course materials that become very familiar to students. Road Trip gives students an opportunity to develop their own ways of engaging course content and allows them to model their approaches for each other. Students come to value writing workshops not just for the feedback they receive on their own work but also for the chance to see how others are handling the assignment. Students frequently propose projects and adopt research and writing strategies faculty haven't imagined before. In more traditional courses, instruction tends to flow one way, from teachers to students. Road Trip helps complicate and improve upon this pattern by opening alternative channels.

We all know how much better we learn and perform when we're invested in the work we're doing. I have observed that students quickly become invested in their Road Trip projects. In part this reflects their eagerness to get away and explore. But I believe they also take seriously the task of justifying all the choices they make, explaining how the trips they propose will provide valuable learning experiences and enrich their engagement of course content. Students in Roads and Rivers often see a clear connection between their work on the Road Trip project and their involvement with the course as a whole. One student used her family's annual Rosh Hashanah trip from northern Virginia to New York as an occasion to explore the history of Jewish New Year observances in her family and in Jewish culture generally. She later commented in her self-evaluation that "Road Trip helped me to better understand the focus of the class." A student who wrote on the bridges of Pittsburgh noticed that "after completing my trip I found it easier to relate with characters from our course texts."

The possibility of writing something that future Roads and Rivers students will read may also help spark students' enthusiasm. But a bigger reason for the faculty's pledge to include selected student works on next year's syllabus is to situate the writing they do through this project in the long history of journey-based writing in and about America. Through their writing, students jump into a conversation that began in the fifteenth century. They can't simply eavesdrop from the margins. Thus the context in which they write goes well beyond the boundaries of our class, which helps to reduce the arbitrary (or "fake," as one of my colleagues bluntly puts it) quality that tarnishes so many assignments students do. Also, while class discussions and weekly essay assignments promote close analytical reading of course texts, the Road Trip assignment spurs students to read *as writers*. They look to course readings to model research tactics, genres, and writing styles, as well as styles and philosophies of travel.

No successful piece of writing is born overnight. This is why writing teachers around the country have come to embrace the process-oriented approach to writing instruction, which requires students to build a piece of writing in distinct stages and allows faculty to respond to one or more pieces of preliminary work before students submit the draft that receives a grade. Obviously, the Road Trip assignment's structure and extended time frame reflect strong faculty investment in the process-oriented approach to writing instruction. Two years of Roads and Rivers students have voiced unanimous support for the assignment's basic structure, echoing one peer's view that "the stages of the project were beneficial. They kept us working on the project through the semester." Also, many students have reported benefits that speak more directly to writing issues. "My original ideas changed so much from start to end," reported a student who studied the displacement of families during the creation of Shenandoah National Park, "that my essay would have been much less thought-out and evaluated if it weren't in stages." As another succinctly put it, "the stages helped me to figure out what the final paper was going to be about."

The Road Trip assignment underscores the value of the process-oriented approach even for students in New Century College, many of whom are well acquainted with it already. Having a journey at the heart of the project helps to sharpen the outlines of each stage in the research and writing process. The proposal, a standard component of any research assignment, takes on special concreteness when it centers on a journey. For many students, planning a research project can seem far less intimidating and exotic when it is mostly a matter of planning a trip. As the trip takes shape, it gives a student a sturdy peg on which to hang her learning objectives and research plans. A student who investigated the geographical reasons for Richmond's selection as the Confederate capital put it this way: "The proposal gave my trip a focus before I left." Of course, not all travelers stay entirely wedded to their proposals. The student who traced cultural currents along a West Virginia stretch of the New River ended up seeing her proposal as the expendable scaffolding she used in climbing to where the real work was: "It was very interesting to see the differences between what I planned and what I did." No matter how they use the proposal, students can apply their insights about this stage of the writing process to their future research projects.

Research is always an active mode of learning, no matter what form it takes. Students may overlook this while parked at the library table or in front of the computer. On the road, however, they vividly experience research as action. They commonly show great enthusiasm for this "hands-on" work and claim a strong preference for it. Road Trip veterans typically report that going to a place they've read about makes it "come alive," makes it "real." In some cases the journey ignites a burning interest in a topic or piece of territory. For example, a student who researched the C&O Canal had only a lukewarm interest in the topic before she traveled the length of the canal, stopping at various information centers to speak with knowledgeable rangers, one of whom suggested she check out the Paw Paw tunnel. Walking almost two miles of tunnel without the aid of a light was—pardon the pun—a rite of passage that changed this student's whole orientation to her project. The C&O Canal, and the Paw Paw Tunnel in particular, became obsessions for her. She made multiple trips back to the canal, tracked down leads at museums and historical sites around the region, and read everything she could find about the canal. At the end of the semester she wrote, "I know more about the C&O Canal than my grandfather does. That has got to say something!"

What I like most about this student's story is that her time on the canal inspired her to pursue other lines of inquiry. As engaging as field work can be, it's important for students to keep in mind that experiential research is neither an end in itself nor a mere matter of confirming the truth of what they've read. Field work is one among many kinds of research. In teaching the Road Trip assignment, faculty must work to assure that several different kinds of research play into projects so that students have a chance to see how material from different sources can help inform a robust and complicated understanding of a topic. This assignment creates opportunities for students to experience research as a dynamic and often dialogic process of critical engagement with multiple modes of inquiry. Information from one kind of source may confirm, clarify, amplify, question, discredit, or otherwise affect one's understanding of information from another kind of source. When reading students' self-evaluations, I'm always on the lookout for evidence that this is happening. Thus I was encouraged when the student who wrote an amusing and well-researched personal essay on the commercialization of the Amish country reported that his time in the field caused him "to see the information in books differently." I was also heartened to hear from a student who wanted to know when and why Baltimore supplanted Annapolis as Maryland's premier city. He admitted that he "really didn't know what I needed to read until I'd gone on the trip." Finally, I was intrigued by the reflections of the student who researched the people displaced by Shenandoah National Park. She had hiked into several active excavation sites as a way of "creating a connection with my subject." This connection ultimately amounted to a moral obligation to investigate her topic carefully, a charge she expressed in a much better pun than mine: "After my trip I couldn't take the superficial approach to library research. It caused me to dig."

The follow-up report due after conclusion of the trip basically serves the same purpose as an evaluation of research, a crucial thing to do before one begins drafting a research-based piece of writing. In this case, students mainly look upon the follow-up report as a chance to tell their stories, refining their "front-line" journal entries into coherent accounts of where they went, what they saw, what they learned. This recounting creates a natural context in which to report on their success (or lack of it) in meeting learning objectives, to identify new lines of inquiry their trips have suggested to them, to evaluate the research they have done to date, and to discuss any follow-up work that awaits them. All of this sifting through the material prepares students to do some productive thinking about what genre suits the material best. It also gives faculty an excellent chance to check students' progress and review their work in detail at a stage when students still have plenty of time to respond productively to clarifying questions and suggestions about research or writing strategies.

As we have seen, some students will repeat their trips to do follow-up research. But in most cases they have finished traveling once they begin drafting the more formal piece of writing the assignment requires. Still, I try to ensure that travel continues to figure into what they write, not only at the level of content but also through analogy to the writing process. The Road Trip project creates all kinds of natural opportunities to bring up the analogy between writing and travel. What I like most about this analogy is that it helps to characterize writing as an *activity*, a means by which we can explore, investigate, wander, seek, tour, survey, roam, and discover without having to leave our chairs. I doubt I'm the only writer who sometimes daydreams about skipping over what some composition specialists call the "discovery" process, wishing I could arrive at the end product without going through the false starts, treacherous turns, alluring cul de sacs, bewildering intersections, hard hills, lazy interludes, and other familiar features that lengthen the writer's road. Those who share my affliction tend to be more patient (or accepting, at least) when they can relate writing to a semi-improvisational mode of travel in which the traveler maps out a basic itinerary, has a destination in mind, but remains open to promising side-paths, unexpected events, new company, and surprising discoveries. Like many writing teachers, I wish far more of my students had a realistic grasp of the time it takes to develop a successful piece of writing. Students tend to better hear my claims about the time writing takes when travel is involved. One can no more produce a rich piece of writing in a couple of hours, I tell them, than one can expect to reach Okracoke Island in the blink of an eye. Writing projects, like journeys, unfold in stages. Students can profit from thinking of their projects as things with legs.

The Road Trip project also helps students to see the integral role writing often plays in the thinking process and creates excellent opportunities for students to experience writing as a powerful and versatile way of knowing. In their proposals students use writing to frame and structure a learning experience, creating a preliminary map for themselves before departure. On the road they do extensive "front-line" work, using their travel journals to capture observations, record lived experience, answer the questions they came with, and form new questions triggered by unfolding events. The follow-up report requires that they use writing to narrate and evaluate their trips, which means they must pore back through and refine the raw material in their journals. Writing is also the means by which students revise learning objectives and research strategies based on their findings so far.

To me some of the most intriguing thinking and writing students do in the follow-up report revolves around selecting a genre for the more formal piece of writing they will produce next. Genre selection really highlights writing's versatility as a way of knowing. How is a short story different from a research paper? What can I do in a personal essay that I can't do in a short story? What is a travelogue, anyway? Which of these genres best fits the research I've done, my writing interests, my intellectual goals? Many students have never confronted such questions. While they probably have some experience writing in multiple genres, past teachers have always told them what they are going to write. Leaving the genre open thus lifts the veil from a part of writing that many students have never seen or considered before. This can be an empowering experience, or a bewildering one. As I like to say, independence has two faces.

Student reactions to having a choice of genres have ranged from indifference to strong enthusiasm. A significant portion of the class typically decides early on to do a conventional research paper. They explain this choice as a matter of doing what's already familiar or, more persuasively, of choosing the genre they see as most suitable for conveying their material. "A research paper was the best way to communicate all the history," explained a student who wrote an exceptional essay on the Cumberland Gap's role in United States history. Not surprisingly, a main challenge facing the people who opt to try another genre is working researched material into a piece of writing they think of as "creative" and "personal." One of our fiction writers made masterful use of an early colonist's voice (and spelling) to recount an exploratory trip up the James River. He struggled to cover his own tracks, allowing that "the most difficult part of the assignment was deciding how to incorporate so much history and factual information into the journal entries of a fictional character without sounding too fake." Several students who attempted personal essays encountered similar difficulties. "I have never written a personal essay that contained research," said the student who wrote about a trip to Harper's Ferry. "It was hard tying in my research." The student who wrote on the New River reported wanting "to provide history and a personal account. I changed the order a million times."

My reaction to news of such struggles is mostly proud and positive. When a writer is changing the order a "million" times, she is deeply involved in what she's doing. Moreover, this writer's struggle to find the best way to present "personal" with "historical" material demonstrates how a problem in the writing process can mirror a stage in the process of intellectual development. The challenge of effectively weaving "academic" research into a "personal" story causes many students in our course to work against and perhaps question the restrictive compartments that have traditionally shaped their learning habits and defined their capacities. Sometimes this struggle makes for awkward patches in the writing, but these are easy to forgive when one considers what's at stake.

Forgiveness is of course good, but faculty would better serve student writers by providing more concrete help at an earlier stage in the process. Probably the biggest change we need to make in Road Trip is the way we teach the past student writing we include in the syllabus. It's not enough to refer students to these writings as models of the kinds of work they might strive to produce. We need to spend substantial class time discussing diverse examples of student work. This would help students start the project with a better feel for what the assignment is asking them to do and some basic familiarity with the various genres available to them. They ought to have a good idea of the challenges one faces while writing in a particular genre, as well as the potential rewards. This will help reduce the stress-level and probably improve the writing of those trying something new. It should also reduce the number of students who choose to do the conventional research paper only because it's the safest option.

There are other matters we should foreground better as well. Without dampening students' excitement about doing their own trips, we need to warn them about the potential dangers of self-directed field research. While many students do their very best work on Road Trip, a small but significant number have done their poorest work on this assignment. Apparently these students have a hard time functioning productively without the structure that more conventional assignments and courses provide. In some cases this can't be avoided; but I think certain students who are at risk of getting tangled in the slack Road Trip offers might be able to respond if greater attention were paid in class to practical matters such as the importance of planning and choice of travel company, along with more abstract matters such as the "two faces" of independent field work. Some students get so swept away by the attractions of self-directed travel that they never consider the responsibilities that come with their freedom—until it's too late. With all the readings and films we have to discuss in class, it's easy to let the experiential part of the course remain "off-stage." We need to make more effort to ensure that students' experiences with Road Trip become a visible thread in the week-to-week fabric of the course. We let students down if we don't capitalize on the opportunities Road Trip creates for discussing the nuts and bolts of travel as well as the values, challenges, and potential pitfalls of independent experiential learning.

Thus far, the only formal opportunities Roads and Rivers students have had to learn about their peers' travels are when they workshop early drafts and when they give their brief presentations on their trips the last day of class. These events provide strong evidence in favor of increasing the amount of class time devoted to student road trips. Students delight in sharing their adventures and misadventures with peers, and they like hearing about the kinds of trips others are taking and seeing the kinds of writing that classmates are doing. Here we see a surprising and somewhat paradoxical benefit of incorporating an independent project like Road Trip into a college course: the research and travel students do for this project ends up making us more of a community than we would be otherwise. Like denizens of a small town or village, students return from their journeys with news about what's happening elsewhere, about places to avoid and places that mustn't be missed. They offer advice on how—and how not—to travel. They teach each other and learn from each other. They laugh. They commiserate. They are what members of every college course probably ought to be—a community of travelers.

Notes

1. Quoted in Walter Benjamin, *Illuminations* (New York: Schocken Books, 1969), 84.

2. Bruce Ballenger, "Teaching the Research Paper," *Nuts and Bolts,* ed. Thomas Newkirk (Portsmouth: Boynton/Cook, 1993), 129–50.

PART III: Field Considerations

Issues to Consider in Planning and Execution

Introduction to Part III

The selections in Part III, "Field Considerations," focus on issues instructors face when planning and teaching courses that take students outside the classroom. We begin with "Facing the Challenge: Overcoming the Common Obstacles to Running a Successful Field Studies Course," by Corey Lee Lewis. This article discusses practical considerations to take into account when planning and executing field-studies courses, with a focus on administrative, logistical, managerial, academic, and ethical factors. Instructors new to the practice of teaching in the field and those who wish to move from day trips to multi-day overnights in wilderness areas will find this essay particularly valuable.

Organizing such trips can seem straightforward in theory, but as Allison B. Wallace reminds us in her essay, "In Thoreau's Wake on the West Branch," ensuring that they run smoothly in the field is no simple undertaking. Her account of bad weather, troublesome locals, and hard-to-manage students provides a cautionary tale. Those who do take or are considering taking students outdoors for more than a few hours will want to read this essay for its insights into the real-world intrusions on learning in the field.

Overcoming gender stereotypes in outdoor education is another aspect of field teaching that should concern us, say Britain A. Scott and Steven M. Hoffman. Their article, "Woodswomen and 'Super Studs': Gender Issues in a Northwoods Environmental Studies Program," provides an insightful analysis of outdoor education's "manly" beginnings. The essay makes instructors aware of how gender issues affect group dynamics.

The question of student demographics is another major consideration for instructors planning field sessions. As Barbara "Barney" Nelson makes clear in "Building Community on a Budget in the Big Bend of Texas," not all students can afford the time or money to take extended trips in high-profile wilderness areas. Her essay helps us rethink how questions of environmental justice impact teaching outdoors and the types of trips we can offer our students.

"Urban Nature as a Scene of Instruction," by John Tallmadge, is the final essay in Part III and the last in the collection. It reminds those teaching in urban or suburban settings that city landscapes are valuable "outdoor laboratories" and that the excursion model—taking students into "remote, idealized landscapes"—can limit their desire and ability to understand those outside their front doors. Cities, Tallmadge observes, are ideal places to engage with the physical world, and we would be wise not to neglect such places in our understanding of what it means to teach outdoors.

❋ COREY LEE LEWIS

Facing the Challenge

Overcoming the Common Obstacles
to Running a Successful Field Studies Course

The star-streaked sky turned above us, as a crescent moon dropped by degrees behind a distant granite ridge. We lay back, resting our weary muscles and sore feet from a long day on the Pacific Crest Trail, and basked in the restorative waters of a natural hot spring. As the thermal water pooled around our weary bodies, steam rose in wisps and whorls through the still night air. We pillowed our heads on rocks and began to relive the events of the past few days, sharing our stories with each other and sending them skyward to follow the hot spring's steamy prayers into the night.

From inside the warm embrace of the hot spring's waters, we watched the sky and the landscape open before us, and in turn something inside each of us seemed to open, to blossom and unfold in the night. Looking back, not one of us will recall another class, another educational experience that so greatly affected us, so often caught us by surprise, and allowed us to surprise even ourselves. Never before, and perhaps never again, would we find our minds so open and eager, our stories—those we had lived and were living—so significant and so beautiful when told.

Just as the beauty and power of field studies experiences often come in the form of unexpected encounters with dramatic landscapes and wildlife, the challenges and difficulties presented by teaching in the field often come upon the unwary instructor by surprise. However, with a little foresight and a judicious amount of careful planning, even the novice field instructor can ensure that the challenges most commonly associated with teaching in the field are overcome with efficiency and, perhaps, with a little grace. In this article I would like to outline some of the most common obstacles a first-time field instructor may face and offer a few suggestions for meeting them that should be of service to instructors who are relatively new to field-based education. Even for instructors with years of experience developing and teaching campus-based curriculum, initiation into field-based, experiential education can present a variety of unusual and unexpected difficulties.

Recognizing the unique challenges common to field-studies courses and having a clear plan of action for meeting them, prior to departing from the security of the university campus, is the first step toward ensuring that one is successful in navigating the difficult terrain associated with planning and executing them. The common problems facing most field-studies classes can be divided into five basic categories: administrative, logistical, managerial, academic, and ethical.

ADMINISTRATIVE CHALLENGES

The most important administrative obstacles that must be overcome when developing field-based programs at the university level include deciding how the course will be offered and funded, recognizing the importance of full-time enrollment credits, and assessing the impact of field-based educational opportunities on student recruitment and retention.

At most universities the primary challenge the administration poses is that the instructor find a balance between the maximum number of students he or she can manage in the field and the minimum number of students necessary for running the class without suffering a financial loss. While the average student-instructor ratio at the undergraduate level is approximately fifteen to thirty students per instructor (institutions vary), the number of students that a single instructor can safely and effectively manage in the field is significantly less, ten to fifteen students, depending on the nature of the field course. A candid discussion with one's department head in the very early stages of the planning process will help ascertain, based on the instructor's salary, the minimum number of students who must enroll in the course in order for it to be fiscally sound.

Alternatively, rather than listing a field-based course through a traditional academic department, it is often more feasible to run one through the university's department of continuing education as a self-supporting class. The advantage of a self-supporting class lies in the fact that the instructor's salary is figured on a percentage of student enrollments, and thus fewer students are needed in order to be able to offer the course. However, if necessary, one has to be open to teaching the course at a reduced rate.

A third option, one that I utilized in order to offer the field course on the Pacific Crest Trail described above, was to offer the class through my department as an independent study. The primary advantage of the independent study was that it allowed us to sidestep almost all of our administrative difficulties. However, the major disadvantage was that, since it was an independent study, I received no salary for the instruction. While this is not a viable option for running a sustainable field-studies program, it is a very effective way to run a pilot course or to begin building a successful track record in running field-based courses that can later be used to garner greater administrative and departmental support.

A final option for first-time field-studies instructors who wish to initiate field-based programs in their own university is to add a voluntary field component to a campus-based course. This is often an attractive alternative for new instructors because the field component can be kept short, perhaps consisting of one or two day-long trips that can be offered for variable credit. At the University of Nevada, Reno, we have run a variety of one-credit field components to campus-based classes quite successfully. Some have taken students on a single overnight camping trip; others have consisted of a series of day trips to study sites near campus. Running a successful number of field components to campus-based courses is an effective way to gain experience and convince the administration of the feasibility and efficacy of longer field-studies programs.

A second factor to consider when designing field-based classes is the financial importance of FTEs (full-time enrollment credits) to university departments and administrations. Although summer is often the best time to offer field-based classes, universities receive FTEs only for the fall and spring semesters. These FTEs translate into real dollars for university departments, so spring and fall courses ultimately make the university more money than summer classes. In order to be sensitive to issues regarding FTEs at my institution, for example, I offered the Pacific Crest Trail class as a fall course, even though the field component took place one week prior to the start of the official fall semester. A series of class meetings throughout the fall enabled us to achieve the minimum number of contact hours necessary to list the class during the regular academic year and succeeded in generating valuable FTEs for our department. Regardless of how one decides to run field-based classes, recognizing the financial importance of FTEs to departmental and university administrators is helpful in garnering their support.

A final factor to consider in gaining the administrative support necessary to implement a sustainable field-studies program is the effect that such exciting and unique courses have on student retention and recruitment. For each of the field classes I run, I use a specialized student questionnaire to document the success of the class in recruiting or retaining students at the institution. In general, student responses indicate that they would be more likely to enroll, or remain, at a university that offers field studies and experientially based programs. By gathering such data throughout the inception of UNR's field-studies program, we hope to demonstrate that our field courses actually earn the university money through improving student retention and recruitment rates. Similarly, photographic documentation of the unique educational opportunities provided by field courses should be kept for advertising purposes. In the past, we have used brochures, slide shows, and PowerPoint presentations to inform students and the community at large about the exciting educational adventures available through our field-studies program. Coupled with enthusiastic student testimonials, a few dramatic images of one's classes in the field can be very enticing to prospective students as well as convincing to administrators whose support one seeks.

LOGISTICAL CHALLENGES

After overcoming the administrative challenges that often arise during the planning process, there are four types of logistical problems that must be solved to successfully run a field-based course: supplying food, transportation, and equipment, as well as designing an accurate budget to adequately cover these expenses.

Feeding students adequately and inexpensively in the field is a major factor in keeping student morale high and budgets low. While there are a number of resources available to help plan field-based menus and establish quantities, a simple rule of thumb can be applied for designing an initial budget: $12.00 per student, per day, will cover food costs quite well; each breakfast is figured at $3.00 per student, lunch at $4.00, and dinner at $5.00. Cooking in the field requires a simple but hardy menu, which usually will fall within these budgeting parameters, especially if one purchases inexpensive bulk foods and avoids the more expensive, pre-packaged and freeze-dried items. A primarily vegetarian menu (with a few meat options for omnivores) is usually cheapest and easiest to store and prepare and will not cause problems with students' special dietary needs or commitments. For each of my field courses, students are given a complete menu, broken down by day and meal, well in advance of the field excursion, so that they can supplement the menu with additional items if they deem it necessary. The simplest way to avoid food-related problems is to have clear communication about the menu before the class leaves for the field.

If planned properly, cooking in the field can be one of the highlights of a field-study experience rather than a source of frustration. In the field, students take turns helping prepare and clean up after meals. On large field courses, two or three students can sign up for each meal, while on smaller courses the work can be meted out in a much more organic fashion. Regardless, food in the field always tastes good and disappears quickly.

In order to supply dependable transportation for field-based courses, the University and State Motor Pool Departments are generally the cheapest and most reliable of options. Some universities also have student associations that can supply vehicles for accredited field-based programs. Twelve to fifteen passenger vans are generally the most efficient means of transporting a large group of students with their associated gear, and, unlike buses, do not require a commercial driver's license to operate. The cost of vehicle rental, like food and other expenses, is factored into the budget and covered through student fees. Relying on personal vehicles, either the instructor's or the students', may enable one to run classes more inexpensively but increases the risk of mechanical failure and reduces the sustainability of one's programs.

For most field-studies trips, I furnish group equipment, such as stoves and cookware, while each student is required to supply his or her own personal gear. It is imperative that the instructor creates a comprehensive equipment list, reviews it with students during pre-trip meetings, and checks the suitability of their gear before leaving. I usually include rental information on the equipment list, so students can easily rent any items that they do not already own. Many universities have campus recreation departments that rent camping gear at very affordable prices.

I strongly recommend a gear check during a pre-trip meeting in order to ensure that each student has the appropriate gear. On the Pacific Crest Trail class, for example, where we were backpacking approximately eight miles a day for a week, I neglected such an inspection, which later caused me some regret. One student showed up with her brother's twenty-year-old external-frame pack, which was built for a person almost a foot taller and eighty pounds heavier than she. Needless to say, the poorly fitting pack caused her much discomfort and the rest of us some inconvenience. On the second day of the trip, I had to take the pack straps off and secure them with duct tape and cord in a makeshift way so that the pack would fit her better. Several days later, the bruises on her shoulders and her added fatigue resulted in my having to carry her backpack, in addition to my own, for the entire day so that we could make it to our next camp before nightfall. While we were able to meet that particular challenge with good humor and a sense of camaraderie, it could have been easily avoided by checking each student's gear in advance.

In addition, because many students have had little to no backcountry experience, gear lists should be as detailed as possible, and should include even those items that seem relatively obvious to the instructor. For example, I have found that it is unrealistic to assume students will know that a summer excursion at high elevations will require both sunscreen and a baseball cap during the day, as well as gloves, a sweater, a jacket, and a stocking cap during the evening. Even though I include such items as a field journal and pencils on their gear lists, students have arrived in the field without such basic and seemingly obvious class tools, another reason why pre-trip gear inspections are beneficial.

Pre-trip meetings are also necessary to ensure that the instructor and his or her students have made preparations in advance to handle any safety or liability issues that may arise in the field. I compile a comprehensive list of the students' names, next of kin, and contact information in case of emergencies, and have each student sign a standard waiver-of-liability form. The waiver-of-liability form, while not necessarily a guarantee against all eventualities that could arise in the field, is customarily accepted as adequate protection against litigation by most educational institutions. The first-time field instructor can easily obtain model waivers that are accepted by his or her administration by contacting either the campus recreation or the athletic department. These departments are generally required to have students sign waivers of liability before competing in intercollegiate athletics, participating in intramural sports, or even using the campus gym. Before departing for the field, I leave the student waivers and a copy of our emergency contact list with a supervising faculty member on campus. In addition, I keep my own copy of the emergency contact list with me in the field and put one in our group medical kit. While I have never had the unfortunate occasion to need this list, or the student waivers, such precautions are imperative for running a safe and successful backcountry course, as well as for protecting yourself in the event that a student is hurt.

It is also necessary to have students list their allergies in writing and, if they require one, to have them bring their own epinephrine pins into the field. Being exposed to an allergen, such as a particular type of food or an insect sting, can quickly become a life-threatening situation in the backcountry. Should a student suffer from a severe allergy, without having his or her prescribed epi-pin available for treatment, the risk of anaphylactic shock and death is real and should be taken very seriously.

After the menu has been set, vehicles reserved, and group gear purchased or found, it is necessary to create a budget and establish the cost per student of attending the course. Typically, field-based courses have lab fees associated with them to cover these costs, which are not factored into the students' regular tuition. An efficiently designed course can be run fairly inexpensively for students, however. On the Pacific Crest Trail course, for example, each student paid one hundred dollars in lab fees for an all-expenses-paid, week-long backpacking trip in the heart of the Sierra Nevada range. Their fees paid for every aspect of the trip except for their own personal camping gear and tuition, covering expenses for food, transportation, camping fees, and wilderness permits.

MANAGERIAL CHALLENGES IN THE FIELD

Once the students and instructor make it into the field, an entirely new set of obstacles and potential problems arises. While classroom management is a concern of every instructor, managing student behavior becomes increasingly important when one is teaching in a classroom that contains significant physical dangers, as well as the psychological hazards of being forced to live with a group of strangers in unfamiliar and uncomfortable surroundings. The field instructor must accomplish the following three basic tasks in order to effectively manage student behavior in the field: one, clearly establish rules to ensure the safety of each student; two, properly assess student abilities; and three, anticipate and ameliorate common psychological stresses.

Ensuring the physical safety of one's students should be the central concern of every field instructor. At the start of each field course, I have very frank discussions with my students regarding what types of behavior are allowed and what will not be tolerated. Some of the safety concerns we address include discussing the necessity for students to stay with the group and inform others of their whereabouts at all times, and how to purify water properly, prevent dehydration and heat stroke, as well as recognize common insects, animals, and topographic features that might present a danger.

During these discussions, I use stories from past trips to illustrate to students the necessity of obeying these ground rules. On one field-studies trip to the Jarbidge Wilderness Area in northern Nevada, for example, one young man's early evening ramble failed to bring him back by the time that we were sitting down to dinner. Since he was planning on taking only a short hike, he didn't think it was necessary to notify anyone of his plans. For those of us left back in camp, however, we were suddenly faced with the realization that one of our fellow students was missing. As night was falling, a search party was forced to scour the precipitous cliffs surrounding the area, without dinner and at much risk to themselves, while the errant student sat safe and sound watching the sunset, completely oblivious to the danger and worry he was causing the rest of the group. While he was found, and no one was hurt, such unnerving situations can usually be avoided by communicating very clear and unbreakable ground rules to your students well before any problems can arise.

Field instructors should also take care not to overestimate their students' physical ability to travel and work under adverse conditions, as well as their capacity to cope mentally with stress and fatigue. During our trip on the Pacific Crest Trail, for example, I unfortunately overestimated how many miles we could make each day. This was, in fact, the first course I had run where we were backpacking to a new campsite each day, rather than remaining at one or two base camps and simply taking short day hikes throughout the surrounding area. Figuring that on similar backpacking trips I easily averaged fourteen miles per day, I planned our looping route so that we would need to cover only seven to eight miles each day. I soon found, however, that it took us much longer to make and break camp and that we made much slower time on the trail than I had at first anticipated. We managed to make each scheduled campsite, but we had to sacrifice valuable time that should have been used for field research, class discussions, and academic exercises, as well as simply day hiking and exploring near our campsites.

For many students with little to no camping experience, simply sleeping, eating, and hiking in the backcountry presents them with a host of new, and often daunting, challenges. The stress that some students feel while living under what may seem to them to be such adverse conditions can create discord in the group and detract from the educational experience. In order to avoid potential problems, I speak candidly with the students as a group about how such stress might affect them and ask them to be watchful for signs of it in themselves and to be patient and understanding when it manifests in others. I also make a conscious effort to check in with each student individually throughout the trip, asking how they are doing, if they are sleeping and eating okay, if their gear is holding up, and so on. Such personal attention can do much to ameliorate any undue stress in students before or as it arises. It is also beneficial for field instructors to have a thick skin and to refrain from taking anything personally should a particular student express impatience, anger, or frustration, or act out in a less than cordial manner. Likewise, field instructors should be mindful of how the stress of being responsible for their students' lives and experiences affects them as well. By beginning each class with an honest and supportive discussion of such issues, one can usually avoid problems before they arise, while also having an established forum to return to should the group need to discuss and solve such problems.

While field-studies experiences can present students with a variety of difficult challenges, they also allow students the opportunity to exceed their own limitations and expectations. On a creative-writing class that took us to the high desert country of the Silver Peak Wilderness Study Area, for example, I found myself confronted with a group of students, none of whom had ever camped before. One of the many memorable experiences of the trip was that by the end of the week-long outing, each student had voluntarily opted to spend a night in one of the many caves that filled the canyon walls of the region. Following my lead, these urban students each selected a suitable cave, gave up their tents, and enjoyed the unique experience of sleeping encased in a wild, earthen womb through the long night. Many of the students later wrote about this experience in their journals, spoke about it often with their friends, and saw it as one of the many highlights of the trip.

ACADEMIC CHALLENGES

One of the most common criticisms from those who have never taught, nor participated in, field-based education is founded on the assumption that field-based classes are not academically rigorous enough to compare to a traditional, campus-based course. Depending on one's field of instruction, this critique may or may not pose a challenge. In the sciences, for example, field studies are generally recognized as being tied closely enough with course content to be relevant, useful, and even necessary. Within the humanities, however, especially in the field of literary studies, the legitimacy of field-based education is often questioned. Because literary scholars have traditionally labored under an erroneous assumption of textual primacy—the belief that all meaning resides solely in the text—they often fail to recognize the legitimacy, and in fact need, of studying the extra-textual relationships surrounding a literary work. English professors readily recognize, for example, that in order to understand T. S. Eliot's "Wasteland," or James Joyce's "Ulysses," one must also study the canonical texts and ideas of the Western tradition to which these works so often refer. These same scholars, however, are less apt to recognize that in order to understand John Muir's nonfiction, Gary Snyder's poetry, or Mary Austin's fiction, an analogous study of the extra-textual environments to which they refer, and about which they write, is also necessary. While the students in my field-based English and Literature courses study fewer texts than those in my campus-based classes, they come to a much deeper understanding of the author's aims, ideas, and methods, as well as a better understanding of how the work is received by readers, and how their own process of reception, response, and composition is linked to the text's attempt to make meaning in the world. As a result, while field-studies courses may not offer the breadth of a campus-based class, they offer a much more in-depth understanding of course content and are considerably more effective in teaching students about the methodologies and practices of their field of study, as well as its worldly relevance.

A second perceptual challenge facing many field-studies courses regarding their academic value is that they often appear to contain fewer hours of instruction than semester-long campus-based classes. While it is often true that field-based classes are compressed in time when compared to the college semester, even a relatively short field course easily exceeds the number of contact hours achieved by a traditional campus-based class. Utilizing this time effectively is the key academic challenge facing the field instructor. In order to answer this challenge, I require students to read all of the required texts for the class prior to departing for the field, and I schedule a rigorous field itinerary that consists of multiple classes each day. In addition, I incorporate the use of a field library and focus much of the instruction on field-journaling and researching methodologies.

In order to ensure that my students' time in the field will be spent as effectively as possible, I utilize a series of class meetings before and after the field-based portion of the course. During our pre-trip meetings, students discuss assigned readings, conduct written responses to course material, and begin to engage with important course-related issues and themes. A rigorous schedule of required readings and written responses prior to departing from the university campus can be a very effective tool for ensuring that one's students are able to get the most out of the field-based portion of their studies. After returning from the field-study excursion, students engage in research, write, workshop, and revise their final papers, as well as share their work with each other and reflect upon the overall experience. These post-trip meetings allow students time to take advantage of university research facilities and to intellectually process their field-based experiences with direction and feedback from the instructor and their peers. Pre- and post-trip meetings are useful both for preparing students academically for their field studies and for supplying a sense of intellectual and personal closure to the course.

Once in the field, I utilize a class schedule similar to any campus-based course, with class discussions, assignments, activities, and workshops, except that the schedule is compressed in time. Depending on the nature of the field course, I usually schedule four to six formal class meetings per day in addition to assigning time for individual work and student-instructor conferences. Our time during the course is spent, as in campus-based classes, exploring key ideas and issues, responding to the texts and to each other, and analyzing specific passages and rhetorical techniques. Unlike what we can do in courses confined to the classroom, however, we are also able to explore connections between the text and the extra-textual environment to which it refers, measure our own experience against the author's, and mimic his or her methods in our own writing.

In addition to these standard pedagogical practices, I have come to rely on the use of two innovative strategies to aid students in making connections between their field experiences and the content of the course. The first of these strategies is to incorporate the use of a carefully chosen library of field guides and selected readings, which accompanies us into the field. On backpacking courses, like the Pacific Crest Trail trip, I carry several field guides myself and often assign one for each student to carry. In this way we have a fairly large number of resources to aid in our field research during the trip. With a base camp and vehicular support, I assemble a more comprehensive field library that often includes other useful tools such as microscopes and field glasses. Regardless of the format, it is essential to have a few field guides specific to the region one is studying in and to utilize assignments in the field that encourage students to become familiar with using these resources. Field-based assignments of this type are very effective in introducing students to methods for conducting both textual and field-based research and in giving them practice in synthesizing these two types of information.

A second strategy I use to introduce students to field research methodologies and to connect their wilderness experiences with course material is to focus much of our academic work on the various manners in which a field journal can be utilized as a tool for interpretation, analysis, and research. Through a series of both directed and undirected journal assignments, students learn to use their field journals to collect data, respond to readings, reflect upon significant experiences, synthesize field and textual research, record daily activities and memorable events, and begin drafting final papers.

A field-journaling assignment I often use in the beginning of the course, for example, is to have students pick a particular species or geographical feature and sketch it in their journals. The students are then assigned to write about their subject objectively, linking their own observations with information gathered from research in our field library. Finally, they write subjectively about their particular object of study, recording their own personal feelings, associations, and reflections. We often utilize the work of such natural historians as John Muir and Charles Darwin as models for such field-journaling exercises, studying their rhetorical techniques and practicing their methodologies. In my literature courses, we will then use our journals to analyze how other authors have chosen to present similar species in their work, to deepen our understanding of their extra-textual allusions and references, and to analyze how the process of reception is affected by the reader's own experience.

Nothing engages students with their environment, and their course work, better than a series of instructional field-journaling exercises. In addition, nothing is more rewarding for me as a field instructor than to sit back in the pine duff, lean against the plated bark of an old-growth ponderosa pine, and watch as my students disperse throughout the forest to study and write about the natural world and their place in it.

I still recall our first field-journaling exercise on the Pacific Crest Trail course. The sparkling sunlight fell in drops and streams from the glittering canopy of ponderosa pine and red fir, to pool on the forest floor in a mosaic of bright puddles and shaded shorelines. Scattered throughout the forest, my students sat writing in their field journals and resting their weary feet and sore backs from the toil of the trail. One student sat on a polished boulder next to a small cascading stream, her bare, pink feet soaking in the frigid water as it tumbled down from snowfields in the high country above us; another stood mesmerized by an ancient red cedar, attempting to capture its gnarled branches and massive form on the pages of his field journal. Time passed and we reconvened to share our studies, each student teaching the others about the species he or she had been studying, sharing their new knowledge as well as their personal reflections and feelings. Often on such field-studies trips, I assign a similar exercise each day, ensuring that the students become practiced in the process of field observation and research, while learning about a variety of local species and ecological processes.

ETHICAL CHALLENGES

In order to ensure that one's field-studies classes are more than some form of extractive educational industry, the ecologically aware field instructor must address two important ethical complications that arise from taking a large group of students into sensitive ecosystems and un-trammeled backcountry areas. The first ethical concern that must be addressed relates to teaching students to do no harm to the ecosystems in which they will be living, while the second involves finding ways of giving back to these natural landscapes, teaching students how to be advocates for those special places they have come to know and love.

Whenever I enter the field with a new group of students, one of our first topics of discussion (along with safety and rules relating to student behavior) is to cover the principles of Leave-No-Trace outdoor ethics. We discuss everything from how to dispose of uneaten food, trash, and human waste, to the need for protecting sensitive water and cultural resources, as well as the various steps we can take to minimize our impact on fragile ecosystems and natural areas. While some of the topics the field instructor must cover may strain his or her sensibilities and embarrass some students, a good dose of humor and honesty is always helpful. I can still recall teaching an all-female class how to dig a cat-hole and properly dispose of human waste following Leave-No-Trace principles for camping in the backcountry. It was a little awkward for me, being the only male present, but with some laughter and friendly banter, I was able to demonstrate the proper digging and squatting technique, as well as discuss the various options available for toilet paper in the field.

Likewise, when a student of mine was fortunate enough to find a hand-woven Paiute bowl deep in the heart of the Silver Peak Wilderness Study Area, it was helpful to have the Leave-No-Trace principles to rely on as authoritative support for why we were not allowed to keep such culturally important artifacts for ourselves. I can still recall our excitement, as she emerged from a small, sand-bottomed cave gingerly carrying an ancient relic from that land's long cultural history in her hand. As we studied the bowl, we noted the willow shoot and yucca fiber construction, the tight weave of a master craftsman, and a series of tiny teeth marks left by kangaroo rats along the rim. We debated the bowl's use, pondered how long it had been there and why it was left, and attempted to articulate the strange feeling that we were standing on the edge of a vast chasm of time, gaining a glimpse of history that few people will ever be fortunate enough to share.

I was apprehensive, at first, that the role of discovery would lead my student into the desire for ownership, and I was afraid of the resentment she might feel toward me when I would tell her, as I had to, that the bowl belonged to its maker and the land more than to us. Our earlier discussions, however, about the role of public lands and our responsibility to preserve them for future generations, led her, without prompting, to reenter the low cave on hands and knees, and reverently place the bowl back on its bed of sand and dust. Such experiences have led me to believe that instructing students in the proper manner for recreating in, and protecting, our public lands should be a central part of any field-studies program that seeks to maintain the privilege of visiting these awe-inspiring and fragile places.

In addition to teaching students how to refrain from damaging the natural landscapes they study and live in, a final ethical challenge facing the environmentally aware field-studies instructor is to guide students into becoming environmental advocates who actively seek ways in which they can give back to the places that have given them so much so freely. As Rick Bass asks in the *Brown Dog of the Yaak*, "Can literature help protect a place? Can some reciprocity exist between the real, fixed anchor of a wild place, and the intangible values—chief among them the art—produced from that source?"[1] In order to answer this challenge, I always try to incorporate some aspect of Service-Learning in each of my field courses. In some cases this has taken the form of engaging the students in a small trail reconstruction project, or some aspect of environmental restoration, such as tree planting or the removal of invasive species. In other cases, I have tried to wed the service project with the course content in a more direct manner. During a creative writing course held in the Silver Peak Wilderness Study Area, for example, my students acted as advocates for the recommended wilderness area to receive permanent protection through formal Wilderness designation. After spending a week living in the high desert country surrounding Silver Peak, my students returned to the university campus and put together a grant-funded publication of their own creative writing and photography that demonstrated the unique biological and cultural values of the area and advocated for its permanent protection. The published journal was then sent to key land managers, politicians, and environmental groups to rally support for the cause.

The most enduring benefit for the students who participated in the Silver Peak course came from this particular project where they were able to use their talents to address a critical need and protect a place they had come to know and love. In addition, the service project added much-needed praxis to the students' writing and took them through every aspect of the publication process, as they struggled to design the layout of their publication, revise each other's work, and stay within budgetary restraints. For those young creative writers, the opportunity to have dramatic life experiences, to come to know and love a particular place, and to write and publish in order to protect it, served as an unparalleled educational experience that would be impossible to reproduce within the confines of a university classroom.

Ironically, while field-studies classes offer the best opportunities to utilize course work and student abilities to help others and effect positive change in the world, one of the perceptual challenges field instructors face is that their courses are often viewed as being too much fun or too self-serving to be academically rigorous or beneficial. When making these criticisms of field studies, however, we would do well to recognize that at their very basis all educational activities are inherently self-centered. Through them we seek to develop the self, usually for self-centered motives such as gaining knowledge, securing a career, or increasing our income. Outdoor recreation and wilderness experiences, likewise, tend to be self-centered activities where participants focus on what they will gain from the experience: adventure, solitude, or relaxation. Both activities, however, can be focused and applied in selfless ways, and herein lies the challenge. Field-based courses, due to their very nature, lend themselves more readily to connecting with the community than do campus-based classes. By taking students out into wild places and backcountry areas, we incur a certain obligation to protect and preserve those areas for subsequent generations. Students are generally grateful for having the opportunity, and especially the encouragement, to offer up some form of personal remuneration to the places that have gifted them with such powerful and transformative educational experiences.

Upon returning from the Pacific Crest Trail course, I came across the following passage in a student's journal, written on the last day of the class, as we reluctantly left the PCT trailhead and returned to our waiting vehicles.

When I escape into the wilderness for a few days it is usually from a primarily selfish motive, but I always emerge with more than I expected. I not only return feeling rested, balanced and connected, but I have plenty of all that good stuff to go around. I give extra long hugs to my friends and family. I am especially patient at work. I smile at everyone I pass. I tell stories about the wonderful things I saw. And I remember. . . . I remember the intimate connection I share with the wild animals on the street. I remember to give thanks. . . . And, I remember that I came to the city to remind others of what they forgot.[2]

As a field-studies instructor, what I remember most are those unique stories that can come only from the wild, stories that you cup in your hand like a bird with a broken wing and bring back to care for and to share with others. I remember hiking with my students, deep in the heart of the John Muir Wilderness, and stumbling upon the hulking and grunting shape of a full-grown black bear. Unaware of our approach, she stood, scratching her back on the rough bark of a young ponderosa pine, the slender, thirty-foot-tall tree tracing great arcs in the air above her. Pressed deep in my memory, I can still see her massive, almost-human footprints in the sand beside our trail. And I still recall with fondness the wonder in my students' eyes, as we marveled at her size and strength, and the concern we felt for the rare and disappearing wilderness that was needed to hold her.

In many places, the land itself remembers my students. Protective legislation, newly constructed hiking trails, and recently planted trees stand as testimony to the challenges they struggled to face and overcome. They carry the memories of these victories and defeats with them, knowing (for the first time perhaps) that they have both the ability and the responsibility to give back to the natural world as graciously as it gives to them.

Notes

1. Rick Bass, *Brown Dog of the Yaak: Essays on Art and Activism* (Minneapolis: Milkweed Editions, 1999), 86.

2. Carly Johnson, Student Field Journal, English 490/790. University of Nevada, Reno, Fall 2001.

In Thoreau's Wake on the West Branch

L
ike all rivers, the West Branch has its moods. That weekend it was
feeling weepy. Often it sobbed outright, tossing its bank-side treetops
like hair, as if gripped by wild fits of riparian anguish; other times, drained
and weary, the sky withdrew its whipping rain and left behind a frigid
quiet, the air temperature dropping enough to lacquer our wet shoulders
with ice. With such tantrums does northern Maine often mark the transition from fall to winter, but I wasn't thinking of that when, several weeks
earlier, I told eight college students we'd be making this trip. Soon it
would become clear I hadn't thought about a lot of things.

When the academic year began in early September, the days were
green-gold and warm, the nights just cool enough to make you reach for
an extra shirt or sweater. Even after the first frosts, a long-shadowed Indian summer set in for a leisurely spell—right up until two days before my
Thoreau Seminar headed for the West Branch of the Penobscot River,
known in those parts simply as the West Branch. Tuesday was as beautifully wine-ripe as a Maine autumn ever gets, the last burgundy leaves
slowly drifting earthward; Wednesday broke overcast and chill and disin-
tegrated by nightfall into a pummeling rain. All day Thursday I prayed for
surcease. I was still at it when Friday arrived and our loaded van-and-
trailer outfit departed campus with its crew already damp under the col-
lars, thanks to the half hour we'd spent in the weather securing our canoes
and other gear on and in the trailer. Leaning hard into my paddle on Saturday, our first full day on the river, I kept my head down so the icy water
could pour off my raincoat's hat brim and land in the boat between my
frozen feet. Memo to Self: Henry paddled this very stretch, yes, okay, and
other Maine rivers as well, on several occasions. *Always in summer.*

Not that the trip's timing had been entirely within my control. Summer was out of the question, as the college did not offer the Thoreau

Seminar in its summer session for the very good reason that there was no summer session. Spring term was decidedly off limits, since most waterways north of Augusta don't usually thaw out before May—that is, about when the school year ends and students rush off to summer jobs. For both logistic and academic reasons, we couldn't easily go in early autumn: on the one hand, the college's canoes and three-tiered canoe trailer were tied up till late October by the paddling classes being taught through the Outdoor Wilderness Rec Department, and on the other hand, I wanted my seminar students to get a lot of Thoreau's short essays under their belts before we took up *The Maine Woods* and set out to re-create part of the journey described in its "Chesuncook" chapter. That pretty much left us just the last weekend in October, and thank goodness we had that: on November 1 (or October 31, those years when it falls on a weekend) deer-hunting season begins in Maine. No time to have a passel of students in the north woods, even if they would be mostly on open water. Which was also why there could be no postponing this particular trip in the hope of getting better weather the following weekend.

Using *The Maine Woods* and J. Parker Huber's indispensable *The Wildest Country: A Guide to Thoreau's Maine*, I had determined that a certain thirty-five-mile section of the West Branch could be paddled in one long weekend, travel time to and from the river included (Unity College is located about a three-and-a-half-hour drive southeast of the spot), thus avoiding the problem of taking students away for too long from their other classes. This stretch of river had, I reasoned, other virtues to recommend it: we could put in at the very place where Thoreau vividly describes an evening spent camping with and eavesdropping on his Native American companions, whose conversation mesmerized him while he watched one tan the hide of a moose the party had killed. We could sleep at a couple of the same stream-side places where he had slept, the Forest Service having since established and maintained them as legitimate recreational campsites, complete with picnic tables, fire rings, and rustic privies. (Crowded with recreational paddlers in summer, the West Branch empties out almost completely in fall; across the years, my seminars always had their pick of campsites.) For most of the journey we'd be in flatwater, which meant advanced canoeing skill would be unnecessary (when students enrolled in the seminar, no effort was made to be sure they could handle a boat and paddle). And the take-out spot, near the head of Umbazooksus Stream, would be accessible by logging roads—or so it appeared from my Maine atlas—to our van and the two seniors we'd bring along on the trip to drive shuttle.

Although I had picked our put-in and take-out destinations, I left most of the rest of the trip planning up to the seminar participants, figuring it would be a good learning experience. Early in the semester, before they were assigned to read any of the essays in *The Maine Woods,* I had them bring the book to class so we could examine one of the appendices included in our edition. "Outfit for an Excursion" lists Henry's (we liked to think of him as Henry) suggested supplies for a twelve-day venture of three men, one of them a local Penobscot to be hired as a guide. Our own "outfit" would eventually differ considerably—few among us owned an "India-rubber knapsack," though a couple of us did have wool shirts— and so, of course, would our party, there being few Indians on hand for hire in 1993, and more women (three) than Henry would have ever consented to take along. Nevertheless, all differences aside, looking over his list of supplies as well as some maps of the north woods that he had used (found in Robert F. Stowell's *Thoreau Gazetteer*) helped the students to start organizing their thoughts when I divided them into task-oriented teams. The equipment team would procure, either from the Outdoor Rec Department or from among our own numbers, the necessary canoes, paddles, lifejackets, tents, sleeping bags, Coleman stove and fuel, cooking pots, first-aid kit, and sundry other camping gear. The food team would compose a menu and procure the foodstuffs. Comparing contemporary and nineteenth-century maps, the routing team would determine which portions of the river, within the segment I had identified, were still as Henry had known them and which had "drowned" or otherwise "moved" during the intervening hundred and forty-odd years, thanks largely to dam projects on other parts of the West Branch. This team would also determine the feasibility, given time constraints, of a side excursion on foot into the riverside village of Chesuncook, which we would come to about two-thirds of the way into the journey (Henry had known it in its early days as a logging camp). I would reserve the van and canoe trailer; recruit two non-seminar, upper-class students to drive shuttle; and request of the provost the necessary funds to pay entrance fees at the forest gates—getting to the river entailed passing through privately owned, timber-company land—as well as cash for re-filling the van's gas tank on the way home.

Most of the planning and preparation came off splendidly. Or I should say, the students did a good job with their respective tasks; it was their fearless leader they should have feared, since her very fearlessness unwittingly set them up for potential disaster.

Why she was so confident, so brash, I cannot easily say. True, she had done a good bit of paddling in her time, and she knew how to teach beginners the basic strokes and the basics of canoe safety, should any of the party prove beginners (only one did). True, she'd also done her share of primitive camping, and she could assume most of the class would have as well, since Unity students typically choose to spend more of their days and nights outside than in. And she could swim. But not till the van neared the river that rainy Friday evening did it even occur to her to wonder or ask the obvious, whether everyone else could swim (affirmative). Nor did she know CPR or any other of those other life-saving skills that a wilderness emergency might make necessary. Cell phones weren't so ubiquitous in the early '90s, so she didn't think to take one, nor any flares for signaling distress. In subsequent years, on subsequent Thoreau Seminar trips, she would consider all of these things—chiefly because she'd had such a memorable time, that first weekend, kicking herself for not having done so.

Perhaps most important, that first year, the dim professor hadn't actually made this particular trip before—hadn't scouted the entire route herself ahead of time. Back in the summer she had driven as far as the river's edge, the put-in point she had in mind, but after getting out of the car and having a look around, she'd gone home. And it wasn't just the river route she later realized she should have scouted but also the roads the shuttle drivers would need to use to find the paddlers way downstream, at the take-out. It never occurred to her she could lose those two, the drivers—yet lose them she did, for well over twenty-four hours. Worse, she came frighteningly close to losing them for good. But I get ahead of my story.

Minor hitches arose early in the planning. For example, the student group assigned to work out the food ("Deborah," "Martin," and "Tom"—names have been changed to protect the guilty) ran into a problem. Whereas we had all assumed the cafeteria staff would supply us with provisions—they commonly did so for classes heading out on field trips, filling boxes with peanut butter, bagels, pasta, jars of pasta sauce, coffee, sugar, and so on—they wouldn't do so for us. All the students in the seminar, it turned out, lived off campus and therefore were not on the cafeteria's meal plan. I hadn't realized that the staff made a distinction, though as soon as it was pointed out to me I saw the sense of it. Okay, so I talked to the class: what if we all pitch in, say, eight dollars, which the food team will use to buy groceries; if the total amount falls short of what they need, I'll make up the difference. The students readily agreed, recognizing they'd spend at least that much if they stayed home and fed themselves according to their usual routines.

However, there was one more food issue that proved less tractable. In discussion it became clear that most of the students saw the value of vegetarian meals for the weekend, so we could avoid dragging along a cooler (takes up a lot of room in a canoe) and also avoid the smelly problem of meat scraps. But Vance would have none of it: this tall, broad-shouldered, country-bred fellow in canvas work pants and scuffed boots not only enjoyed eating meat, he had actually worked up, over the years, a firm personal ethos that said if he was going to eat meat, he must be willing to kill and prepare the animal himself. (Oddly, he had this much in common with strict vegetarians, a conviction that one must take full responsibility for one's dietary choices, since eating to live necessarily entails killing of some kind.) He insisted, then, on his right to have meat at least once each day while we were out, since for him it was a right hard-won, a right he expected to exercise whenever he wished. (He really did raise and kill his own chickens and at least one hog a year on the farm near campus where he worked part-time as an extra hand.) And of course he offered to provide the meat—pork chops he had put up in his freezer the winter before. The class half smiled, shook their heads no thanks, but let off arguing with him for the time being. Later in the semester the question arose again, and though Vance once more stood his ground, by the time a third such discussion transpired, just days before the trip, he backed down and agreed to the vegetarian approach, convinced his position was decidedly minority.

Logistics alone suggested to me at the start of this debate that the vegetarian approach would be best, and I could have settled the question sooner by decree. But I chose neutrality so the students would settle it themselves; a tension had evolved between Vance and his Thoreau Seminar professor, so I had to play him carefully to make sure he never perceived me as taking sides with anyone against him.

This tricky relationship of ours ended up having some bearing on ensuing events, so I want to take a moment here to set it up. I had been running the class the way I was accustomed to conducting an upper-level literature course: with a measure of informality—it was a seminar, after all, and thus built largely upon class discussion—but also with a subtle, constant pressure on the students to read and think very carefully, both in oral discussions and in their papers. A somewhat older-than-average senior who had always struggled in academic venues of this kind, Vance found this seminar pretty daunting. Some of Thoreau can be tough for even ordinary students to read (especially their first time), but in Vance's case— as one of the special-needs types that Unity College has, for most of its history, accepted and worked closely with in its Learning Resources Center—much of Thoreau's writing may as well have been in Sanskrit. His discomfort deepened, I think, when he realized that several of the other students were really digging this stuff and saying some near-brilliant things in class; no doubt Vance was also aware that they were writing strong papers, whereas I had to ask him to revise more than once, just to get work of passing quality. If he was not happy with me, neither could it be said that I was thrilled with him. Although I like to think I take great pains to work with a struggling student, making the extra time for him outside of class as necessary to help him with the material, and gently urging him during class—by means of the occasional, direct invitation—to trust that his comments will be valued, this time I found my patience tested by Vance's defiant attitude. It often came out in the form of deliberate attempts to derail group discussions: "Just who decided this guy was Great Literature, anyway?" Okay, that one I could try to take seriously for a minute, overlooking the dismissive tone and offering what I knew of how Thoreau's literary reputation had developed. But then, trying to move things back to a focus on the text before us, I'd have another challenge of some kind, from the same predictable corner of the room where Vance's long legs spilled before him out of his desk, slightly apart from the rest of the group. He may have needed an upper-level seminar like this one in order to graduate, but he was determined to make me understand he resented the fact.

To keep my cool, I'd sometimes recall to myself the words of a professor I'd known in grad school who, gazing out over a campus quad full of students staging some protest or other, had quietly remarked, "These are the souls that try men's times."

Friday finally, and as we gather in the parking lot behind the Outdoor Rec building, where the van and trailer await our burden of gear, I ponder the news I've just had that two class members are backing out, having decided the rain is not likely to let up and that they just don't feel like dealing with it. Apparently my simple assumption there would be full attendance hadn't been good enough; perhaps I should have required the trip as a condition for passing the course. But that approach bothered me, too; might some of the students have dropped the class—thereby forfeiting a chance to read Thoreau in depth and with formal guidance? Did I really want to send the signal that Thoreau could be read with me only if students were willing to paddle a river one weekend, come hell or (literally) high water? Not having anticipated defectors, I had no alternative assignment ready to pitch their way. If I had, in all likelihood those two would have chosen to come with us.

These thoughts occupied me while Martin, Josh, and I packed the trailer, Charlie filled big plastic jerry cans with drinking water, Deborah ran to a friend's dorm room to borrow some Gore-tex rain pants, and Tom took to the campus police a memo from me bearing a complete list of the trip participants (minus two names hastily marked off) as well as outlines of our route and itinerary. Vance came loping up, took in at one glance the packing that had been accomplished so far, and dropped his knapsack to the ground next to the trailer, saying to no one in particular, "If you'll allow me." He pulled out the stuff we had stowed and started over. I didn't even have time to be annoyed—immediately I saw, from the way he was re-doing our work, that I must never have packed a trailer before. He was good, really good, fitting backpacks and sleeping bags into spaces between the thwarts of the lower, overturned canoes, tucking protective tarps over various sections, guiding ropes in and around the gear and the thwarts, the thwarts and the gear.

Once Silas and his girlfriend Jane—the two non-seminar seniors who had agreed to serve as shuttle drivers—showed up, we were ready to roll. All the journey north, our breath steamed the windows, the so-so windshield wipers fought off the steady rain, and I braced myself internally against the hard-rock radio station the students had insisted on, though none of them listened to it, they were in such a chatty mood. In Millinocket—essentially the end of the civilized world before you hit the Golden Road, a major paved, then dirt thoroughfare used primarily by loggers—I suggested we get a quick bite of supper at a truck stop, because I could see we weren't going to make the river before dark. We'd gotten a later start than we should have, given that the autumn days were shortening, so now the idea of cooking out in the rain and the black night both—well, suffice it to say the students quickly agreed with me, and fortunately all of them had a little pocket money along. In the diner a huge black moose head stuck out of the fake-paneled wall just above our table, its nostrils flared as if noting the seasoned, twenty-year-old bouquet of French fries and baked beans.

By the time we reached the muddy track leading to our put-in, the weather had softened to a drizzle; with our stuff unloaded and rinsed in the river of the mud it had picked up in transit, we threw our tents up quickly, having decided to wait for daylight before starting out. Miraculously, the drizzle subsided only minutes later. Soon the clouds even lifted and thinned, enough to show the dull glow of a rounding moon, and someone asked out of the dark whether we could put the boats in the water and paddle around for awhile, just upstream from our camp. It was the first of many times that weekend I would feel strange about being asked to make a decision; as easy as that came to me in the classroom, this seemed different—most of these folks knew as much as I did (and some, I soon realized, knew much more) about what was safe or wise behavior in the wilderness.

Within minutes we were plying our paddles softly upriver, where the air just over the water appeared deeply whitened by fog. We followed as quietly as possible the hooting of two—no, make that three! someone whispered loudly up ahead—barred owls, apparently from opposite banks. Then suddenly—*whapp!*—what the hell? I jumped as if a gun had gone off nearby. Nervous laughter and cries of surprise immediately suggested a beaver was in our midst. *Whapp! Whapp!* Was it to my right, maybe over by Josh and Tom's canoe? Impossible to be sure, squint as I might into the dark and the mist. Martin and I lifted our paddles so we could drift and listen . . . *whapp!* Jeez, there it was at our stern. And obviously unhappy to have a bunch of giggling college students floating long red boats across its river. "Generally speaking, a howling wilderness does not howl," Thoreau had written in *The Maine Woods.* Maybe not, I thought, but it sure makes a boom when it slaps its broad tail.

In subsequent years, on subsequent Thoreau Seminar trips to this river, there would be many wildlife sightings: moose, deer, fox, great blue herons, osprey, grouse, even the occasional loon (common on the river and surrounding lakes in summer, by autumn they have usually headed out to sea to spend the winter just offshore). But on this first trip, there were no sightings—the weather was too consistently foul for any but a foolish professor and her charges to be abroad—only this night's wild *hearings,* as it were. It was a fog-haunted dream, that first hour I ever spent on the West Branch. It would not be so lovely again for the rest of the weekend.

Saturday. We pushed off in the morning with blond, wiry Silas and short, chubby Jane looking on from the bank. Their instructions were to get back on the logging roads with the van and now-empty trailer and to use the map I'd given them to find us later that night at the campsite we'd be aiming for downriver on the west bank, the one just opposite a big island (named, uninterestingly, Big Island). An unorthodox plan, to be sure—shuttle drivers do not usually try to meet up with paddlers partway through the journey. But since the thin gray lines on the map indicated a logging road ran within a half mile of the campsite and that a foot trail linked the two, I thought what the heck, this way we can all be checking in with each other to be sure everyone's okay. In truth I also half feared I might have to load everybody back up into the van a day early to head back to campus: the rain had resumed in the night, and the air was now cool enough to suggest sleet could be next. Though morale had been high the evening before, who was to say that would last?

Saturday stretched into one long, weather-soaked push down the swollen, cola-brown, northeasterly tending stream, with a stop at one campsite for a quickly assembled lunch under a tarp held aloft by the tallest guys among us, Vance and Tom. (While we huddled and snacked, I told the students I'd planned for us to pull out our copies of *The Maine Woods* right about now; they looked at me blankly while rain dripped off the sides of the tarp.) Throughout the weekend Josh and Tom shared one canoe, Charlie and Deborah another, Martin—a mere slip of a fellow— and I the third; thanks to our odd number, someone had to paddle the fourth canoe solo, for which Vance volunteered, taking as well the lion's share of our gear into his more spacious boat. If I wondered at first whether this would prove a chore for him—more weight in the boat with the least paddling strength—it was soon clear that Vance loved the challenge as well as the solitude. Virtually the entire weekend he stayed at least a half mile ahead of us, sometimes more. I called out to him more than once to ease up, to let us catch up to him so we could all more or less hang together, but I may as well have called to the glowering sky for all the good it did. In class his rebellion had been bounded by four walls and an academic culture that precluded certain behavior; up here in the woods, he seemed to relish the freedom he had to sweat his tension right out of his body, with a paddling rhythm steady and strong enough to move him and his laden canoe twice as fast as the rest of us could travel.

During an afternoon rest stop at another campsite (without Vance, who was too far ahead even to know we had pulled over), while we all waited for someone to return from the privy, I stared down for a while at my cheap, rubber-soled "duck shoes." Their low, below-the-ankle cut rendered them practically useless out here, where getting in and out of the boat periodically meant I had to step in water several inches deep, inevitably soaking my socks. Teeth clenched against the cold while I considered this problem, I suddenly realized one of the students was speaking to me, even shaking me by the arm. What, what's the matter? "Your lips are blue—are you okay?" Of course, don't be silly. But Deborah and the others quickly decided I was going hypothermic and thought we should start a fire. Nonsense, I told them, I'm just a wet, dripping daydreamer.

Yet as we piled back into our canoes, I wondered privately if they were right and felt at least as scared of letting them see me weak as I was surprised and a little scared to find I might really be weakening. Memo to Self: Next year, invest in better shoes. Thicker socks and more layers for the upper body. A wool cap to wear under this uninsulated rain hood.

The prospect of hypothermia for one or more of us grew more plausible as the day wore on, the rain slackened, and the mercury fell. As we neared the campsite where we'd spend the night, I determined that a big fire was indeed in order, as well as some attempt to dry our wet clothes—sleeping bags, too, if any had not been fully protected by the dry bags into which they were stuffed.

Still some distance away from Big Island, I could see through binoculars a canoe hauled up on the bank and overturned: Vance had made it fine. And what was this? He had a fire going already (the Forest Service leaves dry, cut logs under the picnic tables) and was tromping around the perimeters of the campsite, pulling downed limbs toward his fire so they could dry out and be used later for fuel. Good man, Vance, even if you are a pain. Disembarking and climbing the short rise to the site, I could see by his expression he was happy—happy for once to be in his element, to be so obviously competent. He pretended not to hear my pleased thanks for the fire.

With all our boats and gear now in one place, Vance dug around for all the tarps we had and some twine and soon turned our paddles into makeshift poles to rig up a generous, open-air tent, stretching high above and just to one side of the fire. Now it wouldn't have to matter too much if the rain kicked in again (it did)—we could still cook over the Coleman stove without much difficulty and even hang a few wet socks and pants from a line that Josh drew taut between the T-handles of two distantly placed paddles.

All of which was such a delight to watch unfold that I could summon only a moment's shock and irritation when, soon after, Vance produced from his backpack a big, heavily wrapped package of—damn it all, thawing pork chops. *And* the platter-sized pan necessary to fry them in.

An hour later: we're all fed, now seated near the dwindling fire—all of us driven by a light rain to the side with the tarp "roof"—on two sizable logs we've pulled up for the purpose. I'm wondering to myself where Silas and Jane are, trying not to worry quite yet; partly to distract myself and partly to accomplish something of the educational goals I'd had in mind when I first dreamed up this whole venture, I pull out of a plastic bag my copy of *The Maine Woods*. While I sift through the pages, looking for the section that describes the eighteen miles or so that we've paddled so far, the students quiet down with mugs of hot chocolate held close to their chests, staring into the embers. "At mid-afternoon we embarked on the Penobscot," I read aloud. As I read I'm aware of the flickering orange light on the young faces around me, aware too of their occasional glance in my direction. I feel strangely self-conscious, a little sheepish even, but keep going:

> It was dead water for a couple of miles. The river had been raised about two feet by the rain, and lumberers were hoping for a flood [a few giggles] sufficient to bring down the logs that were left in the spring. Its banks were seven or eight feet high, and densely covered with white and black spruce,—which, I think, must be the commonest trees thereabouts,—fir, arbor-vitae, canoe, yellow, and black birch, rock, mountain, and a few red maples, beech, black and mountain ash, the large-toothed aspen, many civil looking elms, now imbrowned, along the stream, and at first a few hemlocks also. (Thoreau 1988, 128–29)

I stopped for a minute so we could compare what we'd seen with this account—the high banks and high water, sure, and some but not all of the tree species. We agreed the elms, maples, and ash trees in particular didn't seem prevalent, though we also conceded we'd spent much of the day with our faces tucked too low under our hats to enable much sightseeing. But when Charlie commented that he did think of Henry often as he paddled, trying to picture him on this very river with his white friend and his Penobscot guide Joe Aitteon, a couple of the others allowed that they had, too; for this I felt grateful. Turning back to the book, I handed it off to Tom on my left, who picked up where I'd left off. He got only another page or so farther before the rain suddenly came down in a sodden fury, like a thousand faucets turned full bore all at once. The tarp roof collapsed at one end, everybody jumped and fled toward their tents, I grabbed my book and stashed it in my coat. By the time I dove head first into my tent I was soaked anew, below the knees anyway, trying to get out of my rain jacket without splashing water across my sleeping bag. With my flashlight I quickly checked to see that my rain fly was doing its job—no leaks along the edges of the tent floor. I peered out my door to see what the state of the tarp shelter and fire might be, mentally noting happily that Deborah, who had a tent to herself and therefore more room to spare than the guys, had stowed the dry bags containing all our food in her quarters some time before the deluge. (In clear weather we'd have hung the food bags from a rope strung high between tree limbs to ward off animal pillage; in this weather, however, Deborah was willing to bet she'd have no trouble with animals, and since I'd read this was no longer bear country, I thought it a pretty safe bet myself.) The pans and dishes on the picnic table, washed and set off to one side, would take care of themselves for the night. And the rain handily took care of the last hint of fire.

With bedtime forced upon us, I was now free to worry heartily about Silas and Jane. The muddy logging roads they must have wrestled all day, the general absence of signs and the difficulty of discerning landmarks through wet, gray weather—what a time of it they must be having. And where might they be now? I knew they had food and camping supplies with them, and that they could always sleep in the van if they wished, so I wasn't concerned for them on those counts. But if they'd gotten stuck in mud way out here in the proverbial boondocks, would anyone have come upon them to offer help? Or if they were lost, how might they find their way out of the maze of roads tomorrow? Would they be able to reach the take-out around the time we'd agreed to aim for—4 P.M.? This last mattered to me chiefly because I knew if I didn't have the students back to campus by ten or eleven Sunday night at the very latest, campus police would likely call the wardens up here to come looking for us. I didn't fancy hearing in Monday's news about a search for Unity College students in the north woods, and I figured the provost wouldn't fancy it, either. In my sleep I fought off these and, it seemed, other fears of a nameless, ephemeral nature—to the extent that I was even sure at one point that headlights had just swept over my tent walls. Bolting upright to unzip my door, I stuck my head out and listened intently for the sound of an engine—the rain had stopped, the night was a chill, black, bottomless well— but heard nothing. And as I grew more awake, I knew they couldn't possibly drive right up to our camp anyway: the evening before, while the others cooked supper, Martin and I had gone searching in the fading light for the foot trail indicated by the map but found only a low, boggy collection of mossy hummocks beneath the big hemlocks surrounding the relatively high ground of the campsite. We hadn't been able to get more than fifty yards beyond the picnic table without sinking nearly to our knees in an icy, fragrant forest tea.

What I didn't know that night—for which fact I have been grateful ever since—was that Jane and Silas had contended with far worse than muddy roads: they had been seriously harassed by some country yahoos in a crumpled blue pickup truck. Two grizzled, patently drunk guys whose idea of fun was to chase the van and pull up alongside it on the driver's side, grinning and hooting obscenities. Approaching a junction of gravel roads, they would fall back, turn off as if to give up the game, but twenty minutes later be seen coming *at* the van from the opposite direction. These encounters occurred more than once throughout the day, the last time with some added twists. Again the pickup pulled up alongside the driver—Jane this time—and with both vehicles still in bumpy motion, the empty canoe trailer clanking and swinging slightly behind, the passenger in the truck got himself high up on his seat, turned to the window he'd lowered, and dropped his pants—evidently for Jane's benefit. She and Silas were annoyed but not yet scared exactly—that came a moment later, when the drunk they were trying to ignore now brandished a pistol of some kind, waving it loosely out the window with one hand while the other held his penis up to urinate in a wild arc. Glimpsing the gun, Jane caught her breath and took her foot off the gas, sliding quickly down in her seat and realizing in the same instant the van might be veering too far to the right-hand edge of a road that she now couldn't really see. Silas too hunkered down fast and reached over to push the wheel left—while the truck roared ahead, its driver not yet aware, or simply unconcerned, that the van had lost speed. Silas quickly sat up to try to get the license number: despite the rain he thought maybe he'd seen it, and he concentrated on remembering it with one part of his brain, while the other watched to be sure those guys weren't turning around or backing up. They weren't. While Jane eased the van to a stop, he found a pencil and wrote the number down on a convenience-store sales receipt. They had to get out and walk around for a few minutes to stop shaking.

Later, these two nervous kids would search fruitlessly for the road they hoped would take them near our campsite—they wanted badly to find us, but couldn't. Pulling over finally, they slept in the van with the doors locked.

Sunday. Much as I knew we needed to get going early—we had a very long day ahead of us, at least fifteen miles to paddle, one of them over an open lake—I just had to try once more to see where or if that foot trail came in. Maybe if we found it and followed it to the road, Silas and Jane and the van would be parked nearby. The students all offered to help, and one suggested we split into two groups so as to fan out and cover more ground quickly, to which suggestion I assented without thinking much about it. Peering ahead into the trees now and then as I picked my way carefully from one tuft of moss to another, trying vainly to keep from stepping into water over my shoe tops, I forgot for a spell about the other group of students, the ones who had headed north while the rest of us moved west. But suddenly I stopped short and wheeled around to stare in the direction they'd gone: no sign of them. I shushed the students with me for a second: no longer any sound of them, either. *What was I, crazy?* Here we were, caught up in searching out a path that might lead us to the drivers, yet I'd just divided our numbers and risked losing *more* students in the process. We need to re-group, I told the ones with me, and started immediately in the direction of our north-walking half.

We found them near the edge of a small creek branching off the river, staring down at the skull and tufts of hair left from a deer kill. Vance and the other guys who had found it seemed uncharacteristically quiet and thoughtful . . . they weren't oohing and aahing to quite the extent that outdoorsy Unity College students ordinarily would. It was as though we'd been visited with an omen of some kind. I broke the silence by saying, in a rare moment of decisiveness for me that weekend, that I'd been wrong to let the group split up, that we should all stay together for the duration of the trip, and that, further, we should stay near the main river. It wouldn't do to get lost in the boggy wilderness, away from the canoes that could so easily take us to other people—even if only the residents of tiny Chesuncook Village, some ten or twelve miles downriver from where we stood. Martin picked up the skull and we shuffled back toward our boats, following the edge of the creek. He rigged it up as a prow ornament to his canoe—which was also *my* canoe. I kept to myself the spooky feeling it gave me and even had to laugh inwardly at the *Deliverance*-like turn this trip felt as if it were taking.

Preoccupied though I was by now with the Silas-and-Jane question, I tried to enjoy and share with the students those moments throughout the day when we passed streams that Thoreau had written about: There's Ragmuff, at the mouth of which he did a little fishing; look, the little falls are still there, even. And look over this way, I think we must be passing the mouth of Pine Stream, where Thoreau witnessed his companions' bumbling attempts to kill two moose—they were only wounded at first, and Henry was disgusted. Although I had hoped for a quick hike from the east bank into Chesuncook, where I'd heard we could see in its little cemetery a couple of headstones bearing the names of people Henry had actually met there (it's true, I discovered two years later, on the next Thoreau Seminar trip), by the time we neared it we had no leisure to pay a visit, nor did any of us feel any longer much curiosity in that direction anyway. We were too cold and tired, and still uncomfortably damp, having had showers again today—though not any additional downpours, thankfully. After a quick rest stop at the point where the river met

Chesuncook Lake, we struck out in what I thought might be the north-
westerly direction where the map indicated that the lake would empty
into Umbazooksus Stream. And now I faced up to yet another of my mistakes: no compass, a serious thing to be without when you also have no
sun. On the map the mouth of Umbazooksus looked easy to distinguish
from that of Caucomgomoc Stream and from a small, unnamed bay lying
between them, as well as another little bay just south of Caucomgomoc.
But out here, gazing across the lake, I was stupefied. The students who
had constituted the itinerary team—that is, those who had studied the
maps almost as much as I had—weren't any more sure than I was just
what lay across the lake in several directions. Ahead and to our right (presumably in the northeast) lay what I took to be big, sprawling Gero Island, and to the west that watery expanse way over there would be—what,
the mouth of Caucomgomoc? Impossible to keep the nearer shore of
Gero Island from bleeding visually into the farther shore of the mainland
lying just beyond it, both shores being rimmed by the same kinds of trees;
impossible to be sure that was indeed a stream opening to the west rather
than the crescent of one of the little bays. We needed to find Umbazooksus on the first try—with my watch edging past three already, there was
no time, nor did it seem we had the energy, to head in the wrong direction. It wasn't as if the lake presented a placid face: clearly, we'd be crossing in a serious headwind, forced to paddle hard to make any progress at
all. Whitecapped waves churned the surface, so as we plodded on for the
next hour I feared someone's boat would take on water. But who could
think long about that? I had to concentrate on setting the right course,
which I did with a tip from Vance: keeping the village's church steeple behind me at six o'clock, so to speak, I'd fix at twelve o'clock on a noteworthy tree on the far horizon—the really tall, white pines worked the
best—urging Martin at the stern to keep us moving along that imaginary
line. As we began to round Gero Island on its western side, I'd choose another landmark every few minutes to aim for, gradually turning us to the
left—oh man, is this still northwest?—and soon used only these points before me to steer by, the church steeple having faded from sight. Briefly I
wondered why Vance wasn't charging ahead any longer—he now brought
up the rear. I figured the combination of this wind and his heavier canoe
was the reason, but later I learned he was deliberately staying near Charlie and Deborah in case they should swamp (Charlie was our novice paddler) in this wild, rocking little sea upon which we were foolishly
launched.

Entering what I dearly hoped was the wide neck of Umbazooksus

Stream, I stood up gingerly in the canoe and trained my binos in the direction, a mile or more ahead, where I expected to find our take-out spot and, if all was right with the world, our van and two safe kids hanging out waiting for us. Nothing yet—we were still too far away. With no rain and less wind to fight now, I tried to savor for a moment the woods along this rather different shore from that of the West Branch. Here, many fewer evergreens appeared to break up the generally pale gray look of these deciduous, leafless trees; but the still-gold aspens (more commonly called "popple" up this way) that Henry had noted in *The Maine Woods* stood out a little better than they had on the river, especially where they caught one or two shafts of late-afternoon light just cracking through an otherwise gunmetal sky. (*Now* you show your face, I said to the westering sun.) I warned Martin I was going to stand up again, to look for the take-out and our van. Yes—there it was, parked just yards away from a low beach that seemed to serve as the landing! Thrilled and squealing, I sat down fast to avoid upsetting the canoe. It's there, Martin—a dark green van with Unity College stenciled across its side in gold! I took up my paddle again and fell quiet, aware that this cheerful, tow-headed fellow couldn't appreciate how relieved I felt after a bad night and long day of worrying. Moments later I couldn't help myself—I had to stand up and look again. *What?* Now the van wasn't there at all. Instead, an old white truck was backing a motorboat trailer down into the river. I flashed back to the "headlights" I'd seen sweep my tent; God, am I dreaming again—this time in broad daylight? Shaken, I sank to my seat, seeing again behind my eyes that quick, binocular snapshot—green van, gold lettering. Paddling now became a way to keep my gaze on the water splashing where the boat parted it and on my hands gripping hard black plastic. Anything to avoid looking toward the landing once more. It's a terribly bewildering experience, to wonder for the first time in your life whether you can trust your own eyes, just when you need badly to trust all that your senses can possibly tell you about the situation at hand.

Another half mile covered, and I dared to look again—without binoculars now, I could see for sure that there was no van parked near the landing, where I thought I'd seen it minutes ago. The guy who'd backed a boat in had already parked his truck, launched his boat, and zoomed off across the water; not till he shot past and waved did I realize we might have needed him. With heavy heart I kept digging the water, weary of the work, weary of the worry, yet not done worrying—were they really lost, then? Were they okay? And if they didn't find us, what would I need to do to get this crew of wet students out of the woods?

Tom and Josh were the first to coast their canoe up to the beach; Martin and I were close enough behind to hear the hollow scrape of their keel hitting sand. Just as our boat also hit land, I saw the head and shoulders of someone approaching us on foot—Silas coming out of the woods and down the slope of beach! And Jane too, not far behind.

Memo to Others Contemplating School Canoeing Trips into the Wilderness:

When you get the class to commit to a trip date, have them commit to a rain date as well.

Require the trip, but design an alternative assignment for those who elect not to go; make it a research project, and chances are everyone will go canoeing.

Scout the entire route yourself well ahead of time. Equip yourself with topo maps—road atlases just aren't good enough, not even those very detailed ones published, state by state, by DeLorme, which is what I relied on initially.

Even if your school has the canoes, convince your administration you will have to hire a professional outfitter, who will take responsibility not only for the boats but also for shuttling your group to and from your van or bus. It only makes sense: the outfitters know the roads, and they often know the locals, rowdy ones included.

Take along a cell phone, radio, or flares, and carry the outfitter's phone number with you. Pack a compass; pack two, in case one breaks. Insist that everyone bring appropriate clothing, and plenty of it, even in summer.

Know the signs of hypothermia, and what to do if it arises. Take a course in first aid and CPR, or make sure one of your students has done so.

Set realistic pedagogical goals for the kind of trip you have designed.

Determine which of your students really know what they are doing in the woods and on the water: relinquish to them some of the control you're accustomed to exercising, then enjoy what a different sort of relationship begins to unfold among you. You'll still feel the change once you're all back in the classroom, and for the rest of the term—maybe even the rest of your life.

Upon return to campus, do not let the students leave the van until all the leftover food is cleared out of the dry bags and the bags are rinsed, until every last piece of gear is cleaned up and someone has taken responsibility for returning it to its owner, until the van itself is policed for trash and miscellaneous articles of clothing. I made the mistake of sending my tired crew on home that Sunday night, with promises they'd help me square everything away on the morrow; several didn't follow through.

As it happened, I *had* seen the van when I thought I saw it. But before I stood up to check again, Silas moved it up away from the beach so the guy in the white truck would have room to back his boat down to the water. As luck would have it, Silas parked the darn thing up in the trees where no one on the stream, which lay a few degrees lower than the bank, could see it. Over a snack of peanut butter and bagels, we all swapped stories: that search for the foot trail, the deer skull. "Allison was pathetic, trying to hold class in the rain"—this from Vance, in whose laughter I detected good-natured reconciliation. The nut case with the gun. Great Caesar's ghost, what had I done, sending two kids into the woods, and one of them female? All my feminism fell mute at the horrific thought of what could have befallen her, or for that matter, both of them.

Search the van though we did for a full half hour before starting home, and again the next day in better light, we never found the scrap of paper on which Silas had scribbled that truck's plate number.

References

Huber, J. Parker. 1981. *The wildest country: A guide to Thoreau's Maine*. Boston: Appalachian Mountain Club.

Stowell, Robert F. 1970. *A Thoreau gazetteer*. Edited by William L. Howarth. Princeton, N.J.: Princeton University Press.

Thoreau, Henry David. 1988. *The Maine woods* (1864). Introduction by Edward Hoagland. New York: Penguin.

❋ BRITAIN A. SCOTT
STEVEN M. HOFFMAN

Woodswomen and "Super Studs"

Gender Issues in a Northwoods Environmental Studies Program

Outdoor education is often described as having its roots in the mid-twentieth-century innovations of German educational philosopher Kurt Hahn. When he founded the Aberdovey Outward Bound School in Wales in 1941, Hahn's intent was to "enhance among young merchant seamen the physical and moral requirements for survival at sea after ships went down to enemy submarines" (Hopkins and Putnam 1993, 29). The initial emphasis of Outward Bound programs was to facilitate personal growth in young men through outdoor challenges. Hahn's work set the tone for an educational approach that would later expand from Europe to the United States and would be variously labeled "adventure education," "experiential education," and "environmental education." In its early days, outdoor education was a macho enterprise.

The first Outward Bound programs for women appeared in Europe in the 1950s, were discontinued with the introduction of mixed-sex courses in the 1970s, and were reintroduced in the early 1980s (Hopkins and Putnam 1993). Meanwhile, when Outward Bound came to the United States in the 1960s, it served a broader constituency and included mixed-sex and single-sex programming. Since that time, women's participation in outdoor pursuits has been on the rise (Henderson and Roberts 1998). Today's outdoor educators can expect to see increasing numbers of women enrolled in their courses and may encounter requests from students for women-only offerings. For this reason, we believe that contemporary outdoor educators must be gender-aware and gender-wary. That is, they must be tuned in to the gender-related dynamics and problems that can arise in coed groups, just as they must be attentive to the particular challenges and benefits for women in this traditionally masculine domain. And, they must guard themselves and their students against the pitfalls associated with making assumptions based on sex and in treating gender as something innate and unchangeable.

In this essay, we use a college-level environmental studies program, Superior Studies at Wolf Ridge (SSWR), as a case example through which to explore the implications of outdoor education's "manly" beginnings for educators working with coed or women's groups. We begin with a brief discussion of environmental studies and a history of the SSWR program. We then discuss some ways in which traditional gender stereotypes and roles may negatively impact wilderness learning. Finally, we explore factors unique to women's experiences in outdoor education and describe the potential both coeducational and women-only programs hold for challenging traditionally limiting definitions of gender.

A SUPERIOR PLACE: ENVIRONMENTAL EDUCATION IN MINNESOTA'S NORTH WOODS

Environmental Studies (ES) is generally regarded as a growth sector for academic institutions. Commenting on the growth of ES programs that had occurred in the late 1980s and early 1990s, Benjamin Strauss (1996, 7) concluded that the period marked "a second awakening for environmental education in institutions of higher learning" (see also O'Reilly 1995). Growth has continued since that time, as evidenced by a recent survey of 891 U.S. colleges and universities, which found that some 43 percent now offer either a major or minor degree program in the field (McIntosh et al. 2001, 15).

Accompanying this institutional growth has been an evolving literature on the pedagogical and curricular approaches best suited to the teaching of environmental studies. The most well-known writer in this area is probably David Orr, whose *Ecological Literacy: Education and the Transition to a Postmodern World* (1992) has served to frame much of the discussion over the last decade. Central to Orr's argument is the problem of disciplinarity as the basis for organizing higher education. According to Orr, "Issues facing contemporary society are complex and cannot be understood through a single department or discipline. . . . Excessive specialization is fatal to comprehension because it removes knowledge from its larger context (1992, 90, 101).

While many in the ES field acknowledge the importance of Orr's argument, actually putting into place the "connective" model of education envisioned by Orr has proven to be problematic. Gary Deason[1] (2000), for instance, points out that a variety of pressures, ranging from curricular distribution requirements to budgetary restrictions that limit the creation of new interdisciplinary course offerings, prevent truly effective integration across the curriculum or even within many ES programs. Resource inadequacy also means that ES students receive little opportunity for experiential or field-based work, despite the fact that teaching and learning in Environmental Studies requires first-hand encounters with complex environmental issues as they occur in a specific context. The implications of waste disposal practices, paper mill operations, fishing regulations, off-shore drilling, and wildlife policy, to name a few, extend beyond any one academic domain. Issues of this sort occur at the intersection of ecological, social, political, economic, and cultural systems and are best understood through interdisciplinary learning that integrates theory and practice. While most ES faculty recognize the need for engaging students in this manner, tight institutional resources and rigid campus scheduling make off-campus programs in integrative learning an unaffordable luxury for many individual institutions.

In an effort to develop an educational alternative that "occurs, in part, as a dialogue with a place and . . . is relevant to the challenge of building a sustainable society [that] enhances the learner's competence with natural systems" (Orr 1992, 90–92), some reformers have turned to independent organizations that maintain cooperative, rather than formal, ties with colleges and universities. Examples of such programs include the School for Field Studies (www.fieldstudies.org) and the School for International Training (www.sit.edu). Others, however, prefer to act on a consortium basis and to work in collaboration with faculty and staff from "home" colleges and universities. The collaborative approach allows reformers to draw upon the combined resources of the member institutions while developing alternative educational structures, pedagogy, and curriculum.

An example of the latter is Superior Studies at Wolf Ridge (SSWR). The program is set in the 2,100 forested acres of the Wolf Ridge Environmental Learning Center (www.wolf-ridge.org) on the Sawtooth Mountain ridge overlooking Lake Superior and neighboring the Minnesota-Ontario wilderness. The location offers easy access to the Boundary Waters Canoe Area Wilderness (BWCAW), the Quetico Provincial Park, the Superior National Forest, a variety of Minnesota state parks and forests, as well as the Superior Hiking Trail and the Lake Superior water trail. The region provides a rich resource for woodland, wildlife, stream, and lake ecology; geology, soil, and weather studies; Native American and European history and culture; issues related to tourism, public lands, mining, forestry, and wilderness use; and personal engagement with the natural world through the arts and outdoor adventure. First offered in 1997 by St. Olaf College, the program is now a collaborative of nine liberal arts colleges and universities in the upper Midwest.[2] A wide variety of courses are offered, including environmental policy, ecopsychology, conservation biology, environmental ethics, Minnesota natural history, and nature writing, among others. Open to students of any major, the program averages between twenty-five and forty students per summer semester and has cumulatively served more than 150 students (the majority of them women) in its five years of operation. Twenty-one faculty from ten campuses have participated in SSWR.

A variety of pedagogical approaches are used in Superior Studies. First, students are offered a choice of wilderness and/or outdoor experiences during the initial week of the program: canoeing in the BWCAW, kayaking on Lake Superior, or backpacking on the Superior Hiking Trail. Wilderness trips are also scheduled on the weekends throughout the remainder of the program. Second, students take field trips to a variety of local and regional sites, including the International Wolf Center in Ely, Minnesota, mining and lumber milling operations in the region, and natural-resource agency offices in Minnesota and Canada. Formal classroom work takes place during the week and is complemented by a weekly seminar where the entire community of students and faculty gather to hear invited lecturers on topics of mutual interest.

Classes serve as an integrative forum for these diverse experiences. The Environmental Policy class, for instance, examines a variety of topics relevant to the process and politics of policymaking as well as issues of concern to the north woods, including wolf management, taconite mining in the Iron Range, waste dumping in Lake Superior, fire management policy in the BWCAW, and so on. One issue of particular importance in the region is public land management. The first week's wilderness trip, led by the class instructor, serves as the initial introduction to the topic (a fact of which the students are largely unaware). Given the geography of the area, access to the wilderness requires the students to cross national forest lands, exposing them to the clear differences between land designations, i.e., logging and a variety of motorized uses in the national forest versus non-motorized uses in the wilderness area. On occasion, students paddle across motorized lakes to access non-motorized lakes. They may also encounter motors when paddling in areas adjacent to Canadian lakes where such activity is permitted. Reflecting on these trips during the formal class periods or when discussing assigned readings, or even recounting their experiences with National Forest Service rangers during the site visits, allows students to understand the meaning and impacts of land-use policy in a unique and powerful way. Similar opportunities for "connective learning" present themselves throughout the SSWR curriculum.

SSWR is an innovative effort at integrating traditional forms of higher education with the challenge of wilderness experience. It seeks to use the wild as a classroom and inform students in a way that is unavailable to those confined to the boundaries of the traditional academy. The benefits of the program, however, are not solely academic. The wilderness component of SSWR also offers students opportunities for personal growth. Outdoor education programs like Superior Studies are believed to increase feelings of self-efficacy, improve the self-concept, hone leadership skills, improve social functioning, enhance spiritual connections with nature, and provide a number of other psychological and physical benefits to participants (Hattie et al. 1997; Cason and Gillis 1994). However, it is unclear how generalized such effects are. Most outcome studies have focused on adventure programming in its therapeutic applications, primarily with at-risk adolescents. Empirically, we know very little about the benefits of programs like SSWR that integrate outdoor experience as only one component of an overall educational endeavor designed for presumably well-adjusted college students.

We also know very little about whether and how the effectiveness of outdoor education programs may be related to characteristics of their participants. In recent years, programs have attracted an increasingly diverse pool of participants, and outdoor educators are beginning to recognize that they should consider factors such as sex/gender, age, race/ethnicity, socioeconomic status, and disability when designing and evaluating their programs (Roberts and Rodriguez 1999; Fox, McAvoy, and Young 1998). In its five years of operation, SSWR has not attracted a particularly diverse body of students in terms of any of these factors except sex: cumulatively the program has hosted eighty-six women and sixty-five men. This sex ratio has afforded SSWR faculty and staff the opportunity to observe coed dynamics and to think critically about women's experiences in this historically male-dominated realm. Drawing on theory, research findings, anecdotes, and personal experiences, we now turn to a discussion of some gendered aspects of outdoor education.

WE ALL WANNA BE MACHO MEN:
GENDER ISSUES IN OUTDOOR EDUCATION

In the summer of 2000, two young women guides at Wolf Ridge designed a t-shirt emblazoned with the words "SUPERior STUDies." Admittedly clever, their wordplay makes salient several gender-related issues that should be of concern to outdoor educators leading coed groups. Applying this label to participants in an outdoor education program implicitly links the content of the program to a stereotypical male-gender role. On a male wearer, the label "SUPER STUD" further evokes powerful images of hyper-masculinity and sexual conquest of women. On a female wearer, the label identifies her as a woman apart from her peers and detached from her femininity, a superwoman able to succeed as "one of the boys" on strictly masculine terms. Even without participants (or teachers) sporting t-shirts like this one, these themes may surface in both blatant and subtle ways. We believe outdoor educators leading coed groups should be sensitive to the ways in which gender stereotypes, gender roles, and gender prejudice can negatively impact their programs.

Gender Stereotypes and Gender Roles

On the first author's office wall is a 1950 place mat from the New England Mutual Life Insurance Company that pictures a boy with a rocket and a girl with a doll beneath the header "What is a Boy—What is a Girl." The copy describes how boys are "found everywhere on top of, underneath, inside of, climbing on, swinging from, running around, or jumping to." A boy is "Truth with dirt on its face . . . and the Hope of the future with a frog in its pocket." A girl likes "new shoes, party dresses, . . . dolls, make-believe, dancing lessons, ice cream, kitchens, coloring books, make-up. . . ." The sex-typing evident in this fifty-year-old relic may seem over-the-top by today's standards, but in fact our culture's gender stereotypes have not changed very much (Lueptow, Garovich, and Lueptow 1995). Our stereotypes continue to link masculinity with activity, independence, and strength, and femininity with passivity, dependence, and weakness. Males are assumed to be competitive, while females are considered cooperative. Men are tough leaders, women caring nurturers. Stereotypical masculinity is consistent with traditional outdoor adventure, while stereotypical femininity is not.

Stereotypes are learned mental structures that act as lenses through which we perceive others, make judgments about their behavior, and determine how to behave toward them. Gender stereotypes are learned early and learned well. By the time children are five years old, they demonstrate an understanding of which behaviors and objects go with which gender label, and not long after they ascribe different personality traits to males and females (Szkrybalo and Ruble 1999). Researchers who study sex-related differences in personality, cognitive abilities, and behavior continue to debate the accuracy of gender stereotypes. All acknowledge, however, that research on differences looks only at group averages; therefore, even if gender stereotypes have a kernel of truth, in practice they are overgeneralizations that ignore variability within the sexes and are frequently misapplied to individuals (see Swim 1994, for discussion). Yet, regardless of the degree to which we may intellectually understand that gender stereotypes are simplistic overgeneralizations, we all engage in stereotypic thinking. Stereotypes serve an essential function as mental shortcuts that make our thinking more efficient. If we had to consider the unique characteristics of every individual we encounter in our social worlds, we would not be able to function.

All people are wired to stereotype most of the time. Combating our automatic stereotypical thinking requires motivation and careful attention (Devine, 1989). Outdoor educators, therefore, must be consciously aware of how gender stereotypes may bias their own perceptions and behaviors, as well as those of their students. They must be alert to instances where stereotypic thinking is having preventable negative effects. And, they must make a conscientious effort to challenge gender stereotyping when they see it. Left unchallenged, gender stereotypes and their associated behavioral scripts limit learning and are a potential safety hazard in outdoor education.

Gender stereotypes limit learning. Stereotypic thinking leads to assumptions that men are competent and tough in the outdoors, but women are not. Men are assumed to be physically able experts, while women are perceived as needing instruction and assistance. In truth, of course, we all learn through instruction, assistance, and tapping into our own strengths. If instructors behave in accordance with gender stereotypes, instead of assessing the needs of each student individually, male students will be left too much to their own devices while female students will be over-instructed.

Gender stereotypes are not merely descriptive; they are also prescriptive (Fiske and Stevens 1993). Stereotypic thinking leads to the labeling of certain activities and roles as masculine and others as feminine, and, importantly, there is social stigma attached when an individual engages in behaviors that are labeled inconsistent with his or her gender role. Males especially experience social condemnation when they step out of a masculine role and venture into the territory of femininity. It is much more negative in our culture to be labeled a "sissy" than to be labeled a "tomboy" (Crawford and Unger 2000). Masculinity is constantly suspect, and many men understandably feel pressured to prove their masculinity by hefting heavy packs, paddling at breakneck speed, besting each other on rock climbs, and by offering assistance to the women. One male Superior Studies student described to us that the "guys feel a sort of obligation to ask if the women need help hoisting canoes or whatever" and explained that if they didn't offer, they would feel like they hadn't fulfilled their job as men. There is demand on male participants to live up to the expectation that as men they are naturally inclined to do the heavy lifting.

In contrast, women participants frequently find themselves fending off men's chivalrous offers and fighting to shed their gender role so that they will have the opportunity to use and improve their physical strength, navigational skills, and leadership abilities. Both women and men have difficulty establishing their legitimacy as leaders in contexts that are seen as incompatible with their gender role (Eagly, Karau, and Makhijani 1995). In the traditionally masculine context of outdoor education, women often find that they are asked to take on the roles of peacemaker and group facilitator, but otherwise their leadership is not respected (Henderson 1996). In Superior Studies we have occasionally seen examples of this. A recent trip had two women leaders, one the same age as the students and one a generation older. The older leader quickly became frustrated by the fact that a few of the male students consistently ignored her instructions until a male leader restated them. One of these male students has since confessed to us that, initially, the younger leader was viewed with similar skepticism, but once she had sufficiently proved herself as a real "woodswoman," her authority was unquestioned. Ironically, because women are not expected to display competence in the outdoors, when they do successfully portage canoes or scale rock walls, they may gain respect and status that is not afforded their similarly competent male peers. In psychology, this is referred to as the "talking platypus phenomenon": it's not how well the platypus talks that matters, it's the astounding fact that it can talk at all (Abramson, Goldberg, Greenberg, and Abramson 1977).

A primary challenge for outdoor educators is to "de-masculinize" activities such as portaging canoes, carrying heavy packs, and acting as leader and to "de-feminize" activities such as cooking, tending to bruised bodies and bruised egos, and acting as mediator in disputes. We should encourage all participants to spend some time chopping firewood and some time chopping vegetables. We should emphasize that all of these jobs are essential to the successful functioning of the group.

Sometimes the breaking down of gender roles occurs spontaneously. As described to the authors by Superior Studies director Gary Deason, one

> . . . windy morning paddling from Grace Lake to Sawbill Lake . . . all three students' canoes had women paddling in the stern and men in the bow. Paddling in the stern of a canoe, especially in high wind, is far more difficult than the bow. Moreover, women carried the canoes on every portage. The remarkable aspect of this atypical behavior was that it happened without discussion or argument. The women, in fact, were the better canoeists and everyone in the group had the good sense to recognize it.

The complete reversal of gender roles without discussion may be atypical, but in SSWR we frequently see gendered division of labor blurring after a couple of days out on a trip. In our experience, this is most likely to occur when leaders set an example for students by their own behavior.

Gender stereotypes compromise safety. Gender-based divisions of labor and roles reinforce stereotypes and limit the experiences and learning potential of both women and men participants. They also can put the safety of the group in jeopardy, as was the case on one Superior Studies trip when a first-time male participant assumed a leadership role to which he brought no expertise. Impressed by the confidence he projected and unaware of his novice status, even the more seasoned participants on the trip stood aside while he issued commands to wear life jackets and offered suggestions for paddling techniques. Easily convinced of his outdoor skills, no leaders were present to supervise when he instructed his peers on how to light the camp stoves. Nor did trip leaders interfere with another novice male participant's pyromaniacal approach to building the campfire into a blazing bonfire. Aside from a few burn holes in spectators' nylon pants and fleece vests, no major casualties were suffered at the hands of these non-experts, but the potential was there for the whole trip to go up in smoke.

On another trip, the experienced older female leader mentioned above struggled to establish her authority with a young man who argued with her about staying on the planned route, questioned her ability to read the map, and scoffed at her instructions to get off the water with a thunderstorm immediately overhead. Only when a male faculty colleague (who was less experienced and not in a leadership role) backed her up did she get the young man's attention. Without this extra support, she and the male student might have ended up lost or capsized—all because of his perception that as a woman she had no expertise or clout.

Individual safety, too, can be threatened by gender stereotypes and gender roles. Several experienced trip leaders have told us that they often encounter a reluctance on the part of both male and female participants to ask for help, gracefully accept input, or to admit that they are cold, hungry, thirsty, exhausted, or hurt. The men are reluctant because they know they are expected to be competent, and to show any "weakness" is to crack the masculine veneer. The women are reluctant because they know they are expected to be incompetent, so to show any weakness is to confirm the negative stereotype. Ultimately, trip leaders and participants may find themselves dealing with an individual who is dehydrated, hypothermic, or incapacitated by an injury that has been left untended for too long. Outdoor educators must de-stigmatize novice status, vulnerability, and basic human neediness. We must reject the mentality that equates success with miles covered, defines fortitude as the ability to ignore the body's natural warning signals, and ties both success and fortitude to masculinity and maleness.

From gender to femininity. In our discussion of stereotypes and roles, we have touched upon a few of the troublesome gender-related dynamics that arise in coed outdoor education. In addition to exploring the interactions between gender roles, an important part of a gender analysis is to identify the different implications, if any, for the two genders in the given context. When a context is traditionally defined in terms consistent with one gender role and inconsistent with the other, the experience of individuals in the inconsistent gender role is problematized.

For the masculine gender role, an example would be child care. Stereotypical masculinity is perceived as inconsistent with being a caring, self-sacrificing, empathic nurturer. Men, therefore, find their legitimacy as caretakers of infants and children questioned. One man we know relates a story of having an unknown woman step in his way and take over when he was diapering his baby in a public place! Several men we know have felt invisible in social interactions when all the questions, concerns, and comments about their children were directed at the mothers while they stood there ignored. In a "feminine" realm such as child care, men's situation warrants particular attention.

In outdoor education, we have an opposite situation. Men in the outdoors find themselves doing things that are a natural extension of a masculine gender role—things they are encouraged to do and are reinforced for doing. There is not a conflicted relationship between being masculine and being in outdoor education. Women, on the other hand, find themselves in a very different position. As we will describe below, femininity is inconsistent with many of the expected behaviors in outdoor education. Importantly, the bulk of the inconsistency lies in the physical nature of outdoor education. We know from decades of psychological and sociological research that women in our culture are socialized to have a very different relationship with their bodies than men are. What it means to be in a woman's body in outdoor education is the topic we turn to next.

Challenges and Benefits for Women Participants

Feminist scholars have addressed "women's issues" in outdoor education since the 1970s (see Cole, Erdman, and Rothblum 1994; Henderson and Roberts 1998; Roberts 1998; and Warren 1996), and woman-centered adventure programming has become progressively more popular in the last two decades. Literature generated by both scholars and practitioners highlights several themes that we have heard running through the anecdotes of women participating in SSWR and other programs. Women are challenged by outdoor programming because

Physical strength and athletic ability are inconsistent with traditional femininity;

Women are taught to experience their bodies as observed, rather than as instrumental;

Women are reminded of their status as women by sexism and sexual harassment.

At the same time, these first two challenges are related to how women benefit from outdoor programming in that

Women have the opportunity to redefine femininity and overcome restrictive socialization;

Women have the chance to live in their bodies and make their bodies work for them.

(No women we talked to have experienced sexism and sexual harassment in their outdoor adventures as beneficial.) We will explore these challenge/benefits below, then discuss how educators can detect and deal with sexist attitudes and behavior in their programs, and finally summarize some arguments for the value of women-only outdoor experiences.

Femininity and bodies. A promotional postcard for a local martial arts studio pictures a confident young woman in boxing gloves with the caption, "So much for that weaker sex thing." The postcard is effective because it makes a cultural reference that we all recognize: women as the weaker sex. In *The Frailty Myth: Women Approaching Physical Equality*, Collette Dowling (2000) challenges the widely accepted notion that women are naturally physically inferior to men, instead blaming traditional feminine gender role socialization for the apparent sex disparity in strength and athleticism. Dowling provides numerous historical and contemporary accounts of women's physical potential being systematically thwarted by laws and customs, rules and regulations, dress codes and beauty standards, medical misinformation and misogyny. Combined with her presentation of theory and research evidence from anthropology, sociology, psychology, and sports physiology, Dowling's anecdotes make for a persuasive argument that it is a restrictive definition of "femininity," rather than biology, that creates women as the weaker sex.

Feminine socialization impedes the development of bodily skill and physical self-confidence in girls and women primarily because its dominant message is that female bodies are valuable for their form, not their function. In our culture, girls and women are constantly bombarded by reminders that physical attractiveness is a central requirement of femininity, that (hetero)sexual allure is the source of a woman's worth, and that an appealing appearance requires substantial modification of the natural body through cosmetics, body hair removal, unhealthy dieting, strategic and constraining clothing, and even elective surgery (Scott 1997). When girls reach adolescence, their self-esteem plummets as they find their flesh figuratively and literally squeezed into the culture's rigid, narrow, and unrealistic beauty ideal (Pipher 1994). The body that was once a source of pride, and a means of exploring and engaging the world, now becomes a hostile adversary that must be tamed into submission to an artificial appearance standard. The self of the girl is conquered by the body that defines the woman.[3]

According to psychologists Barbara Frederickson and Tomi-Ann Roberts, girls and women are socialized to

> . . . internalize an observer's perspective as a primary view of their physical selves. This perspective on self can lead to habitual body monitoring,

which, in turn, can increase women's opportunities for shame and anxiety, reduce opportunities for peak motivational states, and diminish awareness of internal bodily states. (1997, 1)

Women learn to live outside their bodies, not in them. The psychological and behavioral consequences of internalizing an objectified sense of self include a chronic preoccupation with self-surveillance that disrupts a woman's connection to her subjective experiences and distracts her attention away from the outside world. Outdoor adventures require that we be both tuned in to the signals coming from our bodies and attentive to our surroundings. Many first-time women participants in an outdoor program will not have lived in their bodies since childhood and so are likely to find the experience simultaneously unsettling, intimidating, and liberating.

Even women who regularly engage in sports or other physical recreation are often not shielded from self-objectification, body shame, and appearance anxiety (Greenleaf, 2001). Physical prowess does not protect women from the demands of the feminine body ideal. In fact, physically active women commonly face added pressure to appear feminine. As Precilla Choi explains in *Femininity and the Physically Active Woman*,

> Because the visibility of a woman with muscles, demonstrating strength, speed and agility, is more consistent with traditional notions of masculinity, we need to be assured of the sportswoman's femininity, hence the emphasis on beauty and heterosexual desirability. This is deemed necessary in both the world of sport and recreational exercise in order to prevent a diminishing of the visible differences between the masculine and the feminine. (2000, 9)

The idealized feminine form does not have mass or muscles. It is not dirty or sunburned or hairy or stinky. It does not assume unbecoming stances or engage in unflattering movements. It is unnaturally dissimilar to a "masculine" form. Modification of the female body serves to exaggerate the physical distinction between the sexes, which, when left to nature, is often not large. Put us all out to survive in the woods for a few months and we all would end up looking and acting a lot less "feminine." (That femininity is a social construction is most compellingly illustrated by drag queens, cross-dressing men who are often more convincing "women" than most women we know!) In our culture, it is the feminine body that is charged with maintaining differentiation between the sexes, and that maintenance demands time, effort, vigilance, and an arsenal of grooming aids not typically found in a backpack. Some women Superior Studies students have told us that once they got past feeling the pressure to maintain a feminine appearance, they found great pleasure in things like "not having to shave our legs for six weeks!"

The competing demands of femininity and outdoor education put women in a double-bind; being successful at one means being unsuccessful at the other. Women who aspire to both find themselves laboring to achieve some sort of balance in the form of an oxymoronic "strong femininity" or "feminine athleticism." At the same time, they may be struggling with the fallout from years of feminine-gender-role socialization: they likely will have had less physical practice than their male peers and will be less accustomed to subjectively experiencing their bodies as functional. This is both an external and internal battle. Women in outdoor education are boldly defying the expectations of the culture, while fighting with their own feelings of obligation to meet those expectations. For women striving to overcome years of counterproductive programming and make up for deficits in their prior experience, the task becomes even more daunting when the immediate environment is one toxic with sexism and harassment.

Sexism and sexual harassment. Although "sexism" is a label that technically may refer to prejudice toward any person based on his or her sex, it is most commonly used to describe negative attitudes and behaviors displayed by men toward women. In historically androcentric arenas, such as outdoor education, sexist attitudes and behaviors toward women are, in fact, the primary concern. They are a concern because sexist educational environments significantly interfere with women's learning (Cortina, Swan, Fitzgerald, and Waldo 1998).

Program leaders must intervene when they detect women being treated with disrespect, disregard, or disdain. Sometimes the offense will be directed toward a specific woman, while other times it may be a general derogatory or dehumanizing remark or behavior toward women in general. Blatant examples of sexism are easily identified. As a society, we have become sensitized over the last thirty years to sexist jokes, sexist labels for women (chick, babe, slut), and sexist comments about women being stupid, worthless, or inferior. We believe instructors should clearly communicate that chauvinistic behavior will not be tolerated, whether or not women are present. It is not enough to suppress these behaviors only in coed settings. If the underlying prejudicial attitudes are allowed to flourish unchecked when women are not around, sexism will prevail in the program and will show up in subtle ways.

It is essential for outdoor educators who are aiming to banish sexism from their programs to realize that sexist attitudes and behaviors do not always manifest in obvious displays of discriminatory behavior or derogatory remarks. At first glance it may appear that a program is free from sex bias because traditional gender stereotypes are challenged (e.g., women students and men students alternate in leadership positions, take turns cooking, and are afforded equal attention by instructors), and no sexist jokes or names for women are allowed. Sexism is insidious, however, and it creeps into our language, our conversational patterns, and our nonverbal behavior.

An obvious example of sex bias in language that is rapidly becoming extinct is the use of the "generic he," i.e., using masculine pronouns to indicate both sexes. Other examples of language bias are less obvious and more pervasive. Using the modifiers "woman" or "female" in cases where "man" or "male" would be understood and unstated is biased (e.g., woman leader, female rock climber). Like the generic he, these modifiers originate in, and reinforce, an unspoken assumption of the male as the norm and the female as the exception (Henley 1989). Even when we attempt to be inclusive, by using "he or she" for example, the order of our words may have the same effect (Brekken and Scott 1998). We challenge instructors to do what we do in Superior Studies and liberally sprinkle their speech with phrases such as "women and men" and "hers and his."

Some patterns in our language are sexist because they infantilize women, thus reinforcing their subordinate status relative to men. This happens when we refer to women as "girls" without referring to men as "boys," and when we add the suffix "-ette" to make a label feminine. (Of course, referring to men as "girls," or accusing them of acting "girly," is also sexist, and demeans women as much as it insults men.) Women are sometimes treated as lower-status not through language itself but through the dynamics of conversation. Men tend to interrupt others more than women do, and men interrupt women more than they interrupt men (Smith-Lovin and Brody 1989). This means that men more often have the floor, especially when the topic is something about which they are assumed to be experts, such as navigation or fire-building. In Superior Studies we strive to ensure that women and men have an equal voice by soliciting input from women and curbing input from men when sexist patterns arise. (And, of course, if a reverse pattern arises where women take the floor about food preparation, for example, we draw out the men).

Not all subtle sexism involves speech. Sexist attitudes are communicated through nonverbal channels as well. We have witnessed instances of men rolling their eyes or grinning meaningfully at each other when a woman was attempting to read a map or lift a canoe. We have also seen male students cross their arms belligerently or avert their gaze when being issued instructions by a woman in authority. We suggest that when such behaviors occur, they be discreetly but firmly admonished in a private conversation with the offender(s) about the antagonistic message this body language is sending out.

Nasty nonverbal actions are more similar to the blatant sexism described earlier than they are to our other examples of subtle sexism in that they represent "gender harassment," defined as "generalized sexist remarks and behavior that convey hostile or degrading attitudes about women" (Crawford and Unger 2000, 506). Gender harassment creates an intimidating environment for women and must not be allowed by outdoor educators who aim to provide a positive and effective educational experience for all their students.

Even more potentially damaging to the educational enterprise is sexual harassment, which is distinguished from gender harassment by its clearly sexual—and not just sexist—tone. Our university policy borrows language from the Equal Employment Opportunity Commission and defines sexual harassment as

"unwelcome sexual advances, requests for sexual favors, sexually motivated physical conduct, or other verbal or physical conduct or communication of a sexual nature" when

1. submission to that conduct or communication is made either explicitly or implicitly a term or condition of an individual's employment or education;

2. submission or rejection of that conduct by an individual is used as the factor for employment or education decisions affecting that individual, or

3. that conduct or communication has the purpose or effect of substantially interfering with an individual's employment or educational environment.

Thus, sexual harassment may run the gamut from sexually oriented jokes or comments to quid-pro-quo demands for sex in exchange for a grade. Based on our experience in Superior Studies, we suspect that most instances of sexual harassment that occur in outdoor education are on the milder end of the spectrum, where the definition of what constitutes harassment is a bit grayer and more open to interpretation. Is it harassment if a male instructor tells a female student that she has "a good body for rock climbing"? What if he uses a hands-on technique to show her how to securely buckle her climbing harness? What if either of these behaviors is displayed by a female instructor toward a male student? What if they occur between peers? Sexual harassment is sometimes a tough thing to pin down, and to prove, if one looks only at the behavior itself.

Some behavior that is experienced as sexually harassing is intended as an expression of earnest sexual interest, while other harassment may seem almost fatherly until the harasser is rejected and turns hostile (Fiske and Glick 1995). Sexual harassment may involve repeated behaviors or an isolated incident. Whether sexual harassment has occurred depends more upon the reaction of the target than upon the intent or the behavior itself. Sexually harassing behaviors cause the target to experience negative emotions such as intimidation, fear, shame, guilt, anxiety, and humiliation. These emotions can make it very difficult for the target to comfortably stand up to the offender, especially if the offender is in a position of authority. The obvious problem that arises, then, is that an offender may continue to offend out of ignorance that the behavior is unwelcome. (Of course, many sexual harassers know full well that their behavior is having a negative effect and persist exactly for this reason.)

We recommend that outdoor educators leading coed groups proactively address sexual harassment as a standard part of their orientations. In Superior Studies we routinely lead students through an afternoon of water rescue drills and feigned first-aid scenarios. The goal of these exercises is to get students thinking about safety and to give them tips on how to identify a hazardous situation, choose an appropriate course of action, and implement it. A similar approach could be taken with sexual harassment, which we view as a threat to the well-being of individual women and the group. For this topic, men and women students should take turns role-playing harassers, targets, and bystanders to become familiar with the types of behaviors that may be construed as harassing and to practice confrontation and intervention. Scenarios should cover a variety of violations, some of which clearly fit the legal definition of sexual harassment, and others that are less evident.

Women-only groups? One surefire strategy for eliminating male-on-female sexual harassment in outdoor education is to offer single-sex groups. Advocates for women-only outdoor experiences cite this along with a variety of other rationales, most of which derive from the gender-related issues we have discussed. Before we discuss justifications for women-only opportunities, we will restate that Superior Studies is a coed program. While the promise of women-only programs lies in the relatively safe, non-intimidating, non-competitive, and supportive environment they may provide, we believe that coed programs hold promise for educating both women and men about gender stereotypes and sexism.

Arguments in favor of women-only outdoor programming tend to focus on issues we have identified above: gender stereotypes and roles, the paradox of femininity and physicality, sexism and sexual harassment. Women participants' own accounts of their experiences in single-sex groups emphasize the sense of security they experience in the absence of men's judgment, intimidation, condescension, and skill level (Jordan 1998). Feeling safe contributes to women's willingness to take risks, such as testing and trusting their bodies on a rock face, or taking a turn as group leader, navigator, or stern paddler (Mitten 1996; Warren 1996). Not having men in the program also increases women's opportunities to take such risks. Of 274 women surveyed by Hornibrook et al., 56 percent had also participated in mixed-sex programs. When asked about the biggest strength of all-women programs, their most common responses were "noncompetitive, a comfortable and safe atmosphere, support and caring, co-operation, and an opportunity to understand one's capabilities" (1997, 156).

Without men present, women may also be better able to get inside their own skins and feel embodied instead of objectified. Rock climbing is made considerably more difficult when one's mind is partly preoccupied with concerns about what one's butt in the harness looks like from the ground. Outdoor educator S. Copeland Arnold explains,

> My experiences in Outward Bound as a young woman deeply affected my sense of self-acceptance, self-esteem, and body image. I gained an appreciation for my strength and agility. . . . Rather than an object to be adorned and perfected, my body became an ally. (1994, 43–44)

But,

> . . . women do not automatically experience increases in self-esteem and more positive body image as a result of participating in a wilderness course . . . by focusing on the needs of women, Outward Bound-type women's courses can provide the tools for transformation. (1994, 47)

For example,

> What if all-women's courses encouraged women to develop a relationship with their bodies? . . . and gaining an appreciation of the beauty and diver-

sity of the female body were objectives for an all-women's course? . . . In my experience, as an instructor, the issue of body image has always arisen in all-women groups. Instead of letting the issue arise by chance, instructors should use it as a theme for the course. . . . (1994, 52)

To the extent that success in outdoor programming requires women to be in their bodies, instead of monitoring them, all-women groups may make success more attainable. This is particularly true given that it is not only the male gaze that is present in coed groups but also the male voice and the male touch.

As described above, women in our culture internalize the observer's perspective on their bodies. They also endure unwanted attention in the form of comments and physical contact. Whether the comments and contact are intentional, or sexual, will not necessarily determine how they feel to the woman experiencing them. For this reason, women-only groups are standard in wilderness therapy with victims of sexual abuse. Even women who have not been sexually victimized in the past may find that residing in a woman's body can be a liability in a coed group. China Galland, co-founder of Women in the Wilderness, relates how when one of her mentees was working as a wilderness instructor,

her final course was a group of teenage boys, ages 14–16. [She] was the only woman on the trip and she was the lead instructor. The first night in camp the boys informed [her] that since she was the only girl around, they were going to have to rape her. (1994, 247)

In this case, the instructor firmly told the boys that she would not tolerate more of this harassing behavior, but of course she had the advantages of authority and age in this situation. Most women in coed groups are not in such a powerful position.

In our opinion, there is no doubt that women-only groups serve a valuable function in the historically male territory of outdoor education. We are persuaded that single-sex experiences have the potential to offer women qualitatively different, and perhaps superior, opportunities for personal growth when compared to mixed-sex experiences. At the same time, we support coed programming because only in mixed-sex groups do men and women have the opportunity to learn from each other while they learn about themselves. In the words of one Superior Studies instructor, "Life is coed."

CONCLUDING COMMENTS

This essay has highlighted some of the gender-related issues that come to mind when we reflect on our experiences in Superior Studies. For fear of fatiguing the reader, we have not touched upon all of the gender-related themes that run through the literature or our own memories. We hope, however, that we have offered ample thought-provoking examples and empirical evidence so as to inspire others to take a critical look at gender in their own programs.

Thinking critically about gender will naturally lead to consideration of other participant characteristics that may impact the effectiveness of outdoor education, such as race/ethnicity, disability, and socioeconomic background. Doing so will, in our view, help correct whatever bias remains in what began as a way to prepare strapping young white European military men for immersion into the cold waters of the Atlantic.

Notes

1. Deason is currently the president and executive director of the Wolf Ridge Environmental Learning Center. Prior to his appointment in 2000, he was professor of history at St. Olaf College in Northfield, Minnesota, and director of the School Nature Area Project (SNAP). Dr. Deason originated the concept of SSWR and brought together the various faculty who now teach in the program. The authors wish to thank him for his generosity and the assistance that he showed us in the writing of this paper. We also thank him for the many fine hours of paddling that we have shared.

2. The seven founding colleges of SSWR were Gustavus Adolphus College in St. Peter, Hamline University in St. Paul, Concordia College in Moorhead, St. Olaf College in Northfield, University of St. Thomas in St. Paul, St. John's University in Collegeville, and College of St. Benedict in St. Joseph. Additional members now include Central College in Pella, Iowa, and University of Dubuque in Dubuque, Iowa.

3. It is important to note that the majority of theory and research in this area is about *Caucasian* women in our culture. In the words of Crawford and Unger (2000), "There is virtually no systematic psychological research on the effects of inappropriate standards of beauty on women of color."

References

Abramson, Paul R., Philip A. Goldberg, Judith H. Greenberg, and Linda M. Abramson. 1977. The talking platypus phenomenon: Competency ratings as a function of sex and professional status. *Psychology of Women Quarterly* 2: 114–24.

Arnold, S. Copeland. 1994. Transforming body image through women's wilderness experiences. In *Wilderness therapy for women: The power of adventure*, edited by Ellen Cole, Eve Erdman, and Esther Rothblum, 43–54. New York: Hayworth Press, Inc.

Brekken, Christy Anderson, and Britain Scott. 1998. The "man as norm/woman as special category" mindset: Effects of non-biased generics on automatic thinking and controlled behavior. Unpublished research report.

Cason, Dana, and H. L. Lee Gillis. 1994. A meta-analysis of outdoor adventure programming with adolescents. *Journal of Experiential Education* 17: 40–47.

Choi, Precilla Y. L. 2000. *Femininity and the physically active woman.* Philadelphia: Routledge.

Cole, Ellen, Eve Erdman, and Esther D. Rothblum, eds. 1994. *Wilderness therapy for women: The power of adventure.* New York: Hayworth Press, Inc.

Cortina, Lilia M., Suzanne Swan, Louise F. Fitzgerald, and Craig Waldo. 1998. Sexual harassment and assault: Chilling the climate for women in academia. *Psychology of Women Quarterly* 22: 419–41.

Crawford, Mary, and Rhoda Unger. 2000. *Women and gender: A feminist psychology.* New York: McGraw-Hill.

Deason, Gary. 2000. Proposal to the U.S. Department of Education's fund for the improvement of postsecondary education. Finland, Minn.: Wolf Ridge Environmental Learning Center.

Devine, Patricia G. 1989. Stereotypes and prejudice: Their automatic and controlled components. *Journal of Personality and Social Psychology* 56: 5–18.

Dowling, Collette. 2000. *The frailty myth: Women approaching physical equality.* New York: Random House.

Eagly, Alice, Steven J. Karau, and Mona G. Makhijani. 1995. Gender and the effectiveness of leaders: A meta-analysis. *Psychological Bulletin* 117: 125–45.

Fiske, Susan, and Peter Glick. 1995. Ambivalence and stereotypes cause sexual harassment: A theory with implications for organizational change. *Journal of Social Issues* 51: 97–115.

Fiske, Susan T., and Laura E. Stevens. 1993. What's so special about sex? Gender stereotyping and discrimination. In *Gender issues in contemporary society*, edited by Stuart Oskamp and Mark Costanzo, 173–96. Newbury Park: Sage Publications, 1993.

Fox, Karen M., Leo H. McAvoy, and Anderson B. Young. 1998. Building the research foundations of outdoor education. In *Coalition for education in the outdoors fourth research symposium proceedings*, edited by Karen M. Fox, Leo H. McAvoy, M. Deborah Bialeschki, et al., 5–8. Bradford Woods, Ind.: Coalition for Education in the Outdoors.

Frederickson, Barbara, and Tomi-Ann Roberts. 1997. Objectification theory: Toward understanding women's lived experiences and mental health risks. *Psychology of Women Quarterly* 21: 173–206.

Galland, China. 1994. A new generation of women in the wilderness. In *Wilderness therapy for women: The power of adventure*, edited by Ellen Cole, Eve Erdman, and Esther Rothblum, 243–58. New York: Hayworth Press, Inc.

Greenleaf, Christy Ann. 2001. Self-objectification among physically active women: Negative psychological and behavioral correlates. Unpublished doctoral dissertation. University of North Carolina at Greensboro.

Hattie, John, H. W. Marsh, J. T. Neill, and G. E. Richards. 1997. Adventure education and Outward Bound: Out-of-class experiences that make a lasting difference. *Review of Educational Research* 67: 43–87.

Henderson, Karla. 1996. Feminist perspectives on outdoor leadership. In *Women's voices in experiential education*, edited by Karen Warren, 107–17. Dubuque, Iowa: Kendall Hunt.

Henderson, Karla, and Nina Roberts. 1998. An integrative review of the literature on women in the outdoors. In *Coalition for education in the outdoors fourth research symposium proceedings*, edited by Karen M. Fox, Leo H. McAvoy, M. Deborah Bialeschki, et al., 9–21. Bradford Woods, Ind.: Coalition for Education in the Outdoors.

Henley, Nancy. 1989. Molehill or mountain? What we do and don't know about sex bias in language. In *Gender and thought*, edited by Mary Crawford and M. Gentry, 59–78. New York: Springer-Verlag.

Hopkins, David, and Roger Putnam. 1993. *Personal growth through adventure*. London: David Fulton Publishers.

Hornibrook, Taflyn, Elaine Brinkert, Diana Parry, Renita Seimens, Denise Mitten, and Simon Priest. 1997. The benefits and motivations of all women outdoor programs. *The Journal of Experiential Education* 20: 152–58.

Jordan, Deb. 1998. Leading outdoor recreation skills in a safe place: Lessons from a single-sex program. In *Coalition for education in the outdoors fourth research symposium proceedings,* edited by Karen M. Fox, Leo H. McAvoy, M. Deborah Bialeschki, et al., 85–91. Bradford Woods, Ind.: Coalition for Education in the Outdoors.

Lueptow, L. B., L. Garovich, and M. B. Lueptow. 1995. The persistence of gender stereotypes in the face of changing sex roles: Evidence contrary to the sociocultural model. *Ethology & Sociobiology* 16: 509–30.

McIntosh, Mary, Julian Keniry, Kathy Cacciola, and Stephen Clermont. 2001. A glimpse into the future: A new report by NWF on campus greening efforts. In *The Declaration,* by "University Leaders for a Sustainable Future." Washington, D.C.: Association of University Leaders for a Sustainable Future.

Mitten, Denise. 1996. A philosophical basis for a women's outdoor adventure program. In *Women's voices in experiential education,* edited by Karen Warren, 78–84. Dubuque, Iowa: Kendall Hunt.

O'Reilly, Douglas, Jacqui Degnan, and Lori Columbo. 1995. *Environmental studies: 2000.* Boston, Mass.: The Environmental Careers Organization.

Orr, David. 1992. *Ecological literacy: Education and the transition to a postmodern world.* Albany: State University of New York Press.

Pipher, Mary. 1994. *Reviving Ophelia: Saving the selves of adolescent girls.* New York: G. P. Putnam's Sons.

Roberts, Nina Suzanne. 1998. *A guide to women's studies in the outdoors: A review of literature and research with annotated bibliography, 5th edition.* Needham Heights, Mass.: Simon & Schuster.

Roberts, Nina S., and Donald A. Rodriguez. 1999. Multicultural issues in outdoor education. ERIC Digest 1989, report number EDO-RC-99-6.

Scott, Britain. 1997. Beauty myth beliefs: Theory, measurement, and use of a new construct. Unpublished doctoral dissertation, University of Minnesota.

Sibthorp, Jim. 1998. Pitfalls to avoid in adventure education outcome research. In *Coalition for education in the outdoors fourth research symposium proceedings,* edited by Karen M. Fox, Leo H. McAvoy, M. Deborah Bialeschki, et al., 79–80. Bradford Woods, Ind.: Coalition for Education in the Outdoors.

Smith-Lovin, Lynn, and Charles Brody. 1989. Interruptions in group discussions: The effects of gender and group composition. *American Sociological Review* 54: 424–35.

Strauss, Benjamin H. 1996. *Environmental education, practices, and activism on campus.* New York: The Nathan Cummings Foundation.

Swim, Janet. 1994. Perceived versus meta-analytic effect sizes: An assessment of the accuracy of gender stereotypes. *Journal of Personality and Social Psychology* 66: 21–36.

Szkrybalo, Joel, and Diane N. Ruble. 1999. "God Made Me a Girl": Sex category constancy judgments and explanations revisited. *Developmental Psychology* 35: 392–402.

Warren, Karen. 1985. Women's outdoor adventures: Myth and reality. *Journal of Experiential Education* 8: 10–14, issue theme: Experiential Education from the Male and Female Point of View.

Warren, Karen. 1996. *Women's voices in experiential education.* Dubuque, Iowa: Kendall Hunt Publishing.

Warren, Karen. 1997. Where have we been, where are we going? Gender issues in experiential education. *Journal of Experiential Education* 20: 117–18, issue theme: Gender Issues in Experiential Education.

✳ BARBARA "BARNEY" NELSON

Building Community on a Budget
in the Big Bend of Texas

Sul Ross State is an open-admissions university one hundred miles north of the Mexican border in Alpine, Texas, and named after an old Texas Ranger, Lawrence Sullivan "Sul" Ross. Our athletic mascot is the Mexican wolf, or lobo. One semester for an environmental literature class, I chose Barry Lopez's *Of Wolves and Men* as a text. Lopez's book includes a sketch of a wolf track, so my students and I noticed that our cheerleaders had painted panther tracks (no claws), instead of wolf tracks (claws) across our parking lots. Indignantly, we sent a copy of the wolf track sketch from Lopez's book to our cheerleaders. Since then we've had no more embarrassing problems with panther tracks in our lobo parking lot. Although I joke about it, the experience serves as a classic reminder of how far removed we are from the natural world.

The last two wild wolves in Texas were killed in 1970 about seventy miles east and fifteen miles southeast of our campus. A few short years later, however, a wolf was killed right on campus. In 1967, a year before I arrived as an undergraduate, a live Mexican wolf, Miss Sully, had been given to the college by the Arizona-Sonora Desert Museum. The coaches and local supporters thought she would inspire our "Lobo" football players to wild and winning ways. Muzzled, Miss Sully bounced around on the end of a leash during home football games. The rest of her days were spent pacing a large chain-link cage on the lawn between what is now the new museum and the hillside where the old museum once stood.

At first Miss Sully, who had been hand-raised, seemed to crave attention more than a domestic dog. But the longer she spent caged and subjected to the unrelenting human gaze, the more sullen, withdrawn, and cranky she became. People watched her eat, watched her pee, watched her circle the cage. They stuck their fingers through the wire to tease her into snapping. They howled at her, wanting her to howl back. She always howled back at the train whistle, but human howlers were never as successful. I imagined that maybe she sensed the urgency and passion of the train whistle warning of its approach and the desire simply for entertainment from the human voices.

On the morning Miss Sully was found dead, the campus erupted in angry protest. Everyone assumed she had been poisoned. Who could have done such a thing? Who could kill such a beautiful and noble animal? Who could be so cruel? But how and why she died, to my knowledge, was never actually determined. I always wondered if the deed might have been a brave act of mercy to relieve her from her life of captivity, but I kept my opinions to myself.

Almost thirty years have passed since Miss Sully died. The university never tried to replace her. The cage was dismantled and grass soon covered the spot where it had stood. But every fall I take my freshman students on what I call a "sense of place" walk. I show them the deer droppings, the alligator junipers, the esperanza, and the dorms with ghosts. I show them where the lobo cage used to be. After I tell Miss Sully's story, my students always say, "How could anyone be so cruel?" I no longer keep my opinions to myself. I try to help my students see what a sad life Miss Sully was forced to lead just for our entertainment. Pacing a wire cage and being trotted out for sporting events is no life for a lady lobo. I want the ghost of Miss Sully's cage to haunt them. Teaching environmental topics at a university in the heart of Texas ranching country whose mascot is the wolf is just one of the many ironies and challenges I face. Including undergraduate majors in environmental science, environmental studies (both arts and science), wildlife management, natural resource management, and a nationally recognized geology program, I find myself heavily involved with the complexities of environmental issues, perhaps especially those dealing with environmental justice, race, and class.

The ratio of Anglo to Hispanic students at Sul Ross is roughly fifty/fifty with a few African-American students and a few from all over the world. Most, even the faculty, come from rural areas and small towns. We have a chemistry professor from India, for example, but he was raised in rural India, wears cowboy boots, and drives a pickup truck with a bumper sticker that reads "America is Indian country." This area of Texas has one of the highest rates of poverty per capita in the nation. Many of my students work their way through school and often support families on the side, so trying to incorporate field trips into my classes has been a challenge. For me and my students environmental justice is not just an abstraction.

When my students decline the opportunity for a camping trip because they don't own and can't afford camping equipment, can't miss work, can't afford a baby sitter, or can't afford the gas, it becomes painfully obvious to me that an extended nature outing is often a class- and race-based privilege. My students are often children of, or related to, those who serve the food, pump the gas, and clean the restrooms for those who *can* afford to travel. Camping is often touted as a democratic excursion, but it's not. In order to solve my students' logistics of work and family responsibilities, and not embarrass those who don't own and can't afford hiking boots, backpacks, and sleeping bags, our field trips are usually short, sometimes even reduced to an hour of class time. We simply walk outside the classroom door. Although those of us who call ourselves "environmentalists" have been conditioned to imagine that nature happens far away from civilization, I have felt compelled to challenge that perspective in order to help my students recognize and value nature in their own backyards. Numerous scholars have stressed that creating hierarchies of beauty in both women and nature has led to devaluing the unbeautiful and objectifying both. Since I preach that we should treat our yards and pastures with the same sacred awe as a wilderness area, perhaps it is best that I can't whisk my students off for a two-week hike in the California High Sierra. Our poverty forces me to walk the talk.

Fortunately, just walking out the classroom door is enough of a journey to help my students engage with the natural world. Deer browse the campus shrubbery nightly, and their tracks and droppings can be found all over campus, around most buildings. Wild turkeys, javelina, and antelope occasionally stroll across corners of our lawns. Cliff swallows nest along the eves of several buildings, and many of the Chihuahuan desert's most beautiful shrubs and trees have been planted as part of our landscape: desert willow, esperanza, alligator juniper, Arizona cypress, mountain laurel, piñon pines, native maples, giant daggers, yuccas, sotol, sacahuista, cenisas, and madroños. Buzzards, vultures, red-tailed hawks, and an occasional golden eagle drift on rising hot-air thermals within view of classroom windows. So, without leaving campus, I can sometimes create the magic of a nature experience with the added bonus of the "trip" being free and easily available to all.

In the summer, when our temperatures may climb to over a hundred degrees, I like to take my nature-writing class outside to the university's cactus garden. An environmental-science technician employed through the biology department maintains an extensive outdoor plant collection with more than a hundred desert species, many of them rare. Here, the assignment might be simply to pick a cactus with which to identify and then try to empathize with it as a writing assignment. One female student who moonlighted as a bartender wrote a beautiful acrostic poem about a night-blooming cereus, scrawny and ugly by day but known as "queen of the night." While students bake in the sun and look longingly toward their air-conditioned classroom, they write marvelous sentences about the endurance and tenacity of the desert plants, sometimes even gaining a glimmer of appreciation for their parents who often hold jobs that require long hours of physical labor in this same hot sun.

During a class on Henry David Thoreau, we met at the campus outdoor theater site for a demonstration and talk by a local surveyor who set up a theodolite and helped give students a Thoreauvian feel for topography and attention to detail. Students were allowed to look through the scope in order to see how deceptive the course of water channels might appear to the naked eye. He showed us an antique "chain" from the 1800s and a stadia rod used for estimating distance and determining elevation. He talked about land laws and explained the more modern electronic distance meter. Outdoor experiences like this cost nothing and involve no travel, yet I believe give students deeper understanding of topographical perceptions than a mountain hike, not to mention a deeper understanding of Thoreau's observational skills and his ability to find nature on the edges of Concord.

Several times I've taken classes into the deep "big bend" of the Rio Grande to visit the settings for books read for two classes that I teach periodically, one an undergraduate and one a graduate class, both called "Reading and Writing the Big Bend." Perhaps the most successful trip was a three-day/two-night traveling research presentation excursion with graduate students. Since the class met regularly on weekends (nine to five Saturday, eight to twelve Sunday), most students were already committed to adjust their responsibilities and jobs. On the last weekend, instead of meeting in our usual classroom, we took to the back roads to weave the big, beautiful desert country into the class.

Since my students' financial situation must always be considered, I obtained funding for motel rooms though my academic vice-president, but I bought the gas. We all carried water, picnics, hats, and plastic bags to pack out our toilet-paper "roses." We laughed at the rules for travel given us by the college administrators, requiring us to carry cell phones (there is no cell-phone service in the deep Big Bend) and road hazard signs. We seldom met another vehicle as we crossed and recrossed Big Bend National Park and the surrounding desert areas. If we had broken down, we might have needed some signal mirrors to send *avisos* and summon help (as we'd read about in W. D. Smithers's *Chronicles of the Big Bend*), but we certainly would not have needed to warn "traffic" to avoid us! Nowhere on the list of travel precautions were hats, water, or the need for a Spanish-speaking translator mentioned.

The students had read eight classic Big Bend books, done extensive research in the Archives of the Big Bend on topics related to the area, and had each read an additional book of their choice for a report. Their oral presentations were scheduled at related stops on our journey. For instance, one student, a local law enforcement officer, gave his book report on Terrence Poppa's *The Drug Lord,* an unauthorized biography about a local drug runner, Pablo Acosta, who was finally killed at Santa Elena Canyon in Big Bend National Park. While the student talked—white male, armed, and wearing his uniform—Santa Elena Canyon loomed behind him. Next up was a Hispanic student reporting on the border bandit era and what he called "the excessive presence of law enforcement" in the Big Bend. The river here divides two countries and represents the sometimes uneasy contact zone where different cultures collide. Between my two students, the old complicated issues of race relations and law and order hung in the desert air. We all quietly remembered that raids, retaliations, and atrocities were committed by both sides, and the vast desert mountains of the Big Bend country concealed or thwarted them all, passing no judgments about who was right and who was wrong.

Traveling on, our next stop was the porch of the old Castolon Trading Post where we heard a creative paper based on trading post research. At the Hot Springs, site of the J. O. Langford book *Big Bend: A Homesteader's Story,* one of the class readings, we met Roland Wauer, author of numerous bird books, including *For All Seasons: A Big Bend Journal,* which was also an assigned reading. The mystique of the Big Bend helps me attract writers and speakers that my small school normally could not afford. Ro loves the area and will return for a much lower fee than he's worth—a fee again supplied by my favorite administrator. Ro took us birding up Tornillo Creek, pointing out the cliffs where the controversial (controversial because their authenticity has never been established) "clay tablets" discussed in his book had been found. At Big Bend National Park's Hot Springs near Boquillas, while students soaked their feet for free, we heard a book report on Pat Little Dog's *Border Healing Woman* about a curandero who used the mud and waters of another local hot spring to cure ailments of neighbors and visitors, as this one had also been used by the J. O. Langford family in pre-park days. In the one-room (today four-room) school at Panther Junction (also site of another assigned reading, Aileen Kilgore Henderson's *Treasure of Panther Peak*) we listened to a guitar-strumming student dressed as a flapper talk about the school marms imported into the Big Bend during the 1920s. Educating the border children has always been a struggle: ninety-mile one-way bus rides, libraries that can't afford books, students who put in an adult day's work before and after school. Even today a local women's club that I belong to buys school supplies every fall for Big Bend area children who can't afford them.

At the old Hallie Stillwell Ranch, we listened to a paper on women ranchers. Research on hunting was delivered under the glass eyes of numerous mounted mule deer "trophies." As a follow-up, a former student and employee of the Stillwell Store and ranch served us venison burritos for lunch for free. And so it went. After the final report on a cartoonist stationed at Camp Mercer, the loneliest military outpost of World War I, we piled into my four-wheel-drive vehicle and headed south to the Adams Ranch. Here we met two ranch employees who spoke only Spanish and who served as our guides down torturous roads to the base of a faint, steep trail, which we climbed to the old Camp Mercer stone ruins.

Another memorable trip was a three-day/two-night "writing retreat" offered as part of my nature-writing class. My class is often divided equally between those who call themselves "environmentalists" and those who come from rural areas. One of my ambitions as a teacher is to foster understanding between these two groups, the "greens" and the "rurals," that I firmly believe share common goals and should be partners rather than enemies. It seems that the media have been intent on promoting the idea of a world where rural resource "users" oppose urban resource "protectors" and vice versa. The rurals often feel threatened by environmentalists who want to stop hunting and to turn cowboys into tourist guides. The greens in turn often feel threatened by rednecks who will obviously shoot or poison everything that moves and turn grasslands into desert. Neither side's perception is whole or accurate, of course. Since I think of myself as having "dual citizenship" and know they share much common ground, I simply try to expose the students to each other, bring up the volatile subjects, and encourage them to talk it out. They quickly discover that they all want the same things—grass, clean water, healthy ecosystems. Their differences center on how best to accomplish those goals. In order to help them understand each other, I include several nature writers in my syllabus who write with strong rural themes: Wendell Berry, Linda Hasselstrom, Bill Kittredge, Gretel Ehrlich, Richard Nelson, Larry Littlebird, Mary Austin, Ed Abbey, Gary Paul Nabhan, Robert Frost. We also read mystery writers whose work foregrounds nature and presents rural values: Tony Hillerman, Alana Martin. Sensitive to the environmental-justice issues important to our large Hispanic population, I'm constantly on the alert for rural Hispanic nature writing: Fabiola Cabeza de Baca, Rudolfo Anaya, Denise Chavez, Alberto Rios, Ray Gonzalez.

Permission to take college students onto private property has sometimes been hard to come by. Since the Endangered Species Act was passed, landowners fear they will be punished, rather than rewarded, if endangered species are found on their property. But since I have one foot in both "green" and "rural" worlds (consequently neither side quite trusts me completely!), I'm occasionally allowed into places most people can't go. Sometimes, also, I rely on students who have connections and expertise that can help. During this particular nature writing class, a well-liked local cowboy, Casey Adams, was enrolled. Between the two of us, we were able to get access to the old Dude Sproul hunting camp located deep in the Davis Mountains. I had leased grazing land and run some of my own cattle on neighboring Sproul family land. Casey had day-worked for the ranch enough that he could guide us in and out of the confusing maze of seldom-used, steep mountain roads. Since Texas is almost all private land, roads are unnamed, unmarked, and unmaintained.

Casey's most important contribution to the trip was probably the fact that he is also a great camp cook in the old cowboy tradition—he volunteered to do all the cooking. Casey and a friend, Scott Meiers (a student in another of my classes who desperately needed some "extra credit"), claimed to have swept the "widder" nests out of an old cabin and chopped plenty of wood. Again my deus ex machina administrator came through with grocery money and rent for the hunting camp. The rest of our necessities were donated by Casey and Scott, working-class rural cowboys who make fifty dollars a day when they find work but sometimes go for weeks with no work at all, as during the ten-year drouth we'd been having. They had made countless trips up the mountain on their own gas and tires, trying to get a water line working and then finally hauling water in along with bedrolls, groceries, folding chairs, chuck box, and cooking paraphernalia. They donated days of free hard labor, spinning months of life off their tires on the steep, rocky roads. (I've heard it said that if you want something done, ask a busy person. I would add to that, if you want something done for free, ask a poor one.)

Most of the students staying in camp the first night were cowboys. The others had listened to the weather report forecasting the dense fog, chilly north wind, and cold drizzle greeting us the next morning. The cowboys had designated the cabin as the women's camp (because it boasted the modern convenience of an indoor toilet one could "flush" with a bucket of water—if one didn't mind bumping knees with spiders), so they had all rolled out their bedrolls on the ground around the fire. I had pitched my range teepee tent a few hundred yards away and crawled out to find the weather had rooted the cowboys from their bedrolls early. They stood around drinking coffee, letting the drizzle drip off their hat brims, trying to convince me they were too miserable to write. Unfortunately for them, this was not my first day around cowboys. I knew that nothing made them happier than rain, unless it was standing around a campfire during a rain with plenty of groceries in the chuck box. I was not convinced by their claims of phony misery.

My nature-writing class is not a required class, so the rural, working-class students who enroll do so voluntarily. The common perception is that these students take nature for granted when in reality they have deep appreciation for the natural world, as their reluctance to sweep the "wider" nests out of the cabin had eloquently and perhaps a little nervously proved. Another misconception is that they are circumspect, private, and don't like to write. As a scholar of rural literature, however, I've uncovered over seventy-five published books, plus numerous short stories, essays, dramas, and poems written by my students' parents and grandparents. Like their elders, my students are often natural storytellers and astute observers, but, like most undergraduates, they begrudge putting pen to paper. That cold, damp morning, I tried not to give orders and to set a good example instead. Enthusiastically, I dug out my own journal and wrote until the page curled and the ink ran in the drizzle:

I'm sitting in my old familiar camp chair, and weather has blown in as usual. So, I'm feeling at home. It's foggy, about 45 degrees, misting, with gusts of cold wind. . . . The trees here are alligator juniper. Last night around the fire, several of the students were telling alligator stories—I wonder if the trees wondered what on earth they were talking about. . . . No birds are singing, just the wind in the trees and the sound of the fire being whipped by the wind—some of my favorite sounds. I like weather if I'm in camp—wind, fog, cold. I like to look off and see trees gradually become greyer as they disappear in the fog. The fog is blowing through camp like smoke or clouds. . . .This place is bringing back memories of some good times in my past. Once they might have been painful memories, but now I guess enough time has passed that I can enjoy them again.

More students arrived in camp after breakfast, as one of my female Hispanic students, April Poissant, explained:

> We finally reach the campsite where a few other members of the class are already waiting. They had stayed on the mountain, in the freezing temperatures and mist from the storm that blew in overnight. The fog seems to be even thicker at this higher elevation. I look across the campsite and can barely make out the trees in the not too distant grove. The wind is fiercer up here than in the valley. I layer on another jacket to try and keep out the cool, wet chill. Everyone gathers around the campfire to converse. The warmth of the crackling fire gives much needed relief from the damp cold. Our camp cook, Casey, offers me a hot cup of cowboy style coffee. With a little sugar, it's not half bad.

As soon as everyone had warmed up and finished at least one cup of coffee, I sent them off on their first writing assignment. It was a dismal failure, as April described it:

> We are to go off by ourselves, into the trees, and write about our surroundings. This is our first exercise about writing in the moment, a concept our instructor has been trying to explain to us throughout the semester. I wander off only a few steps, when I realize I'd rather be closer to the fire. I return to warm my hands so they can grasp onto my pencil and try again. After writing for about fifteen minutes by the fire, my fingers begin to cramp from the exposure to the chilly temperatures.

Whine, whine, whine! Here we are on a "nature-writing retreat" and all that my students want to do is burn wood (I was beginning to wonder now if Casey had chopped *enough*), eat (I was beginning to wonder if three pickup loads of provisions were enough), drink coffee, and talk to each other. Some students I suspected were hiding in one of the nearby barns instead of writing about the beautiful foggy weather. So I called them all back to the fire and asked them to read their passages. Scott had created only one sentence, which seemed to sum up the feelings of the group: "A lot happens around a cup." Everyone paused thoughtfully for refills and dubbed his weasly creation a classic cowboy haiku, outvoted me, and granted him double credit over my head. What was going on here? I expected to have to serve as referee between the "rurals" and the "greens" but instead they had joined forces and were plotting against me!

I suspected that true to the old cowboy tradition, the dang cooks had slyly usurped my leadership and control. April gave it away in one tell-tale passage:

> Casey scatters out coals from the fire and begins assembling lunch. I have never seen someone cook over an open flame before. This is an entirely different experience. He lays a griddle over the coals for his cooking surface. He periodically checks for just the right temperature, by running his hand just inches from the surface in a fluid sweeping motion. Steak quesadillas soon begin to sizzle on the griddle as my mouth begins to salivate with the wonderful aroma permeating the air.

Casey and Scott were feeding the other students much too well for their loyalty to remain with me.

I'm being funny here, or trying to be. Actually what was happening is what always happens when I can actually bring my working-class rural and urban students together. They discover that they genuinely like each other.

In previous classes, during previous semesters, the "greens," as they call themselves, had often inspired us to be more appreciative of the beautiful desert grasslands surrounding us. They had often inspired us to explain our meaning in more modern and carefully chosen ways so that we didn't misunderstand each other so badly. Sometimes they had created the right perspective to change minds, broaden horizons, and influence behavior.

On the other hand, on this trip especially, the "greens" are passionate and want to be effective nature advocates but often lack the practical knowledge and skills to keep themselves comfortable in inclement weather, often fear spiders and snakes, and sometimes have trouble figuring out a way to "shit in the woods," as one recent camping guide so poetically put it. My rural students will just make a joke about it while slyly explaining what to do. Everyone soon relaxes. Cowboys know how much wood it takes to keep a camp comfortable during a drizzly weekend, and they know how hungry people can get when they get a little more fresh air than they're used to. They also know most people are scared of spiders, so they *claimed* to have swept them out of the cabin but obviously hadn't. They knew that after spending a little time in close quarters, everyone would realize that the spiders meant them no harm and minded their own business. The cowboys loved the weather as much as I did but simply thought we should be spending it swapping good stories around the fire instead of humoring the professor by trying to write on soggy paper. Soon they had the rest of the class rebelling with them. But it was all part of my plan. Nothing builds a friendship faster than adopting a common enemy.

Still more students arrived after lunch. A personal friend, Felicia Martinez, who teaches classes for the gifted at area high schools, also arrived to lead a "curandero" hike—identifying native plants and explaining old Indian and Hispanic cures and uses. Parents and grandparents of my Hispanic students are often experts at plant identification and know their medicinal uses well, but that knowledge is often lost to the younger generations. Cowboys usually know them all, which is another nice surprise to the greens. Because of the weather, Felicia also brought along a mounted botanical collection, but I insisted on the hike and sent them off into the fog while I waited warm by the fire. After another short, chilly walk in the drizzle and fog, Felicia and the students informed me they were back and were moving into the cabin to study her mounted specimens around the ticking woodstove. They allowed me to join them.

By Saturday evening, the women's "widder" camp had been converted to a coed camp and I was the only one left sleeping in the drizzle. I think the situation did, however, earn this old, overweight, out-of-shape, grey-haired professor a kernel of respect from one of the female "rurals." Rancher's daughter Dolly Jean Eppenauer, who's five feet three inches tall, wrote such glowing words about her "tough" English professor who could camp out in the cold rain in a bedroll and teepee that I didn't want to wimp out in front of her, so I spent the second night in the drizzle as well. Actually, I was quite warm and dry and my teepee was much quieter than the cabin, I'm sure. Now that I look back on it, though, it was probably just another of their sly ploys to get rid of me.

The trip was a total failure as far as producing reams of fresh new pages of good nature writing, but the understanding and friendships forged between my students were more important. A campfire never seems to lose its magic power. As story after story had unfolded between them, the greens and the rurals and the Hispanics discovered their common goals. Although the stories were traded orally instead of being written on paper as I had hoped, I felt the purpose behind nature writing was being accomplished. Nature writing (or stories) gives the readers (or listeners) vivid vicarious experiences that deepen appreciation for the natural world, instill a code of ethics toward the non-human, and help to identify with the writer's (or teller's) perspective. Powers of observation increase and plants and animals take on both symbolic and real meanings. People begin to develop a sense of place that transcends race, gender, economic and political boundaries.

As we broke camp on Sunday morning, the sun finally began to peek through the clouds. While "flushing" the now also coed toilet one last time, and leaving the "widders" totally undisturbed, I noticed that only two sticks of wood remained in Casey's and Scott's enormous woodpile, and the grocery boxes were almost empty. With a little outdoor exercise, fresh cold air in their lungs, and weather controlling their lives, my students had eaten like a pack of wolves and had formed what I hoped would prove to be lasting friendships. Instead of labeling themselves as "greens," "rurals," or Hispanics, my students had become, I hoped, a single pack of lobos.

References

Henderson, Aileen Kilgore. 1999. *Treasure of Panther Peak*. Minneapolis: Milkweed.

Langford, J. O., with Fred Gipson. 1952. *Big Bend: A homesteader's story*. Austin: University of Texas Press.

Little Dog, Pat. 1985. *Border healing woman: The story of Jewel Babb as told to Pat Little Dog*. Austin: University of Texas Press.

Lopez, Barry. 1978. *Of wolves and men*. New York: Charles Scribner's Sons.

Poppa, Terrence E. 1998. *Drug lord: The life and death of a Mexican kingpin*. Seattle: Demand Publications.

Smithers, W. D. 1976. *Chronicles of the Big Bend: A photographic memoir of life on the border*. Austin: Madrona Press, 1976.

Wauer, Roland H. 1997. *For all seasons: A Big Bend journal*. Austin: University of Texas Press.

❋ JOHN TALLMADGE

Urban Nature as a Scene of Instruction

Mention "nature," and most people think of hills, lakes, and forests with more wildlife than people. Mention "wilderness," and places like the Grand Canyon or the High Sierra come to mind. Hardly anyone thinks of the cities or suburbs where most of us actually live. And therefore urban nature remains an invisible landscape. We have little sense of its biological vitality or cultural promise and only the most rudimentary concept of its environmental value.

Nor is it hard to understand why. City dwellers do not depend on the local ecosystem for food, clothing, energy, or medicine, and have thus lost the physical and spiritual intimacy experienced by tribal people. Moreover, our culture has not developed ethical or aesthetic categories for interpreting nature in city landscapes. A view of the Tetons across the Snake River is easy to understand and admire; not so the backyard or the edge of a neighborhood park. Our philosophers and nature writers have done a wonderful job of teaching us how to value nature "out there" in remote, exotic environments but have offered few insights for dealing with it "right here," in the mixed, ambiguous landscapes where we live and work. Yet common sense would suggest that we must take all landscapes into account if we are to build honorable and sustainable relations with the rest of life.

I became interested in urban nature reluctantly. As a teacher and environmentalist, I had always sought wild places as a way to escape city life. Inspired by writers like Thoreau, Muir, Abbey, and Dillard, I envisioned a spiritual practice of the wild that repudiated the comforts and addictions of civilization in favor of ascetic, visionary journeys in pure, untrammeled places full of grand vistas and native species. As a teacher, I sought to combine the classroom study of great nature writers with field trips to regions they had described, so that students could experience the spirit of place directly and thereby appreciate the writer's art and insight with critical and emotional depth.

This approach is widely practiced today. I believe it works so well because it mirrors the structure of both the literature and the experience, a pattern that might be called the "excursion model." In this scenario, the protagonist leaves a center of civilization and goes out into nature where he or she encounters wonders, challenges, or epiphanies that yield wisdom, strength, or personal transformation, then returns home to give a prophetic account of the experience. Archetypal in its simplicity, this pattern is recognizable in tribal initiation rituals worldwide, in the Hero Journey described by mythologist Joseph Campbell, in various forms of chivalric romance, and of course in the work of seminal nature writers. We find it in Thoreau's Walden sojourn and Maine-woods travels, in the Sierra journeys of Muir, in the desert adventures of Abbey, in the Arctic travels of Marshall and Lopez, and in Dillard's visionary walks along Tinker Creek. In works like these, which have largely informed environmental thought and activism in America, wilderness is the primary scene of instruction, and the protagonist is a traveler from civilization, a "visitor who does not remain."

So deeply embedded is this pattern that we generally take it for granted. I did not become aware of it myself until work took me to Cincinnati, a town that, as you might imagine, was never high on the list of choice living for wilderness lovers. At first the city hardly seemed natural at all. I experienced it as a gray world of concrete, glass, engine noise, and debris. What little there was of the green world seemed dirty, sick, or abused. I retreated into fantasy, thinking of myself as a wilderness person trapped inside pressed slacks, thin-soled shoes, and a grinding administrative job.

But after the initial shock and withdrawal symptoms wore off, urban nature slowly began to take on a different light. Perhaps it was due to walks with my young children, who notice *everything*, or perhaps it was just curiosity getting the better of depression, but one day I started paying attention to what was going on down the street. In two weeks I counted twenty-four species of birds, not just the usual cardinals and house sparrows, but broad-winged hawks, great blue herons, and even a pileated woodpecker. One night a possum crossed the back yard. Deer tracks appeared in the nearby woods. Red admiral butterflies swarmed the brambles in the park. Fireflies floated to the treetops on hot June nights. I began to realize that we were surrounded by buzzing, flapping, chewing, photosynthesizing life forms that were all pursuing ultimate concerns far different from our own.

This was wildness up close and frequently personal. It was shocking to one accustomed to dreaming of wilderness "out there." But once the turn had been made, everything began to look different. The doors of perception were opened a crack, not only to immediate and particular things, but also to the aesthetic and spiritual presentation of the larger landscape. Urban nature began to appear as a scene of instruction every bit as rich and promising as remote wilderness, albeit in different ways. And I also began to appreciate how the excursion model, useful and powerful as it is, may reinforce habits of mind and action that limit our ability to conceive and enact truly sustainable patterns of life. Now, in addition to wilderness trips, I use urban landscapes as outdoor laboratories for exploring the interactions—physical, historical, and spiritual—between humans and other beings in nature.

THE CIRCULATION OF WILDNESS

Since we customarily think of nature as something apart from humanity, something "out there," I like to begin urban field trips indoors. After all, we spend most of our lives inside buildings, separated from the outdoors by walls, doors, and windows, surrounded by objects whose surfaces reflect our imagery and concerns, and swathed in a climate maintained for uniform comfort. The more barren and sterile the classroom, the better. I began one trip in a windowless aeronautics lab at Santa Rosa Junior College in California, asking the students where nature began. Most pointed to the door, but then one pointed to the dirt on his shoes, wondering about spores and bacteria, another said her cold germs had to be part of nature, a third spotted a fly on the wall, and a fourth noted the slate tops of the lab benches and the plastic composition chairs, made from petroleum that had formed from ancient organisms. Nature, it appeared, was not only circulating through the air and through our bodies but also lurking (as it were) beneath the surface of artifacts. To regard this room as a part of culture and therefore separate from nature was like staring into a mirror.

Crossing the threshold onto a concrete sidewalk outside felt to the students like passing through a membrane. Like a cell wall, the walls of the building permitted some things to pass while keeping other things out. Just beyond the door a well opened to the sky through the cantilevered second floor of the building. Beneath it was a six-by-six-foot patch of soil where shrubs had been planted. We spent half an hour studying this plot and counted more than twenty species in addition to the six that had obviously been installed by the gardener: not only the algae, molds, and mushrooms in the mulch but also centipedes, spiders, insects of all sizes, mosses, and flowering plants. We could easily distinguish various microclimatic zones: the center's abundant sunlight and moisture contrasted with partial to full shade near the edges and bare soil where the overhang of the building created a rain shadow. The vegetation line marking the sun's passage could have been drawn with a ruler.

The students were quick to infer that this small plot was being colonized by the same process that populates denuded islands or volcanic slopes. Species migrate in from outside and settle where conditions permit. Even in the artificially sterilized environments of cities, tides of "aerial plankton" continually waft across the landscape, dropping seeds, pollen, bacteria, spores, encysted protozoa, or viable crumbs of lichen. Things lodge and grow wherever they can. Even a rain pool on a tar-paper roof can turn green and wriggling after a few cloudy days.

Thus sensitized, the students took another half hour to cross the parking lot, whose decaying asphalt was webbed with cracks ideal for moss and flat-spreading weeds, and the debris lodged against concrete car-stops had formed a rich, black soil where wild flowers had already appeared. By the time we reached the fence line tangled with vines, weeds, and woody shrubs, people were panting a bit, overwhelmed by so much life in places they used to pass with hardly a glance. We took a break at the fence, watching birds flit in the shrubs and noticing larger insects, such as butterflies and wasps, that cruised the leaves and blossoms. Someone spotted a rabbit twitching beneath a bush.

From here we could see into adjoining yards and look down streets lined with trees, shrubbery, and flower beds. It was evident that the neighborhood was a complex mosaic of small patches of land that manifested every degree of wildness, from the sterile or manicured to the unkempt and ignored. If you were a rabbit, you could travel a long way undercover along hedgerows and fence lines and find plenty of hiding places in weedy, unmowed corners or along the edges of garages; you'd probably find lots of sweet, herbaceous meals along the way. The whole neighborhood was infiltrated with threads of wilderness; it was a tissue of domesticated cells around and through which wildness circulated like plasma. It was no longer so easy to draw the line between the wild and the human worlds.

THE NEIGHBORHOOD AS MUSEUM

Since most of my students grew up and still live in residential neighborhoods, I like to use the sidewalk as a nature trail. Most environmentally oriented people enjoy hiking in favorite landscapes where, after a few trips, they begin to learn the flowers, the rocks, and perhaps even rudiments of the local ecology. It's a fair bet they know more about such places than about their home ground. I certainly did. Because, after all, the trees along the street were planted, pruned, and taken care of, so they weren't really part of nature. And, how could the laws of ecology apply to a region where the flows of energy, nutrients, and information are all skewed by human activity?

Well, step outside, and sniff the air. Aside from the faint tang of pollution, stronger on some days than others, it's the same climate as in the wild forest two counties over: same mean temperatures, same yearly rainfall, same growing season, same annual solar load. Certain plants thrive here while others never will. Walk down my street in Cincinnati, and you will note that some trees, like silver maple, river birch, or sycamore, are native to this area; some, like Colorado blue spruce, are native to North America but not to this area, while others, such as eastern hemlock or white pine, were once native but have since retreated north; still others, such as Chinese elm, Norway spruce, or gingko, are imports from other continents. But all thrive in this climate and this sort of landscape. In fact, if you travel to other American cities at this latitude, you are likely to find the very same mix of species. It's characteristic. But what explains it?

Classical ecology would say that resident species have co-evolved or co-adapted over time so that the energy and nutrient resources of the landscape are fully, sustainably utilized. An ecosystem is defined in terms of food and energy exchange. But in cities, there seems to be something more at work. For one thing, there has not been time enough for evolution and adaptation to work their course; most American cities are less than three hundred years old. For another, it's clear that many species have been imported. To account for their presence and persistence requires a human factor.

Of course, we don't eat the trees on the block. They provide shade, comfort, and a pleasing view. These are aesthetic fruits. But there often seems to be a hidden dimension of personal meaning. Near my home is a house with a large lot and a dozen mature white pines. The pine flourished here about six thousand years ago but retreated northward as the climate warmed. Every time I walk by this house, I smell their resinous fragrance; I hear the whisper of wind through their fine needles and see the green stain of algae on their bark. For a moment, I'm transported to a wild, fresh landscape far from Cincinnati. And I am sure that whoever planted these pines must have missed the north woods too. There is a story here that I shall probably never know. It surely explains the presence of this pine grove so far from its normal range.

Such manifestations of stories in the land reveal an emotional, psychological, or spiritual dimension to the ecology of the place. The biodiversity of Cincinnati, so much greater than that of surrounding woods, reflects this human factor. To interpret these sorts of landscapes requires an ecology that incorporates both culture and individual human actors. Even a field trip down the sidewalk can illuminate the unconscious presuppositions and limitations in our thinking about such cherished concepts, and so deepen and revitalize environmental practice.

WILDERNESS AS A MATTER OF SCALE

It is a human characteristic to bring all things to the test of oneself, and this is notably true of wilderness. We think of big animals, big scenery, and big acreage: whole watersheds or ranges, intact, pristine ecosystems, wide open spaces in general. We also think of predators, animals large or strong enough to threaten an unarmed person—bears, wolves, mountain lions, that sort of thing. We don't think of smaller animals like squirrels, birds, or insects as markers of wilderness; nor do we think of herbivores like deer. The wild has to have elements of sublimity, provoking awe and fear by virtue of its power and size.

From this point of view, the Cincinnati landscape manifests little wildness. You won't find bison, bear, elk, or wolves here any more. On the other hand, you will find white-tailed deer, coyotes, possums, raccoons, foxes, squirrels, and assorted smaller mammals all cheerfully pursuing their ultimate concerns in relative abundance. In fact, there are more deer now than ever before, as evidenced by the grim fact that we lead the state in the number of deer-vehicle collisions every year! Nevertheless, I suspect that both deer and humans would agree that being hit by a Mercury Cougar is not the same as being taken down by the real thing.

To show how much the sense of wildness depends on a human viewpoint, I often take students on a short walk out the back door and into the woods behind our local park. After we cross the lawn (where, I admit, there's been some chemical alteration of the microflora), the woods close in with their tall pin oaks and hickories surrounded by decomposing leaves. Turn over a dead log, and you'll expose a crowd of centipedes, pill bugs, ants, and beetles scrambling for cover. White mycelial threads of fungi lace the soil, perhaps accentuated by a yellow patch of slime mold. If there's time, I like to scoop a teaspoon of dirt and take it back to the kitchen where we can look at it under a microscope. Between the grains are tiny insects, thrips and mites, along with spiders, and perhaps, if the soil is moist, tiny crustaceans, rotifers clear as jelly flexing and jostling, or protozoans like ciliates barreling along or flagellates whipping about, not to mention clots of bacteria and blue-green algae that do the lion's share of decomposing, fermentation, and nitrogen fixation.

In fact, as you go down the scale from humans to smaller mammals, birds, and insects, life grows increasingly abundant and diverse. As you approach the soil, with its teeming microbial populations, it becomes harder and harder to distinguish this urban biota from what you would find in a wilderness. Where does one draw the line? To see the landscape from a scale compatible with the viewpoints of other creatures is to recognize that wildness may be as much a perspective as a condition. It is certainly not anything absolute. Who can say that the squirrel eating acorns from the pin oaks out back is any less wild than the one who feasts on the same nuts in the mountains of West Virginia or Kentucky's Red River Gorge?

We find the same thing when considering nature's processes as well as its creatures. Fifteen thousand years ago, Cincinnati was covered with ice all the way to the present Ohio River, which more or less marks the line where the glaciers melted as fast as they advanced. A warming trend sent torrents of mud and gravel pouring into the river, scouring and chiseling each crease in the land to a deep ravine. Our valley bottoms are now filled with sand, pebbles, and boulders sorted and deposited by these ancient streams. Pick up a handful of this debris, and you will find not only fragments of the local limestone with its ancient shells but also granite, hornblende, and smoky quartz plucked by the ice from landscapes in Michigan or Ontario. The geologic record shows that Ohio endured periodic glaciations separated by spells of warmth. There is every likelihood that the ice will return.

If it is winter, I like to take students into the gutter to observe how the same geologic processes that shaped the ice-age landscape are still at work. Cincinnati winters see-saw between frost and thaw, which plays havoc with pavement of any kind. Road builders have mined the local valleys for sand and gravel to make concrete, and so you'll find the same mix of pebbles in our streets: fossils and limestone jumbled with granite, schist, gneiss, and other erratic rocks. A January snowfall soon congeals to hard, gray ice which, as it melts down, exposes and concentrates all manner of wind-blown debris, just like the surface of a glacier. The noon sun creates streams that eat into the ice, carving miniature canyons and carrying off debris that gets deposited in deltas where the water drops into a grate or crack. During the night, frost wedging loosens sand grains and pebbles from the concrete, and these, come morning, are also carried off and deposited downstream.

A brief walk down the street on a winter day can therefore reveal how natural processes manifest self-similarity across scales. The seeds of future glaciations lie at one's feet. From this perspective, the landscape's present condition appears less absolute. It's not a bitter end but a phase in history. This makes us think of wildness not as a state but as a direction, less a matter of space, perhaps, than a matter of time.

REPLACING EDEN

To think of wilderness as a matter of time means seeing things from within the landscape. This seems, on the face of it, a most natural and pertinent view. How else could it be done? And yet, the classic American view has been to look at wilderness from without, from a distance, and to see it as a matter of space, a location or condition rather than a process or direction in the flow of life.

I believe that several factors account for this deep and often unrecognized habit of mind. First, our most influential writers and thinkers have depicted wilderness as a kind of earthly paradise, where all things are connected in a harmonious, largely unconscious (and therefore innocent) system of relations that subsume violence and individual death into an enduring, sustainable (and therefore good) economy. For writers like Thoreau, the wilderness was a source of virtue and beauty; for Muir, its grace and beauty were a continuous revelation more healing and redemptive than Scripture. For Dillard, each walk was a long visionary moment sparkling with horrors and angels. For Abbey, the austerity, clarity, and energy of the desert provided the most intense possible experience, which for him was paradise enough.

The excursion model has also played a part. So many nature and wilderness writers describe adventures in places remote from home, visited for a period of days or weeks during pleasant times of the year. Remoteness, exotic locations, and short-term visits all reinforce the tendency to idealize and extrapolate, to think of the wilderness as a kind of park, a place where things persist and endure without interference from human history or, for that matter, any kind of history at all. In classic ecology, the concept of a "climax community" has also reinforced the Edenic view of wilderness by positing a state of equilibrium in the energy and nutrient flows that will be achieved naturally over time and then persist indefinitely. Like the earthly paradise of Scripture, nature in a climax state was supposed to be harmonious, stable, enduring, healthy, and beautiful forever—unless, of course, it was damaged by human beings.

Living in the city makes it harder to see nature this way. For one thing, you live right next to things; they are not exotic or remote, but right here, and sometimes in your face. For another thing, you live here all year round. Therefore, you always see urban nature from within the landscape itself, as a resident rather than as a visitor who does not remain. The excursion model does not work so well. Sometimes, I begin a field trip by asking students to think about how they experience time and nature in their neighborhoods. After a few moments, someone will mention the change of seasons, then someone will comment on migrating birds or the appearance of certain insects such as fireflies. Patterns soon begin to appear, and people realize that they carry a sort of personal almanac marked by more natural features than they would have thought.

Once we get outside, the next step is to think about ecological succession. We commonly regard urban land as disturbed, impacted, degraded, or otherwise diminished from its natural wild state, chiefly as a result of human activity. As proof, we point to the weeds that flourish here: dandelions, plantain, and clover along the sidewalks and park paths, poison ivy and raspberries crowding the edge of the playing field. Interestingly, up north in Minnesota's Boundary Waters Canoe Area Wilderness this group of plants is known as the "Portage Community" because they flourish along portage paths. These species are adapted to disturbed ground, and to them it makes no difference whether the ground is disturbed by a falling tree, a lawn mower, or a canoeist's tramping feet. They grow where conditions permit and mark a pioneer stage in the succession that leads toward old-growth woods. From this point of view, urban landscapes are favorable environments. Moreover, with respect to wilderness, these landscapes are no less natural than a caterpillar is compared to a butterfly.

Running an informal transect across town gives students a vivid picture of urban nature as a patchwork of plots in every stage of succession, from the bare earth of construction sites to the managed equilibrium of gardens and lawns to the remnants of actual old growth preserved in parks and nature centers (even in Cincinnati!). The longer a piece of land has been let alone, the further succession will have advanced; a quick plant check will almost give you the year. Students realize at once how the apparent stability of landscaped areas such as yards, parks, or cemeteries reflects continuous human intervention, so that the successional clock gets set back repeatedly. The result is a false sense of order and permanence, an "artificial climax" if you will. It is not hard to connect this with the aspirations and values underlying an Edenic concept of wilderness.

Observations like these complicate and undermine any environmental ethic or practice based on a clear separation between human beings and nature. The city, with its mosaic of small plots at different stages of succession, is only a figure for the country as a whole, where all land is owned by someone. Moreover, students realize that succession always proceeds in the same direction, no matter the size or location of the plot where it occurs. Succession is a process of sorting out relationships among resident organisms over time. At each stage, certain organisms dominate the biota, and they do not entirely disappear as the process goes on. The biodiversity that grows with succession reflects the remnants of previous stages. As a piece of land accumulates history, we experience it as increasingly wild, that is, increasingly complex, diverse, and saturated with information. Succession always moves in the same direction, and therefore wilderness is always growing back, even in the midst of cities. Our "damaged" landscapes clearly reveal that wildness is the arrow of biological time.

CONCLUSION

I have endeavored to suggest some of the ways that urban nature can serve as a scene of instruction as we enter an ecological age. It is a perfect venue for studying the interactions between human culture and the local landscape and for illuminating the often subconscious choices and beliefs that guide our environmental acts. It also offers variants and alternatives to the excursion model as a guide to environmental experience, thought, and practice. This model, as we've seen, tends to project all value outward toward remote, idealized landscapes, thereby fostering ignorance and neglect of the near-at-hand. Moreover, wilderness trips take time, money, and energy to pull off, and all these must be weighed against the fun, adventure, and learning to be gained.

Urban nature as a scene of instruction offers tangible benefits in terms of accessibility and cost. Moreover, it remains the nature that everyone knows, regardless of race, class, or income. In today's America, the true commons is not the glorious wilderness of national parks but the modest, mixed, and ambiguous nature of cities. This is a good place to start in our journey to understand and appreciate the wild. Urban nature offers the best venue for raising our consciousness to the concealed assumptions and values that inform our ecological behavior; these are the root causes of environmental trouble, and we can't have a sustainable world without addressing them. Nor can we have such a world if we don't deal honestly and affectionately with the landscapes in which we actually live. Fortunately, this is not so hard. A walk through the yard or down the street reveals that there really is a lot going on. The world comes right up to the front door, chock full of flapping, buzzing, fragrant, illuminating lessons.

❋ ANNOTATED BIBLIOGRAPHY

RESOURCES FOR TEACHING

The entries in this section point readers to resources relevant to the practice of teaching outdoors.

Association for the Study of Literature and the Environment (ASLE) Syllabi and Teaching Resources. The URL http://www.asle.umn.edu/archive/syllabi/syllabi.html has links to a syllabi collection edited by Laird Christensen and Peter Blakemore and many other additional syllabi and teaching resources. Not all material focuses on teaching outdoors, but there is a wealth of information here.

Association for Experiential Education. The website www.aee.org contains a list of relevant publications in the field of experiential education as well as information on upcoming conferences. This is a good starting point for those wishing to learn more about the principles and practices of experiential education.

Elder, John. *Stories in the Land: A Place-Based Environmental Education Anthology.* Orion Society, 1998. Contains accounts from secondary teachers using place-based environmental education strategies; many lessons applicable to college courses.

Fuller, David G. "Thoreau in the Wilderness." In *Approaches to Teaching Thoreau's Walden and Other Works*, edited by Richard J. Schneider, 183–86. New York: MLA, 1996. Discusses a course on Thoreau that includes a ten-day canoe trip in Minnesota's Boundary Waters Canoe Area Wilderness.

Gordon, Greg. "Wilderness U." *Orion Afield* 3 (Spring 1999): 10–15. This essay discusses an eight-week Sierra Institute course taught in Montana focused on "conservation issues, nature writing, and wilderness education." The article illustrates how field-studies programs can meld experiential and academic education.

Greenway, Robert. "The Wilderness Effect and Ecopsychology." In *Ecopsychology: Restoring the Earth, Healing the Mind*, edited by Theodore Roszak, Mary E. Gomes, and Allen D. Kanner, 122–35. San Francisco: Sierra Club Books, 1995. Explores the "profound transformations that take place during extended stays in the wilderness." The article helps us consider the effects on individuals in a class who participate in long trips.

Gruchow, Paul. "By Light of the Winter Moon." In *Boundary Waters: The Grace of the Wild*. Minneapolis: Milkweed Editions, 2000. Evocative, thoughtful essay relates author's trip in January with a small group of students to a cabin in Minnesota's north woods. The essay immerses the reader in the beauty of a northern winter and discusses the author's struggle to cope with different personalities and physical abilities.

Harper, Steven. "The Way of Wilderness." In *Ecopsychology: Restoring the Earth, Healing the Mind*, edited by Theodore Roszak, Mary E. Gomes, and Allen D. Kanner, 183–200. San Francisco: Sierra Club Books, 1995. Discusses the idea of wilderness therapy and how it helps individuals cultivate sensory awareness and a better understanding of their own wildness.

Ingram, Anne Merrill. "Service Learning and Ecocomposition: Developing Sustainable Practices through Inter- and Extradisciplinarity." In *Ecocomposition: Theoretical and Practical Approaches*, edited by Christian R. Weisser and Sidney I. Dobrin, 209–33. Albany: State University of New York Press, 2001. Discusses the merits of service learning components in ecocomposition courses. It provides guidelines for incorporating ecologically relevant service learning into courses and includes a syllabus.

"In Pursuit of a·Bioregional Curriculum: An Interview with John Elder." *Orion Afield* 3 (Spring 1999): 26–28. This focused interview discusses the impact teaching outdoors has on students, perspectives on the value of place-based education, and ideas for how to overcome administrative obstacles that limit opportunities for bioregional learning.

ISLE: Interdisciplinary Studies in Literature and Environment 3 (1996). Special issue contains articles on teaching environmental literature and on environmental education; many include syllabi.

The Journal of Environmental Education 11 (Spring 1980). Contains a special section on wilderness education edited by Roderick Nash. An editorial by Nash and seven other short articles on the intersection of wilderness and higher education discuss characteristics of successful wilderness field trips, the benefits of wilderness teaching, and various extended courses that take place on the Mississippi and in the Southwest, Montana, and the Adirondacks.

Journal of Experiential Education. Publishes peer-reviewed articles on environmental education and outdoor adventure programming.

Keller, Christopher J. "The Ecology of Writerly Voice: Authorship, Ethos, and Persona." In *Ecocomposition: Theoretical and Practical Approaches*, edited by Christian R. Weisser and Sidney I. Dobrin, 193–208. Albany: State University of New York Press, 2001. Insightful essay asks us to consider how assignments involving retreat narratives raise issues of race, gender, and class. Through a discussion of the essay topics chosen by African American and white students, the author critiques the idea of retreat narratives and assignments involving a return to nature.

Leslie, Clare Walker, John Tallmadge, and Tom Wessels. *Into the Field: A Guide to Locally Focused Teaching.* Nature Literacy Series. Great Barrington, Mass.: The Orion Society, 1999. Three instructional essays offer ideas for taking students out of doors.

Lindholdt, Paul. "Restoring Bioregions Through Applied Composition." In *Ecocomposition: Theoretical and Practical Approaches*, edited by Christian R. Weisser and Sidney I. Dobrin, 235–52. Albany: State University of New York Press, 2001. The focus of this article is on the importance of place and connecting to bioregions; it includes suggestions for doing so as well as a critique of that practice.

The Literature of Nature. A special issue of *The CEA Critic* 54 (Fall 1991). Though not devoted to teaching outdoors, this issue provides twenty-three articles on topics related to nature and the environment that could easily be adapted to courses with field components. Most focus on approaches to teaching these topics or on relevant literary criticism. Barbara Lounsberry's "'Accuse Not Nature, She Hath Done Her Part': Ten Writing Assignments Involving Nature" provides a list of ten assignments that involve students outside the classroom.

Monsma, Bradley John. "Writing Home: Composition, Campus Ecology, and Watershed Environments." In *Ecocomposition: Theoretical and Practical Approaches*, edited by Christian R. Weisser and Sidney I. Dobrin, 281–90. Albany: State University of New York Press, 2001. An intriguing essay describing an ecocomposition course designed around the compilation of the natural history of Woodbury University, in Burbank, California.

Orr, David W. *Ecological Literacy and the Transition to a Postmodern World.* Albany: State University of New York Press, 1992. "Part Two:

Education" of this important book outlines a new model of education; several chapters discuss the importance of place and of educating the whole person.

Polson, Sheila. "'Environmental Studies 101' on a Travelling School Bus." *Christian Science Monitor,* October 31, 1995, vol. 87, issue 235, 10. Discusses the Audubon Expedition Institute's (AEI) semester by traveling school bus experiential education program for undergraduate and graduate students.

Roorda, Randall. "Sites and Senses Of Writing in Nature." *College English* 59 (April 1997): 385–407. A critique of the notion of solitary individual writing in nature; provoking reading for those teaching nature writing outdoors. A version of the essay also appears in Roorda's *Dramas of Solitude: Narratives of Retreat in American Nature Writing.* Albany: State University of New York Press, 1998.

Sewall, Laura. "The Skill of Ecological Perception." In *Ecopsychology: Restoring the Earth, Healing the Mind,* edited by Theodore Roszak, Mary E. Gomes, and Allen D. Kanner, 200–215. San Francisco: Sierra Club Books, 1995. Provides a discussion of "five perceptual practices that can help us" establish a close connection with our senses, which in turn helps us connect self to the physical world.

Sobel, David. "Border Crossings: A Review of *Green Teacher* and *Clearing* Magazines." *Orion Afield* 3 (Spring 1999): 37. A review of two K–12 environmental education journals that may be of interest to college teachers: *Green Teacher* and *Clearing: Environmental Education in the Northwest.*

Tallmadge, John. *Meeting the Tree of Life: A Teacher's Path.* Salt Lake City: University of Utah Press, 1997. The book contains several thoughtful chapters on teaching outdoors, including "The Dark Side of Katahdin," "In the Mazes of Quetico," and "Meeting the Tree of Life."

Thomashow, Mitchell. *Ecological Identity: Becoming a Reflective Environmentalist.* Cambridge, Mass.: The MIT Press, 1995. This fine book is, in part, a guide to learning experiences, both practical and theoretical, that deal with the idea of ecological identity. Though not directed exclusively toward those interested in teaching outdoors, the contents are easily applicable to the practice of teaching outdoors. Especially relevant is a list of hands-on learning activities.

Waage, Fred., ed. *Teaching Environmental Literature.* New York: MLA, 1985. This ground-breaking collection helped to introduce college instructors to courses in environmental literature and to provide suggestions for teaching in the field. Part 4, "Environmental Literature in the Field," contains four essays discussing courses taught wholly or partially outside the traditional classroom.

FIELD MANUALS AND OUTDOOR GUIDEBOOKS

Whether taking students outdoors for one month or one hour, guidebooks and field manuals can enhance the experience. Though they are no substitute for experience and common sense, used wisely they provide helpful suggestions and tips for new and veteran instructors.

Bechdel, Les, and Slim Ray. *River Rescue*. Boston: Appalachian Mountain Club Books, 1989. The authoritative book on river rescue, written by two veteran paddlers; essential reading for those considering river trips that include even small amounts of whitewater.

Bennett, Jeff. *The Complete Whitewater Rafter*. Camden, Maine: International Marine/Ragged Mountain Press, 1996. For instructors considering rafting trips as part of a course or class session this is a comprehensive resource covering trip planning, gear selection, and river-running technique.

Curtis, Rick. *The Backpacker's Field Manual: A Comprehensive Guide to Mastering Backcountry Skills*. New York: Three Rivers Press/Random House, 1998. A comprehensive manual covering everything from trip planning to camping, weather, and first aid, written by the director of Princeton University's Outdoor Action Program.

Davidson, James West, and John Rugge. *The Complete Wilderness Paddler*. New York: Knopf, 1983. A classic covering all the essentials of planning extended canoe trips; called the "best canoe book ever" by *Canoe* magazine.

Gorman, Stephen. *Winter Camping*. Boston: Appalachian Mountain Club Books, 1999. A thorough guide to planning, outfitting, traveling, and camping in winter environments.

Graham, John. *Outdoor Leadership: Technique, Common Sense & Self-Confidence*. Seattle: Mountaineers Books, 1997. A practical, readable, and essential guide for anyone taking groups on trips longer than a few hours. Contains chapters on women in leadership, decision-making, communication, team building, conflict resolution, and dealing with stress.

Harvey, Mark, and Peter Simer. *The National Outdoor Leadership School's Wilderness Guide*. New York: Simon and Schuster, 1999. A National Outdoor Book Award winner, this book contains advice for those planning and conducting backpacking trips and provides instruction on low-impact wilderness travel.

Huser, Verne. *River Running*, 2nd ed. Seattle: The Mountaineers Books, 2001. Another excellent river rafting resource. Contains chapters on the history of river running, organizing trips, emergencies, and river conservation. Also includes an extensive and thorough bibliography pertaining to river running.

Jacobson, Cliff. *Expedition Canoeing: A Guide to Canoeing Wild Rivers in North America*. Guilford, Conn.: Globe Pequot Press, 2001. Another option for those planning extended canoe trips. This first-rate book is full of pictures and diagrams covering all aspects of wilderness canoe trips.

National Audubon Society Field Guide Series. Provides leading illustrated guidebooks on such topics as birds, trees, flowers, insects and spiders, and reptiles and amphibians.

National Audubon Society Regional Field Guide Series. A new series focused by region: California, Florida, Mid-Atlantic, New England, Pacific Northwest, Rocky Mountain, Southeastern States, and Southwestern States. Each includes sections on flora and fauna, geology, weather, ecology, and best parks, trails, and preserves.

Petersen's Field Guide Series. Another quality series of illustrated guidebooks on birds, trees, insects, plants, and animals.

Schimelpfenig, Tod, and Linda Lindsey, eds. NOLS *Wilderness First Aid*. Mechanicsburg, Pa.: Stackpole Books, 2000. Developed by the highly respected National Outdoor Leadership Schools (NOLS), this book is an essential take-along manual for any field trip.

ALAN BREW teaches composition and American literature at Northland College, an environmental liberal arts school in Ashland, Wisconsin. Like Thoreau, he believes that it is absurd "to attend chiefly to the desk or schoolhouse, while we neglect the scenery in which it is placed."

ROBERT E. BURKHOLDER is Associate Professor of English at Penn State University, University Park. He is a former president of the Ralph Waldo Emerson Society and a longtime Emerson scholar. Most recently he has been engaged with inventing and teaching outdoor courses at Penn State, including the Penn State Wilderness Literature Field Institute, which he began in 2000, and courses on the Appalachian Trail and the Grand Canyon.

KATHERINE R. CHANDLER is Assistant Professor of English at St. Mary's College of Maryland. An originating member of the college's interdisciplinary Environmental Studies program, she teaches courses in composition and literature, including environmental literature. She has published in *Philological Quarterly* and *English Language Notes*. Her scholarly interest is now in contemporary nature writing, most recently that of Terry Tempest Williams and Linda Hogan.

LAIRD CHRISTENSEN's unruly résumé ranges from lumber grader to environmental activist, park ranger to professor. His poems and essays have appeared in a variety of journals, including *Wild Earth*, *Northwest Review*, and *Whole Terrain*. He is currently Assistant Professor of English Literature at Green Mountain College, Vermont's environmental liberal arts college.

HAL CRIMMEL teaches writing and literature at Weber State University in Ogden, Utah. He writes on environmental and outdoor topics for popular and scholarly publications. His articles, essays, and reviews have appeared in *Pacific Northwest Quarterly*, the *South Dakota Review*, *Minnesota Conservation Volunteer*, and *Western American Literature*. He will serve as a Fulbright scholar to Austria in 2004.

BRENT CUTHBERTSON, JANET DYMENT, LESLEY P. CURTHOYS, TOM G. POTTER, AND TIM O'CONNELL all work, teach, and learn about the role and meaning of nature in their lives with the students of the Outdoor Recreation, Parks and Tourism program at Lakehead University in Thunder Bay, Ontario, Canada.

TERRY GIFFORD is Reader in Literature and Environment at the University of Leeds, United Kingdom; Secretary of ASLE UK; and Director of the annual International Festival of Mountaineering Literature, now in its seventeenth year. He is the author of *Pastoral* (1999) and *Green Voices: Understanding Contemporary Nature Poetry* (1995). He has five collections of poetry, the most recent of which is *Whale Watching With a Boy and a Goat* (1998). His *New and Selected Poems* (2003) is titled *The Unreliable Mushrooms*.

ED GRUMBINE is Director of the Sierra Institute, an undergraduate wilderness field studies program at University of California Extension, Santa Cruz. He is the author of *Ghost Bears: Exploring the Biodiversity Crisis* (1992), editor of *Environmental Policy and Biodiversity* (1994), and has worked for wildlands protection for many years.

BOB HENDERSON teaches Outdoor Experiential Education at McMaster University. He is co-editor of *Pathways: The Ontario Journal of Outdoor Education* and writes a regular heritage travel feature for *Kanawa: The Magazine of the Canadian Recreational Canoe Association*. He can regularly be found both inside and outside the classroom.

STEVE HOFFMAN, Professor of Political Science and Director of Environmental Studies at the University of St. Thomas in St. Paul, Minnesota, and a Senior Policy Fellow at the Center for Energy and Environmental Policy (University of Delaware), teaches Environmental Policy in SSWR, and has published several books, numerous journal articles, and technical reports on energy and environmental policy.

COREY LEWIS is currently a Ph.D. candidate in the Literature and Environment program at the University of Nevada, Reno. He also helps manage, and instructs for, the Great Basin Institute (a nonprofit, interdisciplinary field-studies program based at UNR), teaching field-based courses in Environmental Literature, Science, and Wilderness Survival.

CHARLES MITCHELL is Associate Professor of American Studies at Elmira College. His book, *Individualism and Its Discontents: Appropriations of Emerson, 1880–1950*, was published by the University of Massachusetts Press in 1997. His essays have appeared in *ISLE, Whole Terrain,* and *The McNeese Review.*

BARNEY NELSON, an Associate Professor of English at Sul Ross State University in Alpine, Texas, is widely published in both popular and scholarly presses. Her most recent publication is an anthology from the University of Texas Press, *God's Country or Devil's Playground: The Best Nature Writing from the Big Bend of Texas* (2002).

LIZ NEWBERY teaches outdoor education at the Canadian Outward Bound Wilderness School and at McMaster University. She is a doctoral candidate in York University's Faculty of Education, focusing on poststructural feminism and critical pedagogies.

BRITAIN A. SCOTT, Assistant Professor of Psychology at the University of St. Thomas in St. Paul, Minnesota, teaches courses in social psychology, gender studies, and environmental studies, including Eco-Psychology in SSWR. Her scholarship focuses on women's bodies, with work on topics such as beauty advertising, pornography, and women's body-building.

JOHN TALLMADGE is Core Professor in literature and environmental studies in the Graduate College of the Union Institute. A widely published nature writer, ecocritic, and wilderness educator, he is the author of *Meeting the Tree of Life: A Teacher's Path* (1997). He has taught at Dartmouth, Yale, Carleton College, and the University of Utah, and conducted seminars in the High Sierra, the Boundary Waters, the Canyons of the Escalate, and the streets of Cincinnati.

FRED TAYLOR is a writer, teacher, and outdoor group leader who lives in southern Vermont. In addition to teaching nature writing at Antioch, he is on the Graduate Faculty of Vermont College. His essays have appeared in *Whole Terrain, Alligator Juniper, The North American Review*, and Scribner's *American Nature Writers.*

ALLISON B. WALLACE was born in southeast Louisiana and educated at the University of Mississippi and the University of North Carolina, where she wrote a dissertation on ecocentric thought in American nature writing. After nine years on the faculty of Unity College in Maine, she accepted a position in American Studies within the Honors College at the University of Central Arkansas. She is a former Fulbright scholar to Japan, a gardener, beekeeper, essayist, and (of course) a paddler.

ANDREW WINGFIELD is on the faculty of New Century College, an integrative studies program at George Mason University in Virginia. His essays and reviews have appeared in *Western American Literature, The Antioch Review, The Amicus Journal,* and other magazines. His novel, *Hear Him Roar,* is forthcoming from Creative Arts Book Company.

58, 150, 182, 242, 243, 266;
thought, 278; trouble, 287;
understanding, 86; values, 9, 147,
149, 150, 277; writers, 104; writing,
147, 149, 150
environmentalism, 126
environmentalists, 267, 270, 277
experiential —, 21, 24–25, 81, 86, 111:
education, 15, 87, 90, 115, 152, 156,
168, 169, 193, 208, 241; learning,
84, 87, 90, 202; research, 198
field-based —, 6, 9, 22, 23, 24, 80,
208, 211, 216, 217: education, 208,
215; learning, 6,7,11
field: and classes, 111, 215; and
classroom, 54; and courses, 8, 16, 35,
210, 213, 221; and ecology, 53; and
experience, 21, 159, 163, 168; and
program, 58; and research, 201, 214,
217, 219; and sessions, 88; and studies, 10, 23, 205, 207, 208, 209, 210,
211, 214, 215, 216, 217, 218, 220,
221, 243; and study, 22, 23, 25, 26,
211, 216; and teaching, 205; — trip,
3, 4, 6, 10, 18, 20, 27, 81, 84, 93,
102, 119, 152, 156, 157, 166, 168,
226, 277, 285; and work, 9, 198
Finch, Robert, 125, 180
Finger Lakes (N.Y.), 36
Finnegan, William, 37
First Nations, 91
Fleischner, Thomas Lowe, 29
Florida, 1
Florida Keys, 1, 2
Four Corners, 39
Fowles, John, 177–178
Franklin, Benjamin, 37, 38
Friedan, Betty, 37
Fromm, Harold, 137
Frost, Robert, 18, 33, 34, 45, 271

Galland, China, 259
Gathland State Park (Md.), 19
gender stereotypes, 205, 246, 247, 249,
250, 255, 258
Glen Canyon National Recreation Area,
73
Glotfelty, Cheryll, vii, 125, 137
Golden Road (Me.), 229
Gonzalez, Ray, 271

Gordon, Greg, 22, 23
Grace Lake (Minn.), 249
Grand Canyon, 66, 277
Grand Gulch (Utah), 51, 52, 53
Great Plains, 5, 36, 39
Great Salt Lake, 54, 130
Grumbine, R. Edward, 23, 24, 25
Gulf of Mexico, 1, 39

Hamilton, Alexander, 36, 37, 38
Hamilton, Ontario, 165,166
Harper's Ferry, 18, 19, 200
Hasselstrom, Linda, 271
Hawaii, 33, 34, 45
Hawthorne, Nathaniel, 3
Helderburg Mountains (N.Y.), 3
Hemingway, Ernest, 3
Hickory Creek Wilderness (Penn.), 18,
20, 24, 27, 28
High Sierra, 267, 277
hiking, viii, 18, 66, 88, 93
Hinning House, 138,150
Hispanic, 266, 269, 271, 273, 275, 276
Honolulu, 33, 34
hooks, bell, 166
Huber, J. Parker, 224

International Wolf Center, 244
Iron Range (Minn.), 244

James River (Va.), 200
Jaques, Florence Page, 71
Jarbidge Wilderness Area (Nev.), 214
Jeffers, Robinson, 69
Jefferson, Thomas, 18, 37
Jewett, Sarah Orne, 34
John Muir Wilderness, 222
journaling, 84, 93, 107, 216, 218
journals, 50, 89, 108, 112–113, 115–
116, 177, 183, 185, 186, 187, 188,
199, 200, 215, 218, 220, 221, 272
Joyce, James, 216

King, Stephen, 18
Krutch, Joseph Wood, 103

LaBastille, Anne, 24
Labrador, 158
landscape, 3, 8, 15, 18, 22, 23, 33, 34,
35, 36, 37, 38, 39, 40, 41, 42, 44,